N.Y. Dutchess County Board of Supervisors

Proceedings of the Board of Supervisors of Dutchess County

N.Y. Dutchess County Board of Supervisors

Proceedings of the Board of Supervisors of Dutchess County

ISBN/EAN: 9783337302214

Printed in Europe, USA, Canada, Australia, Japan

Cover: Foto ©Suzi / pixelio.de

More available books at **www.hansebooks.com**

PROCEEDINGS

——OF THE——

BOARD OF SUPERVISORS

——OF——

DUTCHESS COUNTY, N. Y.

FOR THE YEAR 1890.

" ENTERPRISE " STEAM PRINT, POUGHKEEPSIE, N. Y.

COUNTY OFFICERS,

1890.

County Judge, - - -	DANIEL W. GUERNSEY.
Surrogate, - - - -	CYRENUS P. DORLAND.
Sheriff, - - - -	J. WESLEY VAN TASSELL.
County Clerk, - - -	THEODORE A. HOFFMAN.
County Treasurer, - - -	ISAAC W. SHERRILL.
District Attorney, - -	MARTIN W. HEERMANCE.
Superintendent of Poor, - - -	MYRON A. SMITH.

SUPERVISORS.
1890.

Amenia................ ....Wm. H. Bartlett.
Beekman........................Kromline Andrews.
Clinton..........................Edward Herrick.
Dover...........................Sheldon Wing.
East Fishkill....... ....Isaac S. Genung.
Fishkill..........................Samuel B. Rodgers.
Hyde Park......................David E. Howatt.
La Grange......... ....Wm. H. Austin.
Milan ....Cyrus Morehouse.
North East......................John Scutt.
Pawling..........................G. Frank Lee.
Pine Plains......................John A. Herrick.
Pleasant Valley..................E. Wright Vail.
Poughkeepsie Town..............A. B. Gray.
Poughkeepsie City, 1st Ward......John J. Mylod.
  "   "   2d   "   .....Wm. Krieger.
  "   "   3rd   "   ......Guilford Dudley.
  "   "   4th   "   ......Charles W. Swift.
  "   "   5th   "   ......Fred W. Pugsley.
  "   "   6th   "   ......Charles Williams.
Red Hook........................Edward Sturgess.
Rhinebeck ....John C. Milroy.
Stanford.........................Chas. H. Humphrey.
Union Vale......................John U. Able.
Wappinger......................George Wood.
Washington ....Lewis D. Germond.

ANNUAL MEETING.

THURSDAY, November 13, 1890.

The Board of Supervisors of Dutchess County, convened on the above date in Annual Session at 10:30 A. M., in the Supervisors' Room, Court House, in the City of Poughkeepsie, the roll being called by the Clerk of the previous Board, the following Supervisors answered to their names :

Amenia	Wm. H. Bartlett.
Beekman	Kromline Andrews.
Clinton	Edward Herrick.
Dover	Sheldon Wing.
East Fishkill	Isaac S. Genung.
Fishkill	Samuel B. Rodgers.
Hyde Park	David E. Howatt.
La Grange	Wm. H. Austin.
Milan	Cyrus Morehouse.
North East	John Scutt.
Pawling	G. Frank Lee.
Pine Plains	John A. Herrick.
Pleasant Valley	E. Wright Vail.
Poughkeepsie Town	A. B. Gray.
" City, 1st Ward	John J. Mylod.
" " 2d "	Wm. Krieger.
" " 3d "	Guilford Dudley.
" " 4th "	Charles W. Swift.
" " 5th "	Frederick W. Pugsley.
" " 6th "	Charles Williams.
Red Hook	Edward Sturgess.
Rhinebeck	John C. Milroy.
Stanford	Chas. H. Humphrey.
Union Vale	John U. Able.
Wappinger	George Wood.
Washington	Lewis D. Germond.

Mr. Pugsley moved that the Board proceed to elect a Chairman.

Motion carried.

Mr. Germond nominated Wm. H. Austin for Chairman.

Mr. Pugsley nominated John U. Able for Chairman.

Mr. Able thanked his friends for the compliment, and withdrew his name as a candidate for Chairman, and on his motion Wm. H. Austin was unanimously elected Chairman.

Mr. Austin upon taking the Chair addressed the Board as follows :

Gentlemen of the Board of Supervisors of Dutchess County :

For the honor you have conferred upon me in selecting me as Chairman to preside over your deliberations, accept my thanks. As a Board of Supervisors, when I look over this assemblage, I do not think it becomes me to make any extensive remarks. With these gentlemen assembled I know they mean to do their duty, and will do their duty, and I will discharge mine as Chairman. What is the pleasure of the Board ?

Mr. Scutt moved that the Board proceed to elect a Clerk.

Motion carried.

Mr. Scutt nominated Smith Heroy for Clerk, and moved that his election be made unanimous.

Motion carried.

On motion of Mr. Vail, Dr. John P. Wilson, was unanimously elected Jail Physician.

Mr. Krieger nominated Wm. Cruger for Janitor.

Mr. Williams nominated Hiram Sleight and on his motion the Board proceeded to ballot for Janitor.

Whole number of votes cast 23, of which

Wm. Cruger received   13
Hiram Sleight "   10

Mr. Cruger was declared elected Janitor.

Mr. Mylod moved that the Board proceed to elect a County Sealer, and nominated Edward Englehart as such.

Mr. Bartlett nominated S. J. Farnum, and moved that the Board proceed to ballot for County Sealer.

Motion carried.

Whole number of votes cast 21, of which

Edward Englehart received   13
S. J. Farnum   "   8

Edward Englehart was declared elected County Sealer.

Mr. E. Herrick offered the following :

Resolved, That the Clerk be authorized to procure the necessary Stationery for the use of the Board.

Resolution adopted.

Mr. Pugsley moved that the Rules of the last Board be adopted for the government of this Board.

Motion carried.

On motion of Mr. Pugsley the hours for meetings of the Board were fixed at 10:30 A. M. and 1:30 P. M.

Mr. Germond moved that the Board proceed to draw for seats.

Motion carried.

No. Drawn.

Wm. H. Bartlett.. 15
Kromline Andrews.. 2
Edward Herrick.. 24
Sheldon Wing.. 12
Isaac S. Genung... 23
Samuel B. Rodgers.. 16
David E. Howatt.. 25
Cyrus Morehouse.. 4
John Scutt... 14
G. Frank Lee... 8
John A. Herrick.. 9
E. Wright Vail.. 10
A. B. Gray... 3
John J. Mylod... 6
Wm. Krieger... 7
Guilford Dudley.. 18
Chas. W. Swift.. 20
F. W. Pugsley.. 17
Chas. Williams.. 13
Edward Sturgess... 21
John C. Milroy.. 22
Charles H. Humphrey.. 5
George Wood... 19
Lewis D. Germond.. 1
John U. Able.. 11

On motion of Mr. Pugsley the Board adjourned to
meet on Monday, Nov. 17th, at 2 p. m.

.   ———

MONDAY, Nov. 17, 1890.
2 P. M.

Board met.
Quorum present.
Mr. Austin in the Chair.

Minutes of the previous meeting read and approved.

Chairman announced the Standing Committees of the Board, and on motion of Mr. Williams the Clerk was authorized to have the Rules and Standing Committees printed for the use of the Board.

RULES.

I. The Chairman having taken the chair, the roll shall be called, and, a quorum being present, the Journal of the preceding day, which shall be regularly kept by the Clerk, shall be read to the end that mistakes therein may be corrected.

II. The Order of Business shall be as follows :

    1. Presentation of Petitions.

    2. The Reception of Reports.

    3. Motions, Resolutions, Bills and Notices.

    4. Unfinished Business generally.

III. No member shall converse with another, or otherwise interrupt the Business of the Board while the Journal or other papers are being read ; and when the Chairman is putting a question no member shall walk out or across the room, nor when a member is speaking pass between him and the Chairman, nor interrupt him except to call him to order.

IV. Every member, when he speaks, shall address the Chair ; and when two or more members rise at once, the Chairman shall name the member who is to speak.

V. When a question has been once put and decided, it shall not be reconsidered more than once ; and the motion to reconsider shall be made within three days after the decision thereon (such three days being constructed to mean three days that the Board is in actual session), except by a vote of two-thirds of the members present.

VI. No person except a member shall be allowed to address the Chair without the unanimous consent of the Board.

VII. The rules and regulations governing parliamentary bodies shall be observed as far as applicable and consistent with the foregoing Rules.

VIII. No member shall be absent from the Board during any sitting more than half an hour at a time without leave from the Chairman.

IX. No resolution offered by any member of the Board, involving the appropriation of money from the public treasury, shall be voted upon the day on which it is offered.

X. All resolutions offered by members, if objected to, shall lie over one day before being acted upon, except by a two-thirds vote ; and all Reports of the Standing Committees shall be read by the Clerk as soon as received, and be held for the examination of the members of the Board at least forty-eight hours before they are presented for adoption.

XI. All resolutions offered by members of the Board shall be offered in writing, and also all amendments thereto.

XII. Any of the Rules may be repealed, altered or amended by a vote of two-thirds of the members.

The following Standing Committees shall be appointed by the Chair, consisting of three members each, except the Committee on Equalization, which shall consist of nine members ; and the Committee on Charitable Institutions and Asylums, and the Committee to examine the Books and Accounts of the Superintendent of the Poor, shall consist of five members :

1. On Equalization.
2. To examine the Books and Accounts of the Superintendent of the Poor.
3. To examine the Books and Accounts of the Treasurer.
4. To examine the Sheriff's and Jailor's Accounts.
5. To examine the Town and County Clerk's Accounts.
6. To examine Surrogate's Accounts.
7. To examine District Attorney's Accounts.
8. On Public Buildings.
9. On Roads and Bridges.
10. To examine the School Commissioners' Accounts.
11. On Legislative Enactments.
12. On Town Auditors' Accounts.
13. To examine Constables' Accounts.
14. To examine Justices' Accounts.
15. To examine Coroners' and Physicians' Accounts.

16. On Military Affairs.
17. To examine Printers' Accounts.
18. To examine the Books and Accounts of the Commissioners of Loans.
19. On Excessive Taxation.
20. On Miscellaneous Bills.
21. On Officers of the Board's Accounts.
22. On State Asylums and Charitable Institutions.

The Chairman presented the list of Standing Committees :

On Equalization :
> Howatt, Germond, Wing, Humphrey, J. A. Herrick, Pugsley, Rodgers, Williams and Gray.

To examine the Books and Accounts of the Superintendent of the Poor :
> Germond, Wing, Vail, Wood and Bartlett.

To examine the Books and Accounts of the County Treasurer :
> Mylod, Lee and Dudley.

To examine Sheriff and Jailor's Accounts :
> Wing, Krieger and Able.

To examine County Clerk's Accounts :
> Genung, Milroy and Wood.

To examine Surrogate's Accounts :
> Humphrey, Sturgess and Swift.

To examine District Attorney's Accounts :
> Sturgess, E. Herrick and Andrews.

On Asylums and Charitable Institutions :
> Milroy, Krieger, E. Herrick, Williams and Morehouse.

On Public Buildings :
> Mylod, Howatt, Gray.

On Military Affairs :
> Krieger, Mylod, Pugsley.

On Miscellaneous Bills :
> Vail, Lee, Dudley.

On Coroners' and Physicians' Bills :
> E. Herrick, Genung, Rodgers.

On Printers' Bills :
J. A. Herrick, Lee, Swift.

On Legislative Enactments :
Lee, Vail, Wood.

On Constables's Accounts :
Scutt, Rodgers, Lee.

On Roads and Bridges :
Humphrey, Genung, Morehouse.

To examine School Commissioners' Accounts :
Germond, Sturgess, Able.

To examine Justices' Accounts :
J. A. Herrick, Milroy, Andrews.

On Excessive Taxation :
Able, Bartlett, Germond.

On Loan Commissioners' Accounts :
Wood, Rodgers, Krieger.

On Officers of the Board Accounts :
Dudley, Sturgess, Milroy.

On Town Auditor's Accounts :
Gray, Able, Vail.

The Clerk presented and read the following communications, which were referred to Committee on County Treasurer's Account :

STATE OF NEW YORK,
COMPTROLLER'S OFFICE,
ALBANY, September 30th, 1890.

To the Clerk of the Board of Supervisors of the County of Dutchess:

SIR :—I enclose a form of statement of the valuation of real and personal estate required to be made by you, pursuant to Chapter 117 of the Laws of 1836, and forwarded to this office previous to the second Monday in December in each year, under a penalty of fifty dollars. I also enclose a form of return of Incorporated Companies liable to taxation. *It is indispensable that this Report be furnished by the time prescribed.*

The Board of Equalization of Taxes, in pursuance of Chapter 312 of the Laws of 1859, have fixed the aggregate valuation of property in your County at the sum of $47,003,394, upon which amount a State tax of $109,987.94 must be levied for the fiscal year, commencing October 1st, 1890, as provided in said act and amendments thereto by Chapter 351, Laws of 1874, being 2 34-100 mills on the dollar, for the following purposes, viz :

For Schools.............1 4-100 mill, per Chapter 554,   Laws of 1890.
For General Purposes. 7-10   "   "   554,   "   1890.
For Canals..............6-10   "   "   122, 266 and 554,
       Total...........2 34-100 mills.

             Your obedient servant,
                EDWARD WEMPLE,
                   Comptroller.

           STATE OF NEW YORK. ⎞
           COMPTROLLER'S OFFICE, ⎟
            ALBANY, Oct. 3, 1890. ⎠

To Clerk of Board of Supervisors :

SIR :—In addition to the State Tax of 2 34-100 mills, directed to be levied as per circular from this office, dated September 30th, amounting to $109,987 94-100, the Board of Supervisors of the County of Dutchess is hereby required to raise the sum of $2,044,55 for additional compensation of the Justices of the Supreme Court in the Second Judicial District, in pursuance of Chapter 765, Laws of 1868, and Chapter 84, Laws of 1890, and for the Stenographers appointed under said Act, to the 30th of September, 1891, as provided by Chapter 84, Laws of 1890.

         ·   Respectfully yours,
                EDWARD WEMPLE,
                   Comptroller.

A communication was also received from the Home for the Friendless, and a Committee of the Board of Supervisors of Chautauqua Co., were read and referred to Committee on Asylums and Charitable Institutions.

Mr. Swift moved that the box containing the bills

against the County be brought up from the Clerk's Office on Wednesday, Nov. 19th, 1890, at 11 A. M.

Motion carried.

Mr. Pugsley offered the following :

Resolved, That a committee of three be appointed by the Chair to apportion the Grand Jurors to the several towns and wards of the county.

Resolution adopted.

The Chair named as such Committee Messrs. Pugsley, Humphrey, Mylod.

Mr. Williams moved that the Tax Books be placed in the hands of the Clerk, and that no alteration be made in said Books after Dec. 1st, 1890.

Motion carried.

On motion of Mr. Pugsley the Board adjourned.

TUESDAY, Nov. 18, 1890.

10:30 A. M.

Board met.

Quorum present.

Mr. Austin in the Chair.

Minutes read and approved.

Mr. Germond offered the following:

TOWN OF WASHINGTON, Dutchess Co., N. Y.

Lewis D. Germond, Supervisor, &c. :

We the undersigned Assessors of the Town of Washington respectfully state, that in the list of taxable property in said town, made for the year 1890, the property and valuation of the parcel known as the Deuel Mill property was erroneously assessed to Frederick Warner instead of C. F. Dieterick.

We therefore recommend that the said property and the valuation be changed and the same be assessed to Charles F. Dieterick the owner of said mill property.

CHAS. I. SWIFT,

S. D. TRAVI8,

Assessors.

Dated Washington, Nov. 15, 1890.

We, the Assessors of the Town of Washington, recommend that the personal property of the estate of V. D. Holbrook be stricken from the assessment roll of said town.

S. D. TRAVIS,

CHAS. I. SWIFT,

Assessors.

Washington, Nov. 4, 1890.

Resolved, That the personal assessment against the estate of N. D. Holbrook, deceased, be stricken from the Assessment Roll of the Town of Washington, as recommended by the Assessors of said Town.

Resolution adopted.

Resolved, That the assessment of the Deuel Mill property in the Town of Washington, be changed to Charles F. Dieterick instead of Frederick Warner, former owner.

Resolution adopted.

Mr. J. A. Herrick offered the following:

PINE PLAINS, Nov. 4th, 1890.

We, the Assessors of the Town of Pine Plains, being satisfied from statements made before us by William B. Jordan, that he should not be assessed for $2,000 personal property,as appears against him on our town roll, do recommend and advise that the same be stricken from the roll.

WILLARD W. HICKS,
ROBERT D. HICKS,
ADAM A. STREVER,
Assessors.

Resolved, That the Clerk be directed to strike out the personal assessments against Sarah Germain $1,000, and Wm. B. Jordan $2,000, from the Assessment Roll of the Town of Pine Plains as requested by the Assessors of said Town.

Resolution adopted.

The Clerk presented and read the following:

Mr. Smith Heroy, Clerk of the Honorable Board of Supervisors of Dutchess Co.:

DEAR SIR :—At the regular meeting of the Board of Managers of the Home for the Friendless, held Wednesday, Nov. 5th, the following action was taken :

Resolved, That we invite the Board of Supervisors to visit and examine our Institution, they naming the time. Will you please present this to the Board and inform me of the time. A Committee of the Managers will receive them.

Yours truly,
MISS E. G. WHEELER.

117 Cannon St., Pokeepsie, Nov. 15th, 1890.

Mr. Able moved that the invitation be accepted and that Thursday, Nov. 21, 1890, at 3 p. m., be fixed as the time of visiting said Institution.

Motion carried.

Mr. Germond offered the following :

Resolved, That the abstract sheets of the several towns be presented to the Clerk of this Board, on Thursday, Nov. 21, 1890, at 11 a. m.

Resolution adopted.

Mr. Genung offered the following ;

Resolved, That the Supervisors hand their respective lists of Grand Jurors to the Clerk on Thursday, Nov. 21, 1890.

Resolution adopted.

On motion of Mr. Pugsley the Board adjourned.

TUESDAY, Nov. 18, 1890.

1:30 P. M.

Board met.

Quorum present.

Mr. Austin in the Chair.

Mr. Pugsley, moved that the Board go into a Committee of the Whole, Mr. J. A. Herrick in the Chair.

Motion carried.

Committee arose.

Mr. Herrick, from the Committee of the Whole, reported progress.

Mr. Mylod offered the following :

Resolved, That a Special Meeting of four be appointed by the Chair, of which the Chairman and Clerk of this Board shall be named as two, for the purpose of collecting any claims that the County of Dutchess may have against persons, Counties and estates, and they be authorized and empowered to do all things necessary for the collection of the same.

Resolution adopted.

On motion of Mr Pugsley the Board adjourned.

WEDNESDAY, November 19th, 1890.

10:30•A. M.

Board met.

Quorum present.

Mr. Austin in the Chair.

Minutes read and approved.

Mr. Austin presented the following which was read and referred to Committee on Excessive Taxation.

To the Board of Supervisors of Dutchess County :

We, Assessors of Town of LaGrange, certify to a mistake made in the assessment of the real estate of Mrs. Fanny Titus in the year 1889, to the amount of $1,000.

JAMES H. LANDON,
ROBERT H. SMITH.

Mr. Rogers presented the following which was on his motion referred to Committee on Excessive Taxation:

FISHKILL-ON-HUDSON, N. Y., Feb. 6. 1889.

TOWN OF FISHKILL :

To LEWIS TOMPKINS, DR.

Feb. 6th, Pd. on Tioronda Hat Wks., assessed 10,000 @ 0131....... $131 00
Should have been   "   "   "   "   "   0087........ 87 00

$44 00

STATE OF NEW YORK, } ss :
DUTCHESS COUNTY.

John I. Schlosser being duly sworn, says that he sat with the Collector of Taxes of the Town of Fishkill, in the month of January, 1890. That the amount collected upon the Tioronda Hat Works, which with other property assessed to Lewis Tompkins was $131, exclusive of the per centage allowed by law to the collector.

That said property is located in the village of Matteawan, and that the amount which should have been collected was $87. That the ratio for property in the village is less than for property outside of the village, that the ratio upon said property was the rate for property outside of the village, and that the difference between the amount collected and the legal tax is $44.

JOHN J. SCHLOSSER.

Sworn to before me, this 11th }
day of Nov., 1890.

J. HERVEY COOK,
Notary Public.

STATE OF NEW YORK, } ss :
DUTCHESS COUNTY.

Amand Miller and Charles E. Bartow being duly sworn, say that they are assessors of the town of Fishkill, and were so doing the years of 1889 and 1890 to date.

That they are well acquainted with property, and the location of property in said town, and whether located in the villages of Matteawan. Fishkill Landing, or in the town of Fishkill.

Deponents also depose and say that there are two tax rates in said town of Fishkill, one for property located in the aforesaid villages, and one for property outside of said villages, was that the rate for property outside of the villages was 131, and for property in the villages, was 87.

That the property mentioned and described as the Tioronda Hat Factory, assessed to Lewis Tompkins, is situated in the village of Matteawan, and should bear the same ratio as other village property. to wit, the ratio 87, and not the ratio of property outside the village, which is 131.

That the said tax so levied and collected as stated herein is excessive in the sum therein stated, as per bill hereto annexed, $44, and should be returned to Lewis Tompkins.

CHAS. E. BARTOW,

AMAND MILLER.

Sworn to before me this 11th day of)
    November, 1890.   (

W. H. WOOD,

Notary Public.

STATE OF NEW YORK,) ss. :
   DUTCHESS COUNTY.   )

William J. Haight being duly sworn, says that he resides at Fishkill Landing, and was collector of taxes of the Town of Fishkill, Dutchess County. N. Y., for the year 1889, and ending March 4, 1890. That he collected the taxes for the said year, and at Matteawan collected the taxes of James Post amounting to the sum of $5.52. That on the tax book of said town there are charged as follows :

James Post, Tax..$5 52

D. H. Post, Tax ....5 52.

That James Post paid his said taxes so assessed to him during said year, but the deponent inadvertently credited the tax so paid to D. H. Post, they both being alike in amount. That the tax so paid should have been credited to James Post and not to D. H. Post, whose tax was not paid to this collector. That deponent in making his return to the County Treasurer returned the tax of James Post as unpaid, and the said County Treasurer has sold the said premises of James Post pursuant to law.

Deponent therefore asks that this Board cancel said tax sale of the premises of said James Post, and the deponent will pay to the County Treasurer the amount of said tax so returned.

W. J. HAIGHT.

Sworn to before me this 15th day }
of November, 1890.

JOHN J. SCHLOSSER,
Notary Public.

The Chair named as additional members of the Committee to collect claims against persons and estates, &c., Messrs. Mylod and Able.

Mr. Dudley offered the following :

Resolved, That in accordance with the requirements of the laws of 1873, Chapter 247, the Supervisors of the respective Towns and Wards are appointed to have charge of the expenses of the burial of honorably discharged soldiers and sailors for the ensuing year, and to serve without compensation.

Resolution adopted.

Mr. Mylod moved that a committee of one be appointed by the Chair, to provide confectionery, &c., for the children at the Home for the Friendless, when the Board visit said Institution.

Motion carried.

Mr. Mylod was named as such Committee.

Mr. Swift moved that a committee of two be appointed by the Chair to bring up the box containing the bills against the County and distribute the same to the several Committees.

Motion carried.

The Chair named as such Committee, Messrs. Swift and Bartlett.

Mr. Vail offered the following :

Resolved, That the Clerk of this Board be, and hereby is requested to present to this Board, in writing, a report of the present number of Lunatics in the several Asylums of the State chargeable to this County for their maintenance, together with a statement of the cost at each Asylum, also stating the number for which the County is being reimbursed wholly or in part.

Said report shall also contain statement of amount of monies collected during the past year or uncollected accounts of previous years.

Resolution adopted.

On motion of Mr. Germond the Board adjourned.

WEDNESDAY, Nov. 19, 1890.
2 P. M.

Board met.

Quorum present.

Mr. Pugsley from the Special Committee to Apportion Grand Jurors, presented the following :

POUGHKEEPSIE, Nov. 19, 1890.

To the Honorable, the Board of Supervisors of Dutchess County :

GENTLEMEN :—Your Special Committee appointed to apportion the number of Grand Jurors to be selected from each Town and Ward, report and recommend the following table. It allowing one Grand Juror for 260 of our population according to last census.

Repectfully submitted,
F. W. PUGSLEY,
JOHN J. MYLOD,
CHAS. HUMPHREY,
Special Committee on Grand Jurors.

TABLE OF GRAND JURORS.

Amenia	9
Beekman	4
Clinton	6
Dover	7
East Fishkill	8
Fishkill	44
Hyde Park	11
La Grange	6
Milan	4
North East	8
Pawling	8
Pine Plains	5
Pleasant Valley	6
Poughkeepsie Town	18
1st Ward City of Poughkeepsie	16
2d " " "	18
3d " " "	13
4th " " "	13
5th " " "	14
6th " " "	13
Red Hook	17
Rhinebeck	13
Stanford	7
Union Vale	4
Washington	11
Wappinger	17
	300

Report adopted.

Mr. Humphrey offered the following :

To the Honorable, the Board of Supervisors of Dutchess County:

We the undersigned Assessors of the Town of Stanford petition your

Honorable body to erase from the assessment the name of Mrs. James D. Miller, assessed for three thousand dollars personal.

STANFORD, Sept. 15th, 1890.

> REUBEN A. HUSTED,
> JOHN H. COX,
> FRANKLIN GERMOND,
> Assessors.

Resolved, That the assessment of Mrs. James D. Miller be stricken from the assessment of Stanford.

Resolution adopted.

Mr. Mylod presented the following :

POUGHKEEPSIE, N. Y., Nov. 19th, 1890.

In pursuance of Chapter 515 of Laws 1886, in relation to selection of papers for publishing Session Laws, we, the undersigned Democratic members of the Board of Supervisors of Dutchess County for the year 1890, hereby designate and select the Poughkeepsie News-Telegraph as the paper for publishing the Session Laws for the coming year.

> JOHN J. MYLOD,
> WM. H. KRIEGER,
> WM. H. AUSTIN,
> SHELDON WING,
> E. WRIGHT VAIL,
> J. A. HERRICK,
> L. D. GERMOND,
> EDWARD STURGESS,
> JOHN C. MILROY,
> ISAAC S. GENUNG,
> EWD. HERRICK,
> G. F. LEE,
> DAVID E. HOWATT,
> CHAS. H. HUMPHREY.

Mr. Pugsley in the Chair.

Mr. Vail moved that the salary of the Jail Physician be fixed at $100, including medicine.

Laid over under the Rule.

Mr. Mylod moved that the salary of the County Sealer be fixed at $25 per year, and the salary of the Janitor be fixed at $2 per day.

Laid over under the Rule.

On motion of Mr. Germond the Board adjourned.

THURSDAY, December 4th, 1890.

10:30 A. M.

Board met.

Quorum present.

Mr. Austin in the Chair.

The Clerk presented the following which was read and accepted, and on motion of Mr. Pugsley the Special Committee was discharged.

To the Honorable, the Board of Supervisors of the County of Dutchess :

GENTLEMEN :—Your Special Committee appointed by the Board of 1889, under the following Resolutions :

Resolved, " That a Special Committee of three be appointed by the Chair, of which the Clerk of the Board shall be named as one, for the purpose of collecting any claim that the County of Dutchess may have against persons, counties and estates, and that they be authorized and empowered to do all things necessary for the collection of the same."

Resolved, " That the Chairman of this Board act as a member of such Committee."

Would respectfully report :

That said Committee met on the 15th day of December, 1889, and from the various matters presented to them, found it necessary to employ Counsel, and on said date employed Hon. Horace D. Hufcut as such, and on said date, your Committee also appointed the Clerk of the Board, to present bills and receipt the same in the name of said Committee.

Also to visit the Asylums in the State and to act for said Committee with the same authority as conferred upon said Committee by the Board of 1889.

The total amount collected and paid to the County Treasurer to Nov. 1st, 1890, is $4,933.88, as will appear by his report in detail. There is still due to Jan. 1, 1891, for which bills have been rendered, the sum of $1,527.84, making a total of $6,460.92, collections for the year.

Your committee, assisted by the Superintendent of the Poor, have had transferred and discharged from the Asylums of the State, 12 patients that were a charge upon the county, whose residence, upon investigation was found to be in other Counties and States.

There has been committed to Asylums as a charge upon the county during the year, 74. Patients discharged and died, 32. Increase during the year, 44.

Your Hon. body will see from the above figures the alarming increase in the number of insane to be cared for, and as informed by one of the physicians in charge of one of the State Asylums, that one of the causes of the increase was alcoholic insanity, and that one quarter of the insane in the Asylums of the State were committed for said cause.

Your Committee in view of the above facts would recommend that your Honorable body take some action in regard to commitments of patients suffering from alcoholic insanity, and that all such patients be temporarily committed to the Almshouses in the County, if the same can be done without conflicting with the State Law.

Your Committee would also call your attention to Act passed by the Legislature of 1889, by which the care and maintenance of insane shall be a State charge, but from information received said Act cannot be effective until additions are made to the several State Asylums, and that Counties shall make appropriations as formerly.

We would also state in relation to the above mentioned Act that several Counties of the State are making an effort to have the said Act repealed by the Legislature this Winter. Your Committee from information received believe that the change proposed by said Act, will increase the cost for care of the insane considerably.

Your Committee would earnestly urge and recommend the designation of some Committee or person to continue the investigation of this matter as we are aware that it requires daily attention.

All of which is respectfully submitted,

JAMES H. RUSSELL,
CLINTON J. ROCKEFELLER,
HENRY BOSTWICK,
SMITH HEROY,
Committee.

To the Honorable Board of Supervisors of Dutchess County :

I report that I have been acting by the appointment of your Committee, to collect in proper cases, for Board and Maintenance of the insane persons supported by Dutchess County, at the several state asylums, and also to prevent improper commitments to be paid for by Dutchess County. As the attorney and advisor of such Committee since January, 1890, I have acted as they have directed within the law.

There is one case now pending in the Supreme Court, against the County of Ulster. Ulster County has appeared by its attorney and answered, denying its liability. It has been thought best to await the action of the Board of Supervisors of Ulster County, at their now annual session, as a settlement of the matter is hoped for.

A great number of cases have been examined, searches made and much work done by the committee and its attorney, and considerable amounts collected. This work has resulted in profit to the County, and should be continued in some form, as the public expenses for support of lunatics by the County, has been for years past greatly increased, and it will be a saving to the County to give the matter close attention.

Nov. 18th 1890.

Respectfully Yours,
HORACE D. HUFCTT,
Attorney.

Mr. Humphrey offered the following :

To the Honorable, the Board of Supervisors of Dutchess County :

GENTLEMEN :—Your Committee would report the following names of persons who are liable for unworked highway labor and would recommend that the amounts named below be added to the assessment rolls of the various towns as named :

	No. Days.	Amount.
John E. Reese, Dover.	7	$10 50
Herman Elsworth, Dover.	1½	2 25
Lewis Allen, N. R., Hyde Park.	9	13 50
Elizabeth Monfort, LaGrange.	1	1 50
Savings Bank, Po'keepsie, Pine Plains.	8	12 50
James Lewis, Pine Plains .	1½	2 25
Jacob Clum, Red Hook.	9½	14 25
Jerome Lyke, Red Hook.	1½	2 25
R. C. Fulton, Red Hook.	1½	2 25
Susan Myers, Wappingers.	2	3 00
Polhemus Myers, Wappingers.	29	43 50

All of which is respectfully submitted,

CHAS. H. HUMPHREY,
ISAAC S. GENUNG,
CYRUS F. MOREHOUSE.

Report adopted.

Mr. Vail moved that Benjamin Lester be allowed $2.70 for excessive tax, and the same be levied and assessed upon the Town of Pleasant Valley.

Motion carried.

Mr. Germond offered the following :

Resolved, That the County Judge be authorized to purchase for the County, Cook's Annotated Criminal and Penal Code and Birdseye Statutes.

Resolution adopted.

Mr. Scutt offered the following :

Resolved, That the sum of $2,717.09, be levied and assessed upon the Town of North East, for highway assessment, exclusive of the Village of Millerton, and the same be made payable to the Commissioners of Highways.

Also the sum of $218 be levied and assessed upon said Town, for bridges, and the same made payable to Commissioners of Highways.

Resolution adopted.

Mr. Vail, That the Clerk of this Board be, and hereby is, authorized to communicate with the Managers of the Gallaudet Home for Deaf Mutes, located in this County, to this effect:

First. That this Board does not see it to be within its proper powers to make any money value donation to the institution as asked.

Second. This Board however does express its willing-ness to pay board for the number of inmates receiving the benefits of the institution, which upon examination are found to be properly residents of this County, and at the price as is charged by other institutions of like character, and that a bill for such maintenance will re-ceive the auditing of this Board for its payment.

Ayes and nays called.

Ayes—Bartlett, Dudley, Pugsley, Swift, Vail—5.

Nays—Able, Andrews, Genung, Germond, Gray, E Herrick, J. A. Herrick, Humphrey, Morehouse, Mylod, Rodgers, Sturgess, Wing, Wood—14.

Ayes 5.

Nays 14.

Motion lost.

Mr. Mylod in the Chair.

Mr. Germond offered the following.

Resolved. That the sum of $200 be levied and assessed upon each of the Assembly Districts of this County, and the same made payable to Messrs. W. R. Anderson and J. A. Vandewater, School Commissioners.

Resolution adopted.

Mr. Pugsley moved to adjourn.

Motion carried.

———

THURSDAY, December 4th, 1890.

1:30 P. M.

Board met.

Quorum present.

Mr. Austin in the Chair.

Mr. Humphrey from the Committee on Roads and Bridges presented the following :   ·

NEW HAMBURGH, Nov. 10th, 1890.

To the Board of Supervisors:

REPORT OF KEEPER OF DRAKE DRAW BRIDGE.

Number of times drawing Drake Bridge for year, 1,546. I hereby make application for keeper of bridge for the year 1891.

Yours respectfully,

PETER H. BROWER,

Keeper.

To the Honorable, Board of Supervisors of the County of Dutchess ;

GENTLEMEN :—The undersigned who was appointed Superintendent of Drake Draw Bridge by the Board of 1889, would respectfully report that he has expended for repairs to said bridge the sum of $111.84 for the following vouchers, viz. :

Robt. J. Stuart	45 33
John G. Harris	11 25
H. Vanostrand	1 50
Caldwell & Garrison	5 75
Millard & Son	48 01
	$111 84

and respectfully ask to be reimbursed to said amount.

I herewith present the report of the keeper Peter H. Brower, who is very attentive to his duties as such, and would recommend that he be re-appointed.

I would report the Bridge in fair working condition.

All of which is respectfully submitted.

P. A. M. VAN WYCK,

Superintendent.

Report accepted and filed.

Mr. Humphrey moved that P. A. M. Van Wyck, be allowed the sum of $111.84 for disbursements made by him for repairs to Drake Draw Bridge, and the same be levied and assessed upon the County.

Laid over under the Rule.

Mr. Andrews moved that the sum of ($10.65) ten dollars $\frac{65}{100}$ be levied and assessed upon the Town of Union Vale, and the same paid to Judson A. Denton, Justice of the Peace of the Town of Beekman.

On motion of Mr. Able, the above was referred to Committee on Justice's accounts for investigation as to the liability of the said Town of Union Vale.

Mr. Scutt offered the following :

Resolved, That the sum of $10.20 be levied and assessed upon the Town of North East for returning election returns for collection, and the

same be made payable to John Scutt, also the sum of $15.00 believed
and assessed upon said Town, and the same be made payable to O. W.
Wakeman for filing election returns to County Clerk's office.

Resolutions adopted.

Mr. Rogers presented the following :

The Standing Committee on Coroners' and Physicians' accounts, move
that the fees of Physicians in cases of lunacy, Post Mortems and Autopsies be fixed by the Board.

Ayes and nays called.

Ayes—Able, Andrews, Genung, Germond, Gray, E.
Herrick, J. A. Herrick, Howatt, Humphrey, Morehouse,
Rodgers, Scutt, Sturgess, Swift, Wing—15.

Nays—Bartlett, Mylod, Pugsley, Vail—4.

Ayes 15.

Nays 4.

Motion carried.

Mr. Gray moved that the above motion be reconsidered.

Ayes and nays called.

Ayes—Andrews, Bartlett, Genung, Germond, Gray,
Herrick, J. A., Howatt, Humphrey, Morehouse, Mylod,
Pugsley, Scutt, Swift, Vail, Wood—15.

Nays—Able, Herrick, E. Rodgers, Sturgess, Wing—5.

Motion carried.

Mr. Pugsley moved that further action on this matter
be postponed indefinitely.

Mr. Gray moved that Mr. Pugsley's motion be laid on
the table.

Ayes and nays called.

Ayes—Able, Andrews, Bartlett, Germond, Gray, Howatt, Morehouse, Pugsley—8.

Nays—Genung, Herrick, E.,Herrick, J. A.,Humphrey, Mylod, Rodgers, Scutt, Sturgess, Swift, Vail, Wing, Wood—12.

Motion lost.

Mr. Gray called up the original motion and moved its adoption.

Ayes and nays called.

Ayes—Able, Genung, E. Herrick, J. A. Herrick, Rodgers, Sturgess, Wing—7.

Nays—Andrews, Bartlett, Germond, Gray, Howatt, Humphrey, Morehouse, Mylod, Pugsley, Scutt, Swift' Vail, Wood—13.

Motion lost.

M. Howatt offered the following :

Resolved, That this Board do hereby refuse to audit, grant or allow any charge, allowance or grant of any monies to any Person, Persons, Incorporations, Societies or for any purpose whatever except by regularly appointed Clerks, the Reporters who report our daily proceedings and otherwise as directed and provided for by Law.

Ayes and nays called.

Ayes—Messrs. Able, Andrews, Genung, Germond, E. Herrick, J. A. Herrick, Howatt, Humphrey, Morehouse, Mylod, Scutt, Sturgess, Vail and Wing—14.

Nays—Messrs. Dudley, Rodgers, Swift and Wood—4.

Ayes 14.

Nays 4.

Resolution adopted.

Mr. Bartlett offered the following.:

Resolved, That the Committee on Coroners' and Physicians' accounts, recommend a scale of fees for lunacy examinations, Post Mortems and Autopsies for this Board to establish.

Mr. J. A. Herrick moved that the above resolution be laid upon the table.

Ayes and nays called.

Ayes—Gray, Herrick, J. A., Mylod, Pugsley, Scutt, Vail, Wood—7.

Nays—Able, Andrews, Bartlett, Dudley, Genung, Germond, Herrick, E., Howatt, Humphrey, Morehouse, Rodgers, Sturgess, Swift—13.

Motion lost.

Ayes and nays called upon the original resolution.

Ayes—Able, Andrews, Bartlett, Genung, Germond, Gray, Rodgers—7.

Nays—Dudley, E. Herrick, J. A.. Herrick, Howatt, Humphrey, Morehouse, Mylod, Pugsley, Scutt, Sturgess, Swift, Vail, Wing, Wood—14.

Resolution lost.

Mr. Humphrey moved that P. A. M. Van Wyck, of New Hamburgh, be and hereby is, re-appointed Superintendent of Drake Draw Bridge, for the year 1891.

Motion carried.

Mr. Humphrey moved that Peter H. Brower be retained as keeper of Drake Draw Bridge for the ensuing year at a salary of $350.

Laid over under the Rule.

On motion of Mr. Pugsley the Board adjourned.

THURSDAY, November 20th, 1890.

10:30 A. M.

Board met.

Quorum present.

Minutes read and approved.

Mr. Swift from the Special Committee to bring up the box containing the bills against the County, presented the following:

We, the undersigned committee of two appointed to open the county box and distribute the bills therein to the respective committees, do hereby respectfully announce that such work has been done, and this Committee very respectfully recommends that said committees use unusal care in examining said bills, especially those of coronors and physicians.

WM. H. BARTLETT,

CHAS. W. SWIFT,

Committee.

On motion of Mr. Williams the report was accepted and Committee discharged.

Mr. E. Herrick offered the following:

Resolved, That Hiram Sleight be allowed $10 for services as janitor during the Canvass, and the same be paid from the Contingent fund.

Resolution adopted.

Mr. Genung moved that the salary of the Clerk of this Board be fixed at the sum of ($600), and the same be paid from the Contingent Fund.

Laid over under the Rules.

Mr. Williams moved that the Special Committee appointed by the Board of 1889, to have an act passed by

the legislature to maintain Drake Draw Bridge as a
State Charge, report as soon as convenient.

Motion carried.

Mr. E. Herrick offered the following :

Resolved, That the sum of two hundred and fifty dollars ($250) for
roads and bridges, be levied and assessed upon the Town of Clinton, and
the same be made payable to the Commissioners of Highways.

Resolution adopted.

Mr. Genung moved that the sum of two hundred and
fifty dollars ($250) be levied and assessed upon Town of
East Fishkill for Roads and Bridges. And the same
be made payable to the Commissioners of Highways.

Motion carried.

Mr. Gray offered the following :

Resolved, That a Summary of the Reports of the Justices of the
Peace of the County, the amount of the fines they have received, and to
whom paid, be spread upon the minutes of the Board.

Resolution adopted.

Mr. Morehouse moved that the sum of two hundred
and fifty dollars ($250) be levied and assessed upon the
Town of Milan, for roads and bridges, and the same be
made payable to the Commissioners of Highways.

Motion carried.

The hour having arrived for the special order, that
being the presentation of Town Abstracts.

Mr. Andrews moved that the sum of $1,488.33 be levied
and assessed upon the Town of Beekman for Town Allowances.

Motion carried.

Mr. Wing moved that the sum of $1,732.04 be levied and assessed upon the Town of Dover for Town Allowances.

Motion carried.

Mr. Austin moved that the sum of $1,116.70 be levied and assessed upon the Town of La Grange for Town Allowances.

Motion carried.

Mr. Morehouse moved that the sum of $1,625.55 be levied and assessed upon the Town of Milan for Town Allowances.

Motion carried.

Mr. Scutt moved that the sum of $579.26 be levied and assessed upon the Town of North East for Town Allowances.

Motion carried.

Mr. Lee moved that the sum of $3.819.03 be levied and assessed upon the Town of Pawling for Town Allowances.

Motion carried.

Mr. Sturges moved that the sum of $3,254.14 be levied and assessed upon the Town of Red Hook for Town Allowances.

Motion carried.

Mr. John A. Herrick moved that the sum of $1,258.34 be levied and assessed upon the Town of Pine Plains for Town Allowances.

Motion carried.

Mr. Milroy moved that the sum of $7,916.56 be levied and assessed upon the Town of Rhinebeck for Town Allowances.

Motion carried.

Mr. Humphrey moved that the sum of $3,445.18 be levied and assessed upon the Town of Stanford for Town Allowances.

Motion carried.

Mr. Able moved that the sum of $1,393.93 be levied and assessed upon the Town of Union Vale for Town Allowances.

Motion carried.

Mr. Germond moved that the sum of $3,083.95 be levied and assessed upon the Town of Washington for Town Allowances.

Motion carried.

Mr. Mylod called up the Resolutions fixing salaries of Janitor and County Sealer, and moved their adoption.

Ayes and nays called.

All members present voting in favor thereof.

Ayes 19.

Resolution adopted.

Mr. Vail called up Resolution, fixing Salary of Jail Physician, and moved its adoption.

Ayes and nays called.

All members present voting in favor thereof.

Ayes 21.

Resolution adoption.

Mr. Vail offered the following:

Resolved, That the sum of $250 be levied and assessed upon the Town of Pleasant Valley for Roads and Bridges, and the same be made payable to the Commissioners of Highways of said Town.

Also, the sum of $100 be levied and assessed upon said Town for the Poor Fund, and the same be made payable to the Supervisor of said Town.

Resolution adopted.

Mr. Milroy moved that the sum of $250 be levied and assessed upon the Town of Rhinebeck for Roads and Bridges the same be made payable to the Commissioners of Highways.

Motion carried.

Mr. Able moved that the sum of $250 be levied and assessed upon the Town of Union Vale for Roads and Bridges, and the same be made payable to the Commissioners of Highways of said Towns.

Motion carried.

Mr. Gray moved that the sum of $500 be levied and assessed upon the Town of Pokeepsie, for the repairs to Bridges, and the same made payable to the President of the Board of Highway Commissioners of said town, and the sum of $3,500 be levied and assessed upon said Town, exclusive of the Village of Wappingers Falls, and that the same be made payable to the President of the Board of Commissioners of Highways of said Town.

Motion carried.

On motion of Mr. Pugsley the Board adjourned.

THURSDAY, Nov. 20th, 1890.

1:30 P. M.

Board met.

Quorum present.

Mr. Austin in the Chair.

Mr. Mylod, the Special Committee appointed by the Board of 1889, to have an Act by the Legislature to relieve this County of the expense of maintaining the Drake Draw Bridge, reported that he visited Albany on March 31st, 1890, and from information received, that there was no opposition to an Act that had been presented for said purpose, and said Act passed the Assembly, and failed to pass the Senate, "for want of time." Your Committee would recommend that a Committee be appointed to urge the passage of said Act this winter.

Mr. Bartlett moved that a Committee of three be appointed to attend to the above matter.

Motion carried.

Chair named as such Committee Messrs. Lee, Mylod and Wood.

Mr. Germond offered the following :

DUTCHESS COUNTY, ss. :

Geo. Wood, of the Town of Wappinger, being duly sworn, says that the following account is correct, and that such services or disbursements have been made or rendered, and that no part thereof has been paid or satisfied.

GEORGE WOOD.

Sworn to before me. this 20th)
    day of Nov., 1890.   )

S. HEROY,

Clerk of the Board of Supervisors.

POUGHKEEPSIE, N. Y., Nov. 20, 1890.

THE COUNTY OF DUTCHESS:

To WOOD & MORSCHAUSER, DR.

To services in preparing and trying case in claim of County agst. estate of Alfred Munger, deceased, and fees paid Referee.

Services........................ ....$25 00

Paid Horace D. Hufcut, Referee................................. .... 25 00

$50 00

Received Payment.

Resolved, That the sum of $50 be levied and assessed upon the county, exclusive of the city, for the payment of the above bill.

Laid over under the Rule.

Mr. Andrews moved that the sum of $250 be levied and assessed upon the Town of Beekman for Roads and Bridges, and the same be made payable to the Commissioners of Highways.

Motion carried.

Mr. J. A. Herrick moved that the sum of two hundred and fifty dollars be levied and assessed upon the Town of Pine Plains for Roads and Bridges, and the same be made payable to the Commissioners of Highways.

Motion carried.

On motion of Mr. Pugsley the Board adjourned.

FRIDAY, Nov. 21, 1890.
10:30 A. M.

Board met.

Quorum present.

Mr. Austin in the Chair.

Mr. Pugsley presented the following:

POUGHKEEPSIE, N. Y., Nov. 26, 1889.

In pursuance of Chapter 515 of Laws 1886, in relation to selection of papers for publishing Session Laws, we, the undersigned Republican members of the Board of Supervisors of Dutchess County for the year 1890, hereby designate and select the Poughkeepsie Weekly Eagle as the paper for publishing the Session Laws for the coming year.

> F. W. PUGSLEY,
> GUILFORD DUDLEY,
> JOHN SCUTT,
> CHAS. WILLIAMS.
> J. U. ABLE,
> C. W. SWIFT,
> GEORGE WOOD,
> WM. H. BARTLETT,
> J. B. ROGERS,
> AUG. B. GRAY,
> CYRUS F. MOREHOUSE,
> K. ANDREWS.

Mr. Austin moved that the sum two hundred and fifty dollars ($250) be levied and assessed upon the Town of La Grange for Roads and Bridges, and the same be made payable to the Commissioners of Highways.

Motion carried.

Mr. Sturgess offered the following :

Resolved, That the sum of $234 be levied and assessed upon the County, to reinburse the Town of Red Hook, for deficiency arising from assessment of the Cheney Towing Co., in said Town.

Laid over under the Rule.

Mr. Howatt offered the following :

Resolved, That the sum of fifteen hundred and seven 50-100 ($1507.50) be levied and assessed on the Town of Hyde Park for Town allowances.

Resolution adopted.

Mr. Genung moved that the sum of $2,036.01 be levied and assessed upon the Town of East Fishkill for Town Allowances.

Motion carried.

Mr. Genung called up the Resolution fixing the salary of the Clerk and moved its adoption.

Ayes and nays called.

All members present voting in favor thereof.

Ayes 20.

Resolution adopted.

On motion of Mr. Pugsley the Board adjourned to meet Monday, Dec. 1st, at 2 p. m.

———

MONDAY, Dec. 1, 1890.
2 P. M.

Board met.

Quorum present.

Mr. Austin in the Chair.

Minutes read and approved.

The Clerk presented the following, which was read and on motion of Mr. Germond was laid upon the table until Thursday, 11 a. m.

The undersigned lady Managers of the Gallaudet Home for Deaf Mutes, respectfully present the following facts to your Honorable Board, which they deem entitles the Home to the consideration of your Board, in the matter of the continuation of the appropriation of previous years :

The Home is supported entirely by charity. More than *two-thirds* of its *income* is derived from the generosity of those living out of this County   *All its income* is expended in this County.

Of the sum received from you, at *least a quarter* is returned into the County Treasurer for taxes. There are among its inmates, *three persons* who are residents of Dutchess County, who must necessarily become inmates of your Alms House, if this home did not afford them a refuge, and their support this year has cost the Institution the sum or *four hundred and seventy dollars and twelve cents.*

MISS ALLEN,
MRS. R. FULTON CRARY,
MARY S. SWIFT,
MRS. JOHN THOMPSON,
MRS. CHARLES ROBERTS,
MRS. EDWARD H. PARKER,
MRS. JOSEPH B. BISBEE,
MRS. D. PORTER LORD,
MISS E. P. NELSON.

To the Honorable, the Board of Supervisors of Dutchess County :

GENTLEMEN :—Pursuant to a Resolution of this Board, adopted Nov. 20th, 1890, I would respectfully report that the total amount collected to Nov. 15th, 1890, from persons and estate who are to reimburse the county, wholly or in part, the sum of $4.985.88.

Amount due to Jan. 1st, 1891, for which Bills have been rendered, $1,275.

The number of Patients chargeable to the County who reimburse the same, wholly or in part, is 42.

The whole number of Patients in the several Asylums and Charitable Institutions of the State, chargeable to the County, are as follows :

Hudson River State Hospital.. 118
Willard Asylum.. 91
Binghamton Asylum.. 33
Auburn Asylum... 4
Utica Asylum.. 2
Middletown Asylum.. 1
Colored Orphan Asylum.. 6
N. Y. Institution for Blind, Batavia... 5
State Asylum for Idiots, Syracuse.. 4
Brunswick Home, Amityville... 1
St. Joseph's Institute, Fordam... 5
N. Y. Institute for Deaf and Dumb, N. Y. City.................................. 7
Home for the Friendless, Poughkeepsie.. 13

Total.. 300

The amounts collected during the past year on uncollected accounts of former years, is $1,514.03.

There is still in the hands of the Special Committee appointed by the Board of 1889, uncollected accounts of former years amounting to about $2,900.

All of which is respectfully submitted. '

SMITH HEROY,

Clerk.

Report accepted and filed.

FISHKILL, New York, November 21st, 1890.

To the Honorable, the Board of Supervisors of the County of Dutchess, New York:

GREETING :—I herewith submit a statement and inventory of all moneys and other valuable things found with or upon all persons on whom Inquests have been held by and before me, the subscriber, one of the

Coroners, in and for the County of Dutchess, between the first day of November 1889, and November 1st, 1890 :

Upon whom found.	Articles found.	Disposition thereof.
Patrick Holigan $2 30		Paid County Treasurer.
Donato Dantono........................ 5 23		.. ..
Michael Swiska........................ 20		.. ..
M. Mc Voy.............................. 50		.. ..
Spencer Mead....................... 2 00		Joshua Mead, father of deceased.
Michael Murray 7 75		" County Treasurer.
collected wages due Murray from Frank Timothy.............22 03		" "
John Gatz............................. 01		" "

WILLIAM J. CONKLIN,

Coroner.

STATE OF NEW YORK, ⎱ ss. :
COUNTY OF DUTCHESS. ⎰

William J. Conklin, one of the Coroners of the said County, being duly sworn, says, that the foregoing statement and inventory of all moneys and other valuable things found with or upon all persons on whom inquests have been held, by and before him, within the time specified in such statement and inventory, and of the disposition thereof, is in all respects just and true to the best of his knowledge and belief, and that the moneys and other articles mentioned in such statement and inventory, have been delivered to the Treasurer of the County of Dutchess, and to the legal representatives of the persons mentioned therein, as stated therein.

WILLIAM J. CONKLIN,

Subscribed and sworn to before me this ⎱
November 21st, 1890.   ⎰

SHERWOOD PHILLIPS,

Notary Public.

Report accepted and filed.

Mr. Vail moved that Ordinance No. 4, adopted by the Board of Supervisors of 1877, imposing a tax upon dogs and bitches, be, and the same is hereby re-enacted.

ORDINANCE NO. 4.

An ordinance imposing a tax upon dogs within the several towns of Dutchess County, to provide for the collection and disposition thereof, and to reenact an ordinance passed December, 1877, "entitled an ordinance to provide for taxing dogs and for the collection of said tax, and to create a fund to pay for injuries upon sheep occasioned by dogs, in and for the County of Dutchess."

[This ordinance is made under authority of Chapter 482 of the laws of the Legislature of the State of New York, passed in 1875, and passed December 11, 1890 by the Board of Supervisors, a majority of all its members voting in favor thereof.]

The Board of Supervisors of the County of Dutchess do ordain as follows :

SEC. 1. There shall be annually levied and collected in the several towns of Dutchess County, the following tax upon dogs :

Upon every bitch, owned or harbored by any one or more persons, or by any family, three dollars ; and upon every additional bitch, owned or harbored by the same person, or persons, or family, five dollars. Upon every dog, other than a bitch, owned or harbored by one or more persons, or by any family, one dollar ; and upon every additional dog, other than a bitch, owned or harbored by the same person, or persons, or family, two dollars.

§ 2. The Assessors of each town shall annex to the assessment roll of real and personal estate therein, annually made by them, the name of each person or persons owning or harboring any dog or bitch, together with the number thereof so owned or harbored by such person, or persons ; and the Board of Supervisors shall impose the taxes thereon, in pursuance of Section One of this Act, at the same time that the other taxes in said county are imposed, and incorporate in their warrant for the collection of such other taxes a provision for the collection thereof in the same manner in which such other taxes are directed to be collected.

§ 3. The collector of each town shall collect the sums of money so specified as the dog tax at the same time, in the same manner, and with the like authority in all respects, as in the collection of the other taxes imposed by said Board of Supervisors ; and shall pay the same to the Supervisor of his town, first retaining therefrom a commission of ten per cent, upon all sums so collected by him for his fees. The same remedies to enforce such collection and payment of the money collected may be had against such collectors and their sureties as is provided in the case of other taxes collected or to be collected by them.

§ 4. Each Collector shall, before receiving such tax list and warrant and within eight days after being notified of the amount of such dog tax to be collected, execute and deliver to the Supervisor of his town a separate bond, with one or more sureties, to be appproved by such Supervisor, in a penalty of double the amount of such taxes, conditioned for the faithful execution of his duties as such Collector, and the payment by him of all moneys so collected and to be paid by him.

§ 5. The moneys collected in the respective towns under this ordinance shall constitute a fund in and for such towns respectively, for the payment of damages done to sheep therein by dogs.

Except that any person or persons may present within one year after paying such tax on any dog, dogs or bitch, to the Supervisor of the town in which such tax was paid, an affidavit showing that for one year previous to the payment of such tax he or she or they did not own any dog, dogs or bitch, and did not within said period, keep or harbor on the premises under his or her control, any such dog, dogs or bitch, for which he or she or they were assessed, and present to the said Supervisor satisfactory evidence that the said tax has been paid, then the said Supervisor shall be authorized to refund to such person or persons out of the dog fund of the said Town the amount of dog tax so erroneously assessed, upon his filing in the Town Clerk's Office of said Town the affidavit and such other evidence as he may have, showing such erroneous assessment.

§ 6. All acts and parts of acts inconsistent with this act are hereby repealed.

§ 7. This act shall take effect immediately,

STATE OF NEW YORK, }
    DUTCHESS COUNTY, } ss:
    SUPERVISOR'S ROOM. }

I have compared the preceding with the original ordinance on file in this office and do hereby certify that the same is a correct transcript therefrom and of the whole of said original.

ATTEST.   SMITH HEROY,
    [L. S.]   .   Clerk.

Mr. Able moved as an Amendment that the whole matter be referred to the Committee on Legislative Enactments.

Amendment carried.

The Clerk presented the following :

To the Board of Supervisors of Dutchess County ;

GENTLEMEN :—You are respectfully invited by the Fabian Society of this City, to visit their Rooms on Tuesday evening, Dec. 2d, 1890, to attend a musicale to be given by the members of said Society

Respectfully yours,

WM. F. Mc GEEN,

Corresponding Secretary.

Invitation accepted.

Mr. Wood moved that the sum of two hundred and fifty dollars ($250) be levied and assessed upon the Town of Wappinger for Roads and Bridges, and the same be made payable to the Commissioners of Highways.

Motion carried.

Mr. Bartlett offered the following :

Resolved, That a Committee of Three be appointed by the Chair, on Public Buildings outside of the City.

Resolution adopted.

The Chair named Messrs. Germond, Wing and Bartlett as such Committee.

On motion of Mr. Pugsley the Board adjourned.

TUESDAY, December 2d, 1890.

10:30 A. M.

Board met.

Quorum present.

Mr. Austin in the Chair.

The Clerk presented and read the following, which was, on motion of Mr. Pugsley referred to Committee on Justices' Accounts.

To the Honorable, the Board of Supervisors of Dutchess County:

Pursuant to the requirements of Law, I have the Honor to report that the whole number of criminal proceedings in the Recorder's Court of the City of Poughkeepsie, from the first day of December, 1889, to the first day of December, 1890, are 745. Of the said number 40 are in relation to felonies, and chargeable upon the County at large, and 705 are for misdemeanors, and are chargeable to the City of Poughkeepsie.

The amount of 705-745 of $1,500. ....$1,419 57

    is chargeable to the city.

And 40-745 of $1,500... 80 43

    is chargeable to the County and payable to the City.

                                                                       $1,500 00

Dated Dec. 1, 1890.

Respectfully submitted,

A. B. SMITH,

Recorder of the City of Poughkeepsie.

Mr. Mylod, from the Committee on County Treasurer's accounts, presented the report of the County Treasurer, which was read and referred to Committee on Treasurer's accounts, and the Clerk was ordered to have 50 copies printed for the use of the Board.

Office of the Treasurer of Dutchess Co., }
POUGHKEEPSIE, Nov. 1st, 1890.

To the Honorable, the Board of Supervisors of Dutchess County:

GENTLEMEN :—I herewith present the following abstract of my accounts as County Treasurer for the year ending with the date of this report.

The items will be found herein, accompanied with the proper vouchers.

Cash on hand Dec. 1st, 1889,		$ 6,021 41
Total receipts .		329,549 13
		$335,570 54
Total payments,	$321.249 42	
Balance,	14,321 02	
		$335,570 54

Respectfully submitted,

ISAAC W. SHERRILL,

County Treasurer.

Receipts.

Balance on hand reported Dec. 1st, 1889,	$6,021	41
Charles Scott, tax sale, Wappinger,	3	39
Receipts from Armory,	72	80
Note, Farmers & Manufacturers Bank	7,000	00
School Tax Dist. No. 12, P. Valley,	20	20
Note, Farmers & Manufacturers Bank,	3,000	00
" " " "	5,000	00
Interest on Deposits,	64	30

Rent, Barber Shop, Court House,	4 00
School Dist. No. 6, Po'keepsie,	13 96
Tax Sale, Redemption Church Immaculate Conception, Amenia, 1888,	25 86
Cash from Dr. Conklin, Coroner in re D. Montano,	5 23
Fine, E. C. Bloomer,	40 00
" F. Sweet p,	30 00
" Cookingham,	20 00
Banks Brothers (over payment),	21 00
Rent, Court House, Barber Shop,	4 00

Taxes Collected to April 1st, 1890.

Amenia,	$9,043 25
Beekman,	3,232 39
Clinton,	5,759 98
Dover,	7,081 90
East Fishkill,	7,636 77
Fishkill,	26,199 58
Hyde Park,	12,904 66
LaGrange,	6,925 14
Milan,	3,559 90
North East	9,498 04
Pawling,	9,266 01
Pine Plains,	5,111 95
Pleasant Valley,	6,226 00
Poughkeepsie,	14,617 54
Poughkeepsie City,	74,769 37
Red Hook,	17,948 37
Rhinebeck,	16,491 77

Stanford,	8,227	65
Union Vale,	3,920	03
Wappinger,	8,983	54
Washington,	9,362	75
Corporation Tax Fees Paid Collectors,	350	75
Fine, Egbert Tripp,	40	00
School Apportionment from State Treas.,	8,256	45
Fees on State Tax,	500	00
Rent, Barber Shop,	4	00
Interest on Deposits,	21	38
School Money, Dist. No. 6, Dover,	48	08
Rent, Court House,	4	00
Interest, F. & M. Bank,	271	98
" Po'k "	118	46
" City "	46	63
Taxes collected to July 1st, 1890,	10,331	34
School Tax, Dist. No. 4, Red Hook,	15	15
Redemption Tax Sale '88, B. T. Shelden, Hyde Park,	36	23
Redemption Tax Sale '88, Pat Murray, Fish-kill,	17	98
Rent, Barber Shop,	4	00
School Tax, Dist. No. 4. North East,	21	88
Fine, Albert Paul,	50	00
" Charles E. Knapp,	50	00
" George B. Abell,	50	00
" Caroline Musterman,	50	00
Redemption Tax Sale, '88, H. Bowman, Fish-kill,	5	10
Interest on Deposits,	14	35
School Tax, Dist. No. 4, Rhinecliff,	113	34
" " " " 2, Pine Plains,	15	10

Redemption Tax Sale, 1888, M. Alexander,
Fishkill, 4 03
Advertising Tax Sales, 128 00
Filing Certificates, Tax Sales, 7 50
Taxes collected to Oct. 1st, 1890, 927 34
Rent, Court House basement, 4 00
H. L. Cookingham, coroner, money found on
body, .99
School Tax, Dist. No. 5, P. Val., Ancram, and
Galatin, 87 22
School Tax, Dist. No. 1, Pine Plains, 27 81
"   "   " 3, Stanford, 53 23
"   "   " 12, " 44 05
"   "   " 10, " 30 77
"   "   " 6, Red Hook, 10 41
"   "   " 6, Rhinebeck, 27 77
"   "   " 2, Stanford, 69 14
"   "   " 2, North East, 37 12
Fine C. W. Hignell, 7 50
School Tax, Dist. 2, Stanford, 41 80
"   "   " 12, Rhinebeck, 28 73
"   "   " 3, North East, 64 70
"   "   " 8, Clinton, Washington
and Stanford, 15 18
"   "   " 5, Red Hook, 43 86
"   "   " 4, " 16 37
"   "   " 3, Milan, Gal. & Clerm't, 57 95
"   "   " 4, Stanford, 28 65
"   "   " 2, Pine Plains, 56 85
"   "   " 2, North East, 55 05
Fine, People vs. Pulver, 100 00

Bail Bond, Geo. S. Root, (forfeit),   200 00
School Tax, Dist. No. 3, Red Hook,   423 26
Tax, Dennis H. Post, Fishkill,   6 14
Tax Redemption, John Mahony, Fishkill,   3 58
Tax Redemption, Geo. S. Allen, Fishkill,   2 92
Sale of 20 Bonds ($1,000 each) Canal and
    General Deficiency Fund Loan-Refunding
    Bonds, Principal, $20,000 00
Premium,   105 00
Poor Fund as Pr. Resolution, Board Supervis-
    ors,   175 00

Hudson River State Hospital.

Board Gertrude Halsted to Jan. 1st, 1890,   52 00
"   Betta Martin to Dec. 9, '89,   58 50
"   John H. Traver, to Jan. 1st, 1890,   55 90
"   Amelia Hilliker to Jan. 1st, 1890,   218 40
"   Mary C. Sackett to Jan. 1st, 1890,   218 40
"   Louisa Miller to Jan. 1st, 1890,   27 30
"   Mary Mawha,   27 37
"   Peter Woodfield,   42 00
"   Mary Powers,   10 85
"   Jas. E. Powers,   13 90
"   Jacob Hutton,   150 00
"   Alex. W. McGibben,   80 00
"   B. G. Smith to May 1st, 1890,   27 25
"   Albert Kiowski to Apl. 1st, 1890,   111 40
"   Mary Kimlin to Apl. 17th, 1890,   261 20
"   Betta Martin to March 9th, 1890,   58 50
"   Minerva J. Conklin to Jan. 1st, 1890,   491 40

Board E. Lawrence,	18	00
" Mary Mawha,	27	37
" John H. Traver to Apl. 10th, 1890,	55	90
" Peter Woodfield to Apl. 20th, 1890,	26	65
" Wm. S. Rowe to Aug. 1st, 1890,	64	60
" Bartholomew Myers,	97	05
" B. G. Smith,	27	25
" Louisa Miller to Apl. 1st, 1890,	27	30
" Anna Mackey to July 1st, 1890,	14	70
" Betta Martin to June 9th, 1890,	58	50
" Mary E. Hall,	43	22
" Mrs. A. W. McGibben to July 1st, 1890,	52	00
" Gertrude Halsted to July 1st, 1890,	52	00
" Isaac Aiken,	34	00
" John H. Traver to July 10th, 1890,	55	90
" Catherine Proctor,	10	50
" Anna Mackey,	27	30
" Mary Mawha,	27	37
" John Bonahan,	16	80
" B. G. Smith,	27	25
" Julia Wickes 3 months from Aug. 9th,	54	60
" Louisa Miller Apl. 1st to Sept. 1st,	48	83
" Robert McNulty,	16	80
" John Bonniconem to Oct. 18th, 1890,	16	80
" Peter Woodfield Apl. 20th to Sept. 1,	39	90
" Betta Martin to Sept. 9, 1890,	58	50
" John H. Traver to Oct. 10th, 1890,	55	90
" Michael Hoban to Oct. 3d,	6	30
" Catherine Proctor,	27	30
" Wm. S. Rowe to Nov. 1st,	77	10
" Mary Kimlin to Oct. 1st,	101	85
" Julia Goodheim to Jan. 1st, 1891,	55	25

Binghamton Asylum.

Board Eliza Ferris,   55 19

Willard Asylum.

Board Peter Massoneau to April 1, 1890,	157	60
" Ella Burger,	35	00
" Mrs. Wetzell to April 1st, 1890,	206	99
" Ella Burger,	25	00
" Rebecca Tripp to May 3d, 1890,	135	97
" Catherine Dean,	10	00
" Ella Burger,	25	00
" Catherine Dean,	24	00
" Ella Burger,	22	00
" Peter N. Massoneau to Jan. 1, 1891,	102	65

Fish and Game Protection.

Fine, Tanner & Brown,	8	23
" Harvey Day,	25	00
" Custer & Tompkins,	10	00
" In re Noble, Marsh, Baxter, Leonard, et al.,	30	00
" Gilbert Hunt,	10	00
" Ira Van Vliet,	30	00

Disbursements.

Salary, Clerk Board Supervisors,	$ 600	00
Lansing, Van Keuren & Brown, Court Calenders,	32	50
C. W. Arnold, Tax Sale Redemption, Wappinger,	3	39
Hiram Sleight, Clerk's Order,	10	00
Morgan Lee, Clerk's Order,	25	00
J. W. Pulver, Burial Soldier,	50	00
W. F. Boshart, Printing Report,	19	50
J. P. Wilson, Jail Physician,	25	00
J. W. Pulver, Headstones,	15	00
Laura Middlebrook, Burial and Headstones,	50	00
Geo. Broas, bill,	6	50
George W. Davids, bill,	30	00
Mark DuBois,	30	00
Derrick Brown,	30	00
R. V. Le Ray,	30	00
L. Count Smith, Dist. No. 12, P. Valley,	20	20
Frank Shay, steam fitting Court House,	1,417	00
Court S. Howland,	10	00
Edward Manogue, Janitor,	78	00
George Esselstyne, Clerk's order,	25	00
W. Morgan Lee, Clerk's Order,	25	00
" " " "	21	00
Frank Gilbert, Witness Fees	12	25
J. M. Edwards, Pleasant Valley,	105	76
A. V. Haight, Sixth Ward,	90	00
James H. Ward, Third Ward,	158	00
George Esselstyne, Rhinebeck,	114	28
John W. Stickle, Milan,	113	50

C. J. Rockefeller, Red Hood,	121	60
James II. Russell, Beekman,	· 116	72
Edward Herrick, Clinton,	109	22
Shelden Wing, Dover,	139	00
Isaac Genung, East Fishkill,	108	55
Samuel H. Sanford, Fishkill,	132	73
David E. Howatt, Hyde Park,	92	28
Wm. H. Austin, LaGrange,	114	36
J. A. Pulver, North East,	130	73
Henry Bostwick, Union Vale,	117	25
A. W. Corbin, Pawling,	127	52
John A. Herrick, Pine Plains,	112	02
A. B. Gray, Po'keepsie,	107	16
Charles H. Humphrey, Stanford,	102	98
George Wood, Wappinger,	108	84
L. D. Germond, Washington,	120	74
John J. Mylod, 1st Ward,	90	00
C. W. Swift, 4th Ward,	90	00
W. H. Kreiger, 2nd Ward,	90	00
F. W. Pugsley, 5th Ward,	90	00
Matthews & Whalen, Bill,	28	85
Interest on note, City Bank,	100	00
A. W. Corbin, Com. Drake's Draw,	2	00
L. D. Germond, " " " .	2	00
Geo. Esselstyne " " "	2	00
Henry Bostwick, " " "	2	00
Wm. Bartlett, Amenia,	128	25
Thomas McGlasson, burial Soldier and Head-		
stone,	50	00
W. J. Finch, Burial Soldier and Headstone,	50	00
Bernard McCabe, Bill,	12	00
Smith Heroy, warrant 1225,	325	00

Matthews and Whalen, repairs Court House,		9	15
Charles McCoy, labor,		1	50
J. A. Redfield, burial soldier,		35	00
Po'k News Co., as pr. resolution,		3	50
John Manogue, janitor,		36	00
Dan'l B. Robinson, Dist. 6, Po'k,		13	96
H. Haubennestel,	Warrant 1218	27	00
A. B. Lewis,	" 843	17	00
"	" 1194	21	00
E. V. Vincent,	" 875	19	00
Po'keepsie News Co.,	" 809	769	35
"	" 1263	79	50
Jos. Morschauser,	" 857	4	00
J. H. Titus,	" 882	21	00
Wm. Haubennestel,	" 1214	5	60
Po'keepsie Gas Co.,	" 1127	58	20
" "	" 1217	37	40
E. White,	" 830	86	61
"	" 1275	50	60
"	" 1213	1	50
City of Po'keepsie,	" 1279	104	65
Andrew Bilyou,	" 1136	192	80
E. S. Hoyt,	" 925	30	00
John A. Bayly,	" 878	23	00
Owen Cook,	" 1131	155	77
"	" 1222	6	25
Po'keepsie Steam Cooperage,	" 1169	60	00
W. H. Sheldon,	" 1151	64	78
J. P. Ambler, Assignee,	" 845	20	00
" "	" 943	341	70
" "	" 942	173	76
" "	" 829	7	15
" "	" 848	17	00

J. P. Ambler, Assignee,	Warrant 1223	514	80
W. W. Smith,	" 1164	167	15
J. Trowbridge,	" 873	17	00
A. Doughty, Assignee,	" 1280	72	20
W. Cramer,	" 839	200	00
Trowbridge & Adriance,	" 1181	42	00
Benjamin Joseph's Sons,	" 1186	29	15
J. Parker Heath, Assignee,	"	400	00
Spross, Quigley & Spross,	" 1137	68	00
E. B. Osborne,	" 941	776	18
P. Lambert,	" 876	19	00
H. S. Acker,	" 1188	193	47
Platt & Platt,	" 1262	60	50
"	" 812	814	00
Van Dyne & Mellady,	" 849	45	00
C. Wetzel,	" 1174	7	50
D. C. Anderson,	" 885	23	00
W. J. Reynolds, Assignee,	" 869	240	00
Lansing, Van Keuren & Brown,	" 811	98	40
C. D. Johnson,	" 1173	1	50
Dr. A. Hasbrouck,	" 837	10	00
E. C. Adriance,	" 879	14	00
R. W. Frost,	" 880	23	00
Dr. T. K. Couse,	" 948	40	00
Hugh Morgan,	" 1246	501	40
Frank J. Decker,	" 1180	891	55
C. M. Colwell,	" 1168	113	00
City Nat. Bank,	" 1146	25	00
S. A. Perkins,	" 887	15	00
John Byrnes,	" 1357	158	00
Electric Light Bill (1889)		30	42
" " (1890)		36	67

Po'k Gas Co. Bills (2)			127	00
J. G. Frost,	Warrant	871	208	57
J. H. Keeler,	"	846	5	00
Dr. R. W. Case,	"	863	10	00
Chas. M. Colwell,	Warrant	1143	11	95
F. A. Faust,	"	867	120	00
J. H. Hickok,	"	888	5	00
Vail & Sutton,	"	1138	29	60
L. Haubennestel & Son,	"	1169	50	50
J. L. Melhado, Assignee,	"	841	288	00
Peter Shields,	"	855	4	00
S. D. McIntosh,	"	872	20	00
J. E. Sadler,	"	1125	20	00
J. Benjamin & Son,	"	1216	15	00
D. C. Foster & Son,	"	1219	46	75
J. Benjamin & Son's,	"	1153	32	00
S. H. Brown, Assignee.	"	859	4	00
Van Wyck & Collins, Headstones,			30	00
Note, F. and M. Bank, Dec. 13, '89,			7,000	00
"		22, '88,	3,000	00
"		31, '89,	5,000	00
Interest Feb'y 19, '90,			125	42
Wm. Mould, Headstone,			15	00
Chas. McCoy, labor,			2	75
W. R. Farrington,	Warrant	1149	11	05
Henry Bostwick.	"	1224	17	80
Dr. R. K. Tuthill,	"	860	115	00
Electric Light Co.,	"	1145	212	94
Dr. H. E. Parker,	"	834	60	00
Pokeepsie Rural Cemetery,	"	836	29	00
C. S. Howland,	"	1148	21	00
"	"	1247	9	45

Wilson Hicks,	Warrant	884	14 00
Shurter & Briggs,	"	1220	65 60
"	"	1134	49 05
D. C. Valentine,	"	883	5 00
Dr. H. R. Powell,	"	835	190 00
Jas. Reynolds, Assignee,	"	1157	30 00
Jas. Maher,	"	1130	40 20
Charles Kircher,	"	1221	66 00
Note, City Nat. Bank,			3,000 00
Int. "			66 67
S. J. Farnum,	"	874	23 00
Smith Heroy, indices, Surrogate's Office,			150 00
W. J. Finch, Burial and Headstone,			50 00
A. G. Tobey,	warrant	810	19 00
Thos. Hammond,	"	926	20 00
Chas. W. Belding,	"	831	1,488 02
Jas. Myers,	"	1243	7 45
Millerton Telegram,	"	827	25 00
Chas. Dresser,	"	1242	35 80
Lansing, Van Keuren & Brown,			360 85
Geo. Huntington,	"	1124	10 00
W. H. Austin,	"	1266	27 43
Jas. H. Ward,	"	1267	24 00
" "	"	886	21 00
Geo. Hughes & Son,	"	944	169 05
Jas. J. Dowd,	"	1255	30 00
Alms House Com.,	"	1147	168 57
S. S Peloubet,	"	1174	25 75
W. C. Little & Co.,	"	1163	22 00
Schou & Phillips,	"	1135	120 93
P. H. Ward,	"	1129	590 89
Dut. Co. Book Bindery,	'	825	304 50

Dr. J. P. Wilson,	Warrant	847	300 00
Geo. Hughes,	"	1168	148 65
Albany Penitentiary,	"	1277	48 30
" "	"	1276	2,872 47
Wm. Keys,	"	853	4 00
Dr. H. Angell,	"	922	10 00
M. Shwartz & Co.,	"	1158	1 25
H. A. Brown,	"	1162	10 60
A. G. Gates,	"	1128	12 00
Banks Brothers,	"	1176	50 00
J. S. Bird,	"	932	10 00
Perkins & Brother,	"	1183	105 65
Jas. Donnelly,	"	1227	2 35
W. H. Hopkins,	"	931	10 00
Wm. S. Johnson,	"	1200	45 43
Smith Heroy, Com. on Claims,			37 45
Pine Plains Herald,	"	820	36 00
Pine Plains Register,	"	819	37 00
Geo. G. Johnson,	"	935	10 00
Dr. G. S. Beckwith,	"	934	10 00
H. C. Wilber,	"	933	74 89
J. W. Tipple,	"	1249	1 60
D. B. Ward,	"	861	50 00
Dr. J. S. Wilson,	"	866	10 00
J. M. Haskins,	"	1233	17 20
Eggleston Brothers,	"	950	22 00
S. L. Buckley,	"	1231	83 30
L. H. Rockwell,	"	927	10 00
I. H. Conklin,	"	1204	4 60
Amenia Times,	"	821	36 00
Electric Light Co.,			36 67
W. S. Watson,	"	906	20 00

Jas. Sunderland,	Warrant	1254	15 40
T. J. McGlasson,	"	1059	1 00
Albert Larger,	"	1123	2 00
E. Coffee,	"	1058	1 00
D. F. Davis,	"	952	4 00
D. M. Ormsbee,	"	891	223 00
H. Freer,	"	1079	1 00
G. W. Cornwell,	"	1074	1 00
Eugene O. Sullivan,	"	1122	2 00
Dr. J. E. Moith,	"	895	110 00
Wm. Brown,	"	1003	7 00
Chas. M. Kittridge,	"	953	30 00
B. H. Murphy,	"	1060	1 00
S. B. Westfall,	"	1120	2 00
Willis Van Beuren,	"	1091	3 00
Walter Lemon,	"	1085	1 00
C. B. Bocock,	"	1093	1 00
Fred. Moith,	"	1050	2 00
T. J. McGlasson,	"	907	54 00
Willis Van Beuren,	"	1250	6 85
A. T. Moith,	"	908	17 20
Theo. Moith,	"	1244	13 65
Fishkill Standard,	"	813	28 00
M. Quick,	"	1057	1 00
W. Phelps,	"	1090	1 00
Dr. W. J. Conklin,	"	894	1,039 15
Highland Hospital,	"	1273	500 00
St Joachim's Church,	"	951	42 00
John Clifton,	"	1009	11 00
Jos. Mosher,	"	1049	2 00
W. R. Brown,	"	1005	3 00
G. Ammermen,	"	1012	4 00

A. Townsend,	Warrant	1002	5	00
W. H. Burlingame,	"	1011	4	00
Clayton S. Cole,	"	1118	3	00
Howel! White,	"	898	80	00
Fishkill Printing Ass'n,	"	814	19	50
Dr. O. K. Strong,	"	897	20	00
John Flannery,	"	911	42	00
" "	"	1089	2	00
T. A. Pollard,	"	1104	1	00
Dr. J. H. Doughty,	"	896	85	00
Fishkill Journal,	"	815	28	00
A. W. Underhill,	"	1080	3	00
C. W. Way,	"	1053	2	00
G. W. Bradshaw,	"	1041	1	00
Samuel Rogers,	"	901	12	00
" "	"	1014	12	00
Benjamin Sullivan,	"	1007	7	00
B. F. Fream,	"	1065	5	00
J. C. Sawyer,	"	1013	2	00
E. Conklin,	"	1103	2	00
M. C. Sanford,	"	1008	13	00
H. B. Bevier,	"	1001	7	00
J. B. Whitson,	"	1000	20	00
Jas. McCabe,	"	1054	2	00
Sherwood & Phillips, Assignee,	"	903	2	00
Geo. S. White,	"	1088	2	00
C. B. Bevier,	"	1047	5	00
Sherwood & Phillips,	"	910	49	20
Dr. J. T. Schenck,	"	893	85	00
Levi Hadfield,	"	1251	31	90
Levi Ellis,	"	1253	7	65
" "	"	909	6	95

Chas. Hoysradt,	Warrant	900	67 00
"	"	1039	1 00
W. H. Southard,	"	1006	3 00
Frank Luther,	"	1086	5 00
E. S. Phillips,	"	1043	10 00
Dr. J. O'Reilly,	"	899	20 00
Dr. J. R. Strong.	"	892	20 00
J. S. Hall,	"	1250	11 30
A. R. Tiel,	"	905	20 00
H. T. Kuryz,	"	1051	2 00
Geo. Whiteman,	"	1103	1 00
Peter F. Clark,	"	1082	1 00
W. H. Miller,	"	1042	3 00
Alex. Hamilton,	"	1067	5 00
Jas. Hunt,	"	1055	2 00
J. F. Larger,	"	1106	1 00
J. L. Hall,	"	1066	8 00
Wm. Smith,	"	1070	5 00
"	"	1045	2 00
S. H. Sanford,	"	1046	6 00
Dr. F. T. Hopkins,	"	949	55 00
Wm. H. Wood,	"	1265	72 00
J. W. Taylor.	"	1063	4 00
Richard Schey,	"	1087	3 00
L. L. Inman,		1071	5 00
R. S. Judson,	"	1069	5 00
A. G. Ormsbee,	"	1119	2 00
Howard Ormsbee,	"	1121	2 00
S. H. Parsons,	"	1004	3 00
C. O. Osborne,	"	1064	2 00
B. F. Stowell,	"	1068	5 00
C. Aldridge,	"	1072	1 00

L. W. Perrine,	Warrant	1044	1 00
Dr. W. J. Conklin,	"	1281	10 00
E. S. Haight,	"	1048	2 00
W. F. Weston,	"	1083	5 00
F. Boos,	"	877	19 00
Dr. W. Baxter,	"	947	40 00
Dr. J. McConnell,	"	946	40 00
Dr. J. O. Pingrey,	"	1196	40 00
Supt. N. Y. & Mass. R. R.,	"	1269	40 00
Luckey, Platt & Co.,	"	1187	15 00
W. Van Etten,	"	1240	15 00
W. H. Robinson,	"	939	12 00
M. Knickerbocker,	"	1257	11 00
D. C. Tripp,	"	928	10 00
Dr. L. C. Wood,	"	940	10 00
Geo. T. Howland,	"	921	10 00
J. W. Elsefer,	"	913	10 00
Dr. E. Losee,	"	936	10 00
Dr. Walter Herrick.	"	19	10 00
H. J. Vail, Assignee,	"	956	6 00
J. S. Ackerman,	"	902	5 00
Thomas Way,	"	1111	2 00
S. B. Knox,	"	1109	2 00
P. V. Robinson,	"	1115	2 00
John Sturges,	"	1112	2 00
Richard J. Morris,	"	1114	2 00
John Constantine,	"	1110	2 00
J. S. Ackerman,	"	1113	2 00
Heman Voorhes,	"	1116	2 00
Chas. Whitman,	"	1032	1 00
A. Redfield,	"	1031	1 00
R. E. Lusk & Son,	"	1170	154 60

W. R. Anderson,	Warrant	1271	200 00
Marvin Safe Co ,	"	1184	315 00
Gallaudet Home,	"	1274	500 00
A. L. Husted,	"	1212	16 50
S. H. Williams,	"	1232	60 80
W. O'Reilly,	"	1133	7 18
Henry Stibbs,	"	1144	11 05
Luckey, Platt & Co.,	"	1154	88 71
Barnes Brothers,	"	1160	111 05
Thos. Maher,	"	1261	152 10
G. D. Underhill,	"	1192	2 27
Wappingers Falls Chronicle,	"	822	36 38
Wm. Carroll & Son,	"	1126	100 00
J. C. Milroy,	"	961	1 00
M. Dedrick,	"	969	2 00
C. V. Coon,	"	1210	2 00
Wm. B. Rynders,	"	983	2 00
Thos. Kirley,	"	971	6 00
Thos. E. Hester,	"	970	6 00
James Larry,	"	972	4 00
Wm. J. Larry,	"	978	2 00
M. V. B. Schriver,	"	1211	4 00
Wm. R. Carroll,	"	966	1 00
Geo. W. Custer,	"	968	6 00
Rhinebeck News,	"	817	12 00
James Barbour,	"	975	6 00
E. Herrick,	"	973	6 00
A. M. Traver,	"	962	1 00
Jas. Brice, Jr.,	"	979	2 00
T. H. Moore,	"	964	1 00
W. T. Simmion,	"	982	2 00
A. L. Moore,	"	963	1 00

E. P. Wheeler,	Warrant 980	2 00
Frank Cline,	" 984	2 00
Murray Diedrich,	" 1229 ·	27 60
Rhinebeck Gazette,	" 816	29 50
Wm. M. Sleight,	" 1259	53 35
Martin Hermans,	" 828	87 06
Geo. Esselstyn,	" 1264	38 00
Ephraim Herrick,	" 918	25 00
C. S. Van Etten,	" 917	20 00
Chas. E. Nolan,	" 1260	36 00
F. J. Cornwell,	" 981	2 00
Water Bill, Court House and Jail,		46 94
M. Lamoree,	" 959	1 00
F. E. Stickle,	" 955	1 00
A. L. Stickle,	" 957	1 00
Gideon Dakin,	" 996	2 00
Orrin Wakeman,	" 1278	2 00
Levi P. Hatch,	" 998	2 00
John N. Pulver,	" 994	2 00
L. H. Wright,	" 1195	2 96
B. A. TenEyck,	" 854	5 00
G. A. Noll,	" 1139	7 50
J. M. Corcoran,	" 1215	8 00
Dr. A. F. Hoag,	" 923	10 00
Dr. M. H. Angell,	" 937	10 00
C. L. Bates, Assignee,	" 824	11 25
Wood & Tittamer,	" 1172	13 68
Amaar Wood,	" 851	15 00
Joseph Morschauser,	" 864	26 00
Charles E. Lane,	" 862	30 00
Dr. J. M. Sheedy,	" 890	65 00
Prof. Leroy C. Cooley,	" 838	280 00

J. W. Van Tassel,	Warrant 832	8,639	39
W. A. Tompkins,	" 1238	6	90
J. E. Barrett,	" 1100	1	00
L. Carry,	" 1099	1	00
J. D. White,	" 1098	1	00
D. Kirk,	" 1097	1	00
Isaac Miller,	" 1096	1	00
P. W. Knapp,	" 1095	1	00
D. Knickerson,	" 1094	1	00
Adriance Bartow,	" 1189	3	44
Dr. J. F. Lamb,	" 833	13	00
Edward Wood,	" 850	5	00
Dr. D. A. Knapp,	" 930	20	00
Dennison & Brown,	" 1175	100	00
Diossy & Co.,	" 1177	10	00
Hud. Riv. Tel. Co.,	" 1150	28	00
" " " "	" 1185	52	00
M. S. Reynolds & Brother,	" 1165	307	94
" " "	" 1166	89	75
T. Suwarrow,	" 1142	52	00
Hiland Rose,	" 1230	75	92
John Hoolihan,	" 1245	91	90
" "	" 1252	19	65
John Olivett,	" 1209	7	40
Thos. A. Guerney,	" 1208	5	10
Cornelius Carpenter,	" 1029	1	00
Wm. A. Lawson,	" 1030	2	00
Wm. Baker,	" 1026	1	00
R. Van Sicklen,	" 1027	1	00
Cyrus Baker,	" 1022	2	00
John G. Harris,	" 1035	1	00
" "	" 1202	9	77

Samuel Ellis,	Warrant 1190	8	25
J. Alverson,	" 1023	1	00
Zachariah Chew,	" 1239	17	30
John Reynolds,	" 1024	1	00
John Matthews,	" 1028	1	00
John O'Farrell,	" 1033	1	00
J. A. Vandewater,	" 1272	200	00
Robert Lawson,	" 1025	2	00
Walter Farrington,	" 1167	100	00
John Ely,	" 1152	23	01
Miss E. L. Northrop,	" 1248	2	50
J. L. Carman,	" 881	7	00
Mrs. E. Dunwoody,	" 1141	7	00
Edwin Barnes,	" 924	20	00
Dr. J. W. Poucher,	" 844	60	00
Theo. A. Hoffman,	" 942	1,622	15
A. G. Gedney,	" 1201	25	70
F. H. Burnett,	" 1203	10	00
J. H. Malloy,	" 1234	26	52
S. Kisselbrack,	" 986	2	00
Uriah Plass,	" 990	2	00
Dr. J. H. Brown,	" 916	10	00
Dr. J. E. Losee,	" 915	10	00
F. L. Stillman,	" 985	2	00
H. L. Cookingham,	" 1270	16	50
" "	" 912	225	25
Red Hook Journal,	" 823	31	00
Benj. Teats, Assignee,	" 1236	42	13
C. L. Rockfeller,	" 914	30	20
S. Holt,	" 967	7	00
D. Minkler,	" 1235	6	85

Geo. Shoemaker,	Warrant	990	2 00
" "	"	1199	10 00
John N. Near,	"	1258	26 75
C. H. Humphrey,	"	1193	3 60
James Maher,	"	—	5 50
Geo. W. Slocum.	"	1228	18 50
Pawling Journal,	"	818	27 00
Geo. B. Van Scoy,	"	1020	1 00
J. B. Whittick,	"	1018	1 00
W. G. Ferriss.	"	1036	1 00
M. Ryan,	"	1017	1 00
D. Van Scoy,	"	1019	1 00
Thos. Welch,	"	1015	1 00
D. H. Stringham,	"	1179	28 80
A. S. Austin,	"	1241	26 30
David S. Chapman,	"	997	2 00
Guy C. Bayley,	"	423	10 00
"	"	1197	15 00
John Scutt,	"	993	2 00
Charles Nolan.	"	976	2 00
W. Daley,			1 00
Jas. J. Oliver,	"	852	24 00
Humane Restraint Co.,	"	2191	8 50
Benj. Hopkins,	"	1205	75
Henry Cook,	"	995	2 00
L. B. Stanton,	"	1155	30 75
A. E. Hauver,	"	954	1 00
Armory Gas Bill,			49 40
St. Peter's Cemetery,	"	889	16 00
M. J. Bonney, Assignee,	"	1198	5 00
Nathan Purdy,	"	1117	2 00
A. Phillips,	"	974	2 00

A. G. Couse,	Warrant 992	2 00
Frank McCoy,		1 50
J. H. Colter,	" 920	10 00
Wesley Gibbs,	" 999	2 00
W. H. Cannon,	" 956	1 00
John Zeigler,	" 1178	5 50
Hudson Riv. Tel. Co.,		36 00
Nicola Kernan,	" 958	1 00
T. J. McGlasson,		50 00
W. Skelly,		50
Pok. Publishing Co.,	" 826	11 50
Silas W. Coon,	" 988	2 00
Van Wyck & Collins,		15 00
John J. Mylod,		25 86
Myron Smith, overcharge Kiowsky	.	20 72

Allowance, Mileage and Percentage on Returned Taxes.

Amenia,	8 08
Clinton,	3 29
Dover,	8 92
East Fishkill,	3 38
Hyde Park,	3 59
Lagrange,	4 35
Milan,	6 76
North East,	5 45
Pawling,	8 42
Pine Plains,	6 92
Red Hook,	13 33

Rhinebeck,		4 39
Stanford,		3 60
Union Vale,		4 81
Washington,		8 98
Amount of Corporation Tax Fees paid Collectors,		350 75
Henry Marks,	Warrant, 1156	590
Dr. J. C. Otis,	" 840	10 00
Electric Light & Power Co.,		36 67
Benj. Hammond,	" 1104	4 00
H. R. Schofield,	" 1040	1 00
Squire Van Buren,	" 1056	1 00
John Robertson,	" 1062	1 00
John J. Bagnall,	" 1132	7 75
John Nephine,	" 977	2 00
Dr. F. M. Pultz,	" 938	10 00

School Apportionment.

Amenia,	1,747 37
Beekman,	683 42
Clinton,	1,279 50
Dover,	1,269 30
East Fishkill,	1,695 41
Fishkill,	6,159 55
Hyde Park,	2,175 68
Lagrange,	1,596 13
Milan,	1,225 71
North East,	1,729 41
Pawling,	1,465 09
Pine Plains,	1,227 94

Pleasant Valley,			1,535 66
Poughkeepsie,			2,362 85
Poughkeepsie City,			12,976 36
Red Hook,			2,591 34
Rhinebeck,			2,787 36
Stanford,			1,540 78
Union Vale,			1,095 92
Wappinger,			2,910 90
Washington,			1,844 38
J. H. Ostrander, Burial Soldier,			50 00
Dr. J. G. Porteous,	Warrant	865	125 00
W. A. Shoemaker,	"	960	3 00
Thos. H. Waters,			74 87
Dr. C. E. Sieger,	"	858	10 00
E. Knickerbocker,	"	1207	5 90
Water Bill, Court House and Jail,			33 28
James Maher,			73 85
Electric Light and Power Co.,			36 67
State Treasurer, Taxes,			116,741 56
Van Dyne & Mellady,			50 00
Jas. Matthews,			4 22
E. C. Morehouse,	Warrant 1206		85
James O'Brien, Bill.			77 89
D. W. Guernsey, Referee,			100 00
J. H. Zahn,	Warrant 1226		4 56
H. F. Bissell, Headstone,			15 00
Van Dyne & Mellady, Burial,			50 00
Poughkeepsie Cab Line,			28 50
James O'Brien, Repairs,			5 90
T. Suwarrow,			25 50
Burnett Brothers, Burial and Headstone,			50 00
Poor Fund as per Resolution of Board,			175 00

C. H. Hoysradt,		50 00
C. B. Cunley,	Warrant 1161	85
W. S. Colwell,	" 1092	3 00
Po'keepsie Electric Light Co.,		36 67
Po'keepsie Gas Light Co.,		7 20
Water Bill, Court House and Jail,		19 80
Gas Bill, Armory,		23 40
A. J. Silvernail, Moving Safes,		20 00
Stanford & McDonough, Bill,		30 00
H. F. Bissell, Headstone,		15 00
Mary McGann, Burial and Headstone,		50 00
James Maher, Bill,		18 40
James Lynch, Headstone,		15 00
J. J. Reynolds, Headstone,		60 00
Po'keepsie Electric Light and Power Co., Bill,		36 67
J. H. Shaffer, Col. Dist. No. 4, Red Hook,		15 15
City National Bank, Int. on Note,		93 33
Hud. Riv. Tel. Co.,		36 00
Van Wyck & Collins, Headstones,		15 00
Cornelius Daley, Bill,		13 00
E. B. Taylor, Bill,		8 68
J. J. Mylod, Tax Redemption, B. T. Sheldon, Hyde Park, '88,		36 23
Frank Englehardt, County Sealer,		25 00
J. W. Van Tassell, Sheriff, In reward of Arthur Pendergass,		250 00
Treasurer Dist. 6, Dover,		48 00
H. F. Bissell, Headstone, -		15 00
Pok. Light and Power Co.,		36 67
Water Bill,		39 70
W. G. Donaldson,	Warrant 989	2 00
Chas. A. Hoysradt, Burial and Headstone,		50 00

H. F. Bissell, Headstone,	15	00
A. Remlein, Desk 19th Sep. Co.,	30	00
J. J. Mylod, Tax Sale Harriet Bowman, Fish-
kill, '88,	5	10
Mary Schuster, Burial and Headstone,	50	00
John Dempsey, Dist. 4, Millerton,	21	88
J. G. Frost, Burial and Headstone,	50	00
H. E. Bissell, Headstone,	15	00
Electric Light and Power Co.,	36	67
P. A. Ward, Bill,	505	66
Shelden Wing, Burial and Headstone.	50	00
Armory Gas Bill,	27	80
1,000 Envelopes,	22	00
Mary Ostrom, Burial and Headstone,	50	00
Hudson River Tel. Co.,	36	00
Electric Light and Power Co.,	36	67
Jas. Brice, Col. Dist. No. 2, Rhinebeck,	13	34
H. W. Watson, Col. Dist. No. 2, Pine Plains	15	10
Jacob B. Dixon, Burial & Headstone,	50	00
Po'k. News-Press, Adv. Tax Sales,	73	00
John Brusie, Col. Dist. No. 2, North East,	37	12
J. W. Tipple, Col. Dist. No. 5, Pine Plains,
Ancram and Gal.,	87	22
Col. District No. 1, Pine Plains,	27	81
L. L. Carman, Dist. No. 2, Stanford.	69	14
Geo. Wurster, Col. Dist. No. 12, Stanford,	44	05
Chas. H. Deuell, Col. Dist. No. 10, Stanford,	30	77
Charles Lown, Col. Dist. No. 6, Rhinebeck and
Red Hook,	38	18
Geo. M. Palmer, Col. Dist. No. 3, Stanford.	53	23
J. B. Monfort, warrant 201	1	00
Platt & Platt, Adv. Tax Sales,	73	00

John Brusie, Col. Dist. No. 2, North East,	55	05
Vail, Sutton & Vail, Insurance,	24	00
Chas. Van Wagner, Col. Dist. No. 3, North East,	64	70
Chas. H. Butts, Col. Dist. No. 4, Stanford.	28	65
James W. Hermance, Dist. No. 2, Pine Plains,	56	85
W. R. Cole, Dist. No. 3. Milan, Gallatin and Clermont,	57	95
J. H. Shaffer, Dist. No. 4, Red Hook,	16	37
R. G. Moore, Dist. 35, Red Hook,	43	86
Wm. Hermans, Dist. No. 8, Clinton, Washington and Stanford,	15	18
L. L. Carman, Dist. No. 2, Stanford,	41	80
H. F. Bissell, Headstones,	15	0
Water Bill, Court House and Jail,	61	46
John Pickett, Bill,	5	75
Chas Van Wagner, Dist. No. 12,	28	73
A. S. Coffin,	7	11
J. H. Halsted,	30	00
G. H. Uhle,	6	80
J. O'Brien,	17	80
A. S. Coffin,	34	06
W. R. Farrington,	28	50
M. M. Vincent,	12	40
J. O. Pingrey,	75	00
Jas. F. Whalen,	23	40
C. B. Cunley,	10	00
W. V. Coe,	20	65
Charles E. Northrop,	7	20
John Doyle,	48	17
Smith Tompkins,	15	00
Albert Knapp,	11	45
Walsh & Griffin,	8	00

W. O. Mailler,	175 91
S. N. Haight,	11 00
J. A. Fitch,	5 60
H. P. Thompson,	59 04
Jane McAllister,	19 50
Jas. H. Russell,	10 00
Myron Smith,	350 00
Olin Cutler,	5 25
S. K. Phillips,	110 10
E. Wright Vail,	17 45
J. L. Hammond,	33 95
John Bates,	63 25
Michael Whalen,	20 00
J. B. Whatson,	15 50
S. H. Cutler,	59 80
Amelia Mitchell,	5 53
Frank Lamoree,	11 25
E. D. Hall,	13 00
Henry Bostwick,	36 90
G. C. Payne,	21 42
Butler, Clapp, Wentz & Co.,	201 70
Helen E. Sherrow,	6 54
C. E. Haight,	16 85
Elias Vail,	18 20
Frank Lawrence,	81 00
D. L. Benham,	28 30
John Shaughnnessy,	39 24
Benjamin Howell,	30 15
A. S. Coffin,	46 01
A. Laird,	96 72
L. H. Osborn,	32 80
D. Warner,	21 89

——Hoffman,	15	0ʋ
Geo. Howell,	22	20
Gurdon Haight,	66	52
John Murphy,	82	34
Jno. M. Edwards,	43	47
David Dixon,	54	84
Geo. E. Rodgers,	245	82
E. R. Knapp,	10	25
Geo. H. Uhl,	167	01
D. White,	15	30
C. R. Haight,	16	50
Geo. Campbell,	56	02
Lorrin R. Traver,	63	42
E. B. Underhill,	23	00
A. White,	21	48
Fallkill Mfg. Co.,	53	50
Jas. H. Ward,	62	83
Geo. Hufcut,	23	30
C. W. Belding,	22	90
F. C. Tompkins,	14	30
Reynolds & Co.,	50	52
W. O. Mailler & Co.,	68	59
G. V. Benson,	20	70
R. G. Coffin,	138	63
J. H. Ward & Son,	29	15
J. B. Carpenter,	23	60
J. W. Butts,	26	50
Peter Bragaw,	18	20
Julia A. Butler,	12	30
Geo. Hammond,	14	30
J. P. Conklin.	11	50
I. H. Halsted,	9	45

J. A. Butler,	15	10
A. S. Coffin,	27	97
J. Sherrill,	6	50
E. Thompson,	80	00
Thorn Duell,	8	05
Mrs. Angus Fowler,	26	00
P. Barron,	6	50
Reynolds & Cramer,	23	71
Geo. O. Benson,	19	30
Geo. C. Payne,	12	15
Wm. Sheey,	12	10
J. N. Bullis,	10	85
E. B. Underhill,	74	15
L. C. Tompkins,	43	50
Joseph Holmes,	5	83
S. W. Haight,	5	50
H. C. Wilber,	28	00
E. Cole,	7	50
W. O. Mailler & Co.,	112	40
Merritt & Colwell,	41	65
Reynolds & Cramer,	61	60
J. C. Haviland,	25	50
H. Pray,	15	00
C. A. Brooks,	67	50
Am. Briggs,	14	65
Arthur Frazier,	16	25
W. O. Mailler & Co.,	41	58
Swift Brothers,	44	88
Howard Haight,	81	13
A. S. Coffin,	34	11
W. E. Scott,	35	40
James H. Russell,	90	00

Hoffman & Co.,	15 00
E. Wright Vail,	9 15
Frank Lawrence,	15 00
James H. Ward & Son,	48 01
J. O. Pingrey,	75 00
H. C. Wilber,	35 49
Thomas Wright,	10 73
Wm. Hughes,	10 83
Jane McAllister,	44 50
Ives & Bonar,	18 33
J. A. Terwilliger,	5 60
A. B. Smith,	15 00
John Tompkins,	34 57
Wm. Gemmel,	19 75
Charles Joseph,	121 15
Reuben Haught,	3 92
Myron Smith,	160 00
W. C. Lester,	9 81
A. S. Coffin,	9 16
Butler, Clapp & Co.,	52 03
W. O. Mailler,	55 78
R. G. Coffin,	59 92
L. Decker,	20 00
Hammond & Brother,	15 00
Timothy Conklin,	11 60
David Liebermuth,	24 25
Fred. Warner,	138 12
P. L. Van Wagner,	145 83
J. H. Ward & Son,	62 23
James Hayes.	13 00
Geo. M. Wellman,	27 00
W. O. Mailler & Co.,	109 95

John Schwartz & Sons,	37	30
A. S. Coffin,	20	53
Timothy Flannigan,	18	00
W. H. Austin,	105	51
R. T. Monfort,	23	74
D. Briggs,	10	10
W. G. Cowee,	16	20
J. O. Pingrey,	75	00
E. S. Devine,	35	00
Vail & Sutton,	57	50
Howard Haight,	51	05
Swift Brothers,	64	85
S. M. Davidson,	22	53
A. ˙S. Coffin,	15	50
B. S. Bayly,	12	40
Jas. M. Clark,	42	00
E. S. Devine,	60	00
Frank Shay,	27	54
James H. Ward,	76	65
Jane McAllister,	19	50
Cole Brothers,	108	00
W. O. Mailler & Co.,	37	04
E. S. Deuell,	73	12
V. Rickes,	29	66
W. O. Mailler,	35	00
J O. Pingrey,	100	00
Wm E Smith,	91	94
C M Benjamin,	6	00
Jas Reardon,	65	82
Richard Vincent,	13	50
A S. Coffin,	10	02
W. O. Mailler & Co.,	45	84

Thomas E. Graecen,	21 17
Hoffman & Co.,	15 00
R. G. Coffin,	67 76
Howland & Dutcher,	57 50
James H. Ward & Son,	95 14
W. O. Mailler & Co.,	69 21
H. S. Vanderburgh,	16 80
John June,	15 75
R. G. Coffin,	94 34
A. G. Coffin,	8 87
Mead & Murdock,	105 45
Charles Joseph,	75 30
Knickerbocker & Wright,	12 75
Kirby. DuBois & Boyd,	6 45
II. W. Fitch,	13 30
R. G. Coffin,	64 09
S. Teachout,	10 50
Myles Doyle,	18 90
A. J. Rogers,	45 55
40 Deficiency Loan Bonds, Nos. 121 to 160 inclusive,	20,000 00
192 Coupons,	3,360 00
W. Morgan Lee, Drawing Bonds,	25 00
E. S. Atwater, Drawing Statute,	25 00
Express,	4 00
Interest on Bonds,	300 00
Circuit Court, Dec., 1889,	646 70
Sessions " Jan.,	529 05
Circuit " Mch.,	856 25
Sessions, " April	923 30
Circuit, " June	921 45
Sessions " Aug.,	983 65

Circuit Court, Oct.,	1,731 46
Hudson River State Hospital to Sept. 30, '89,	7,716 57
" " " " to Mch. 31, '90,	9,338 90
Binghamton " " to Jan. 1, '90,	1,447 98
" " " to Apr. 1,	1,275 72
" " " to July 1,	1,286 40
" " " to Oct. 1,	1,263 64
Utica Lunatic Asylum, to Jan. 1, '90,	171 81
" " " to Apr. 1,	97 53
" " " to July 1,	100 20
Home of Good Shepherd Oct. 31, '88 to Oct. 31, '89,	104 00
Willard Asylum to Jan. 1,	3,081 58
" " to April 1,	3,005 40
" " to July 1,	2,866 91
N. Y. Asylum for Idiots. Bill.	64 00
Auburn Asylum to Oct. 1, 1889,	585 00
N. Y. State Inst. for Blind,	124 24
Po'k Orphan Home, to Jan 1,	260 25
" " " to Apr. 1,	294 07
" " " to July 1,	262 44
" " " to Oct. 1,	312 24
Deaf and Dumb Inst., Bill,	452 51
Middletown Asylum to Jan. 1, '90,	97 50
" " to June 1,	53 10
" " to Oct. 1,	49 65
Colored Orphan Asylum to Jan. 1,	536 57
St. Joseph's Inst to Jan. 1st,	330 00
" " to Oct. 23, 1889,	641 51
E White, City Treasurer,	50 60

Daniel W. Guernsey, Salary to Jan. 1st, 1890,	500	00
" " " to Ap'l. 1st,	500	00
" " " to July 1st,	500	00
" " " to Oct. 1st,	500	00
Horace D. Hufcut, Salary to Jan. 1st, 1890,	500	00
C. P Dorland, to Apl. 1st,	500	00
" " to July 1st,	500	00
" " to Oct. 1st,	500	00
Martin J. Heermance, Salary to Jan. 1st, 1890,	375	00
" " " to Apl. 1st,	375	00
" " " to July 1st,	375	00
" " " to Oct. 1st,	375	00
Isaac W. Sherill, " to June 1st,	312	50
" " " to April,	312	50
" " " to July,	312	50
" " " to Oct. 1st,	312	50
Myron Smith, Salary to Jan. 1st, 1890,	425	00
" " " to Apl. 1st,	425	00
" " " to July 1st,	425	00
" " " to Oct. 1st,	425	00
Mrs. H. F. Butts, Salary to Jan. 1st,	75	00
" " " to Apl. 1st,	75	00
" " " to July 1st,	75	00
" " " to Oct. 1st,	75	00
N. L Heroy, Salary to Jan. 1st,	25	00
" " " to Apl 1st,	25	00
C. Mackey, Salary to July 1st,	25	00
" " to Oct. 1st,	25	00
Smith Heroy, Salary to Jan. 1st, (Surrogate's Clerk)	250	00

J. M. Dorland, Salary to Apl. 1st,	250	00
" " " to July 1st,	250	00
" " " to Sept. 1st,	167	66
C. P. Dorland, Clerk's Salary to Oct. 1st,	83	33
Rent of Armory to Feb. 1st,	375	00
" " to May 1st,	375	00
" " to Aug. 1st,	375	00
J. M. Corcoran, Salary to Dec. 1st,	33	33
" " " to Jan. 1st, '90,	33	33
" " " to Feb.,	33	37
" " " to Mar.,	33	33
" " " to Apl.,	33	33
" " " to May,	33	33
" " " to June,	33	33
" " " to July,	. 33	33
" " " to Aug.,	33	33
" " " to Sept.,	33	33
" " " to Oct.,	33	33
" " " to Nov. 1st,	33	33
Salary Peter H. Brower to Dec. 1st, '89,	87	50
" " " to Mch. '90,	87	50
" " " to June 1st,	87	50
" " " to Sept. 1st,	87	50
J. P. Wilson, Salary to Apl. 1st,	25	00
" " " to July,	25	00
" " " to Oct. 1st,	25	00
Frank Ackerly,	25	00
Frank J. Decker,	8	50
Matthew Kennedy,	35	00
State Treasurer,	69	73
Myron Smith, Bill,	58	25
Mead & Murdock,	71	66

W. H. Austin,	79	27
Wm. E. Smith,	51	84
Bears & Trafford,	159	80
R. H Andrews,	7	40
Jas. Reardon,	71	22
Balance on hand,	14,321	02

$335,570 54

POUGHKEEPSIE, Nov. 1st, 1890.

I hereby certify that there now is a balance of Fourteen Thousand Three Hundred and Twenty-one dollars and two cents standing to the credit of the Treasurer of Dutchess County, (Isaac W. Sherrill) on the books of the Farmers and Manufacturers National Bank of Poughkeepsie.

GEO. H. SHERMAN,

Bookkeeper.

General Fund.

Receipts, $305,316 44

Disbursements.

Overdraft, Dec. 1st, 1889,	$ 3,516	49
Amounts paid to Date, ¯.	234,401	21

Appropriations.

Poor Fund,	8,000	00
Funded Debt,	3,800	00
Court and Jury,	6,000	00

Hudson River State Hospital,	12,000	00
Binghamton " "	6,000	00
Utica " "	500	00
Home of Good Shepherd,	100	00
Willard State Hospital,	11,000	00
N. Y. Asylum for Idiots,	48	00
Auburn State Hospital,	400	00
N. Y. Institute for Blind,	98	00
Poughkeepsie Orphan Home,	500	00
Middletown Homeopathic Asylum,	300	00
Colored Orphan Asylum,	502	79
St. Joseph's Institute,	860	51
County Judge,	2,000	00
Surrogate,	2,000	00
District Attorney,	1,500	00
County Treasurer,	1,250	00
Superintendent Alms House,	1,700	00
Matron " "	300	00
Chaplain, " "	100	00
Surrogate's Clerk,	1,000	00
Rent of Armory,	1,600	00
Armorer,	400	00
Jail Physician,	100	00
Repairs Alms House,	500	00
Balance on Hand,	4,839	44

$305,316 44

Poor Fund.

Balance on Hand Dec. 1st, 1890.		832 71
Transferred from Gen. Fund Pr. resolution		
Supervisors,		175 00
Appropriation for 1890.		8,000 00
		$9,007 71
Superintendent's Orders paid,	$8,233 47	
Balance,	774 24	
		9,007 71

Funded Debt.

Balance on Hand Dec. 1st, 1890,	$	982 50
Sale of 20 Bonds,		20,105 00
Appropriation for 1890,		3,800 00
		$24,887 50
To 40 Bonds 121 to 160,	$20,000 00	
" Coupons,	3,360 00	
" W. M. Lee, Drawing Bond,	25 00	
" E. S. Atwater " Statute,	25 00	
" Express,	4 00	
" Interest on Bonds,	300 00	
" Balance,	1,173 50	
	$24,887 50	

Court and Jury.

Balance on Hand Dec. 1, 1890,		$ 14 94
Appropriation for 1890,		6,000 00
Balance overdrawn,		576 92
		$6,591 86
To Circuit Court, Dec. '89,	646 70	
" County " Jan.,	529 05	
" Circuit " Mch.,	856 25	
" County " April,	923 30	
" Circuit " June,	921 45	
" County " Aug.,	983 65	
" Circuit " Oct.,	1,731 46	
	$6,591 86	

Hudson River State Hospital.

Balance on hand Dec. 1, 1890,	$3,445 47
Board, Gertrude Halsted to Jan. 1, '90,	52 00
" Beatta Martin to Dec. 9, '89.	58 50
" John H. Traver to Jan. 1, '90,	55 90
" Amelia Hilliker to Jan. 1, '90,	218 40
" Mary C. Sackett to Jan 1, '90,	218 40
" Louisa Miller to Jan. 1, '90,	27 30
" Mary Mawha to Jan. 1, '90,	27 37
" Peter Woodfield (20 weeks),	42 00
" Mary Powers,	10 75
" James E. Powers,	13 90
" Jacob Hutton,	150 00
" Alex W. McGibben,	80 00
" B. G. Smith to May 1, '90,	27 25

Board	Albert Kiowsky to April 1, '90,	111	40
"	Mary Kimlin to April 17, '90,	261	20
"	Beatta Martin to March 9, '90,	58	50
"	Minerva J. Conklin to Jan. 1, '90,	491	40
"	E. Lawrence,	18	00
"	Mary Mawha,	27	37
"	John H. Traver to April 10, '90,	55	90
"	Peter Woodfield to April 20, '90,	26	65
"	Wm. S. Rowe to Aug. 1, '90,	54	60
"	Bartholomew Myers,	97	05
"	B. G. Smith,	27	25
"	Louisa Miller to April 1, '90,	27	30
"	Anna Mackey to July 1. '90,	14	70
"	Beatta Martin to June 9, '90,	58	50
"	Mary E. Hall,	43	22
"	Mrs. A. W. McGibben to July 1, '90,	52	00
"	Gertrude Halsted to July 1, '90,	52	00
"	Isaac Aiken,	34	00
"	John H. Traver to July 10, '90,	55	90
"	Cath. Proctor,	10	50
"	Anna Mackey,	27	30
"	Mary Mawha,	27	37
"	John Bonahan,	16	80
"	B. G. Smith,	27	25
"	Julia Wickes, 3 mos from Aug. 9, '90,	54	60
"	Louisa Miller, April 1 to Sept. 11, '90,	48	83
"	Robert McNulty,	16	80
"	John Bonnicone to Oct. 18, '90,	16	80
"	Peter Woodfield, April 20 to Sept. 1, '90,	39	90
"	Beatta Martin to Sept. 9, '90,	58	50
"	John H. Traver to Oct. 10, '90,	55	90
"	Michael Hoban to Oct. 3, '90,	6	30

Board, Catherine Proctor,		27 30
" Wm. S. Rowe to Nov. 1, '90,		77 10
" Mary Kimlin to Oct. 1, 90,		101 85
" Julia Goodheim to Jan., 1891,		55 25
Appropriation for 1890.		12,000 00

$18,662 53

Bill to Dec. 30, '89,	$7,716 57	
" March 31, '90,	9,338 90	
Balance on hand,	1,607 06	

$18,662 53

Binghamton Asylum.

To Balance overdrawn Dec. 1st, '90,		₿ 702 95
Check for Bill to Jan. 1st, '90,		1,447 93
" " " Apl. 1st,		1,275 72
" " " July 1st,		1,286 40
" ". " Oct. 1st,		1,263 64
Balance overdrawn,		78 50

$6,055 19

| Board Eliza Ferris, | $ ⁄ 55 19 | |
| "   Appropriation for 1890, | 6,000 00 | |

$6,055 19

Utica Asylum.

| By Balance Dec. 1st, 1889 on hand, | | $ 14 43 |
| By Appropriation for 1890, | | 500 00 |

$514 43

To Check for Bill to Jan. 1, '90,	$171 81	
" " to Apr. 1, '90,	97 53	
" " to July 1, '90,	100 20	
Balance on hand,	144 89	
	$514 43	

Home of Good Shepherd.

By Balance on hand Dec. 1st, '89,	$104 00
By Appropriation for 1890,	100 00
	$204 00

To Check for Bill to Oct. 31, '89,	$104 00	
To Balance on hand,	100 00	
	$204 00	

Brunswick Home.

By Balance on hand,	$297 76

New York Asylum for Idiots.

Balance on hand December 1st, 1889,		$100 00
Transferred to General Fund per Order		
Board Supervisors,	$100 00	

Albany Orphan Asylum.

By Balance on hand December 1st, 1889,		$77 00
Transferred to General Funds per Order		
Board Supervisors,	$77 00	

Albany Penitentiary.

By balance on hand December 1st, 1889,	$48 38

Willard Asylum.

By balance on hand Dec. 1st, 1889,		$61 33
Board Peter Massoneau to April 1st, '90,		157 60
Ella Burger,		35 00
Mrs. Wetzel to April. 1st, '90,		206 99
Ella Burger,		25 00
Rebecca Tripp to May 3rd, 1890,		135 97
Catherine Dean,		10 00
Ella Burger,		25 00
Catherine Dean,		24 00
Ella Burger,		22 00
Peter N. Massoneau to Jan. 1, '91,		102 65
Appropriation for 1890,		11,000 00
		$11,805 54
To Check for Bill to Jan. 1st, 1890,	$3,081 58	
To Check for Bill to April 1st, 1890,	3,005 49	
To Check for Bill to July 1st, 1890,	2,866 91	
Balance on hand,	2,851 65	
	$11,805 54	

New York Asylum for Idiots.

Balance December 1, 1890,		$16 00
Appropriation for 1890,		48 00
		$64 00
To Check for Bill, March 7th,	$64 00	
		$64 00

Auburn Asylum.

By Balance December 1st, 1890,		$199 13
Appropriation for 1890,		400 00
		$599 13
To Bill to October 1st, 1890,	$585 00	
Balance on Hand,	14 13	
		$599 13

New York State Institution for the Blind.

By Balance on Hand Dec. 1st, '89,		$35 00
By Appropriation for 1890,		98 00
		$133 00
To Check for Bill March 5th, 90,	$124 24	
To Balance on Hand,	8 76	
		$133 00

Repairs to Alms House.

By Appropriation for 1890,		$500 00
To Myron Smith, Bill,	$58 25	
" Mead & Murdock, "	71 66	
" W. H. Austin, "	79 27	
" Wm. E. Smith, "	51 84	
" Beers & Trafford, "	159 80	
" R. H. Andrews, "	7 40	
" James Reardon, "	71 22	
" Balance,	66	
	$500 00	

Poughkeepsie Orphan Home.

By Appropriation for 1890,		$500 00
Balance overdrawn,		672 82
		$1,172 82
To balance overdrawn Dec. 1st, 1890,	$43 82	
To Check for Bill to Jan. 1st, 1890,	260 25	
To Check for Bill to April 1st, 1890,	294 07	
To Check for Bill to July 1st, 1890,	262 44	
To Check for Bill to Oct. 1st, 1890,	312 24	
	$1,172 82	

New York Institute for Instruction Deaf and Dumb.

By balance on hand Dec. 1st, 1890		$609 92
To Check for Bill Mar. 7th, '90,	$452 51	
Balance on hand,	157 41	
	$609 92	

Homeopathic Asylum, Middletown, N. Y.

By Appropriation for 1890,		$300 00
To balance Dec. 1, 1889,	$49 55	
To check for bill to Jan. 1, '90,	97 50	
" " " to June 1st,	53 10	
" " " to Oct. 1st,	49 65	
To balance on hand,	50 20	
	$300 00	

Colored Orphan Asylum.

By balance Dec. 1, 1889,		$22 21
By Appropriation for 1890,		502 79
Balance overdrawn,		11 57
		$536 57
To Check for Bill to Jan. 1; '90,	$536 57	

St. Joseph's Institute.

By Appropriation for 1890,		$860 51
Balance overdrawn,		330 00
		$1,190 51
To bal. overdrawn Dec. 1, '89	$219 00	
To Check for Bill to Jan. '90,	330 00	
" " . " to Oct. 23, '89,	641 51	
	$1,190 51	

Separate Fund.

By balance on hand Dec. 1st, 1889,		$900 78
To E. White, City Treasurer,	$50 60	
Balance on hand,	850 18	
	$900 78	

County Judge.

By balance Dec. 1st, 1889,		$ 500 00
Appropriation for 1890,		2,000 00
		$2,500 00
Daniel W. Guernsey, salary,	$500 00	
" "	500 .00	
" "	500 00	
" "	500 00	
Balance on hand,	500 00	
	$2,500 00	

Surrogate.

Balance on hand Dec. 1st, 1889,	$ 500	00
By Appropriation for 1890,	2,000	00
	$2,500	00

To H. D. Hufcut, Salary,	$500	00		
To C. P. Dorland, Salary,	500	00		
" " "	500	00		
" " "	500	00		
To Balance on hand,	500	00		
			$2,500	00

District Attorney.

Balance Dec. 1st, 1889.	$ 375	00
Appropriation for 1890,	1,500	00
	$1,875	00

Martin Heermance to January 1st, 1890,	$375	00		
Martin Heermance to April 1, 1890,	375	00		
Martin Heermance to July 1st, 1890,	375	00		
Martin Heermance to Oct. 1st, 1890,	375	00		
Balance on hand,	375	00		
			$1,875	00

County Treasurer.

By balance Dec. 1st, 1889,		$ 312 50
Appropriation for 1890,		1,250 00
		$1,562 50
I. W. Sherrill, Salary to Jan. 1st, 1890,	$312 50	
I. W. Sherrill, Salary to April, 1890,	312 50	
I. W. Sherrill, Salary to July, 1890,	312 50	
I. W. Sherrill, Salary to October, 1890,	312 50	
Balance on hand,	312 50	
	$1,562 50	

Alms House Superintendent.

By balance to Dec. 1st, 1889,		$ 425 00
By Appropriation for 1890,		1,700 00
		$2,125 00
Myron Smith to Jan. 1, 1890,	$425 00	
" " to April 1, 1890,	425 00	
" " to July 1, 1890,	425 00	
" " to Oct. 1, 1890,	425 00	
Balance on hand,	425 00	
	$2,125 00	

Matron, Alms House.

Balance on hand Dec. 1st, 1890,		$ 75 00
Appropriation for 1890,		300 00
		$375 00
Mrs. H. F. Butts to Jan. 1, '90,	$75 00	
" " to April 1, '90,	75 00	
" " to July 1, '90,	75 00	
" " Oct. 1, '90,	75 00	
Balance on hand,	75 00	
	$375 00	

Chaplain, Alms House.

By Balance Dec. 1st, 1889,		$ 25 00
By Appropriation for 1890.		100 00
		$125 00
To N. L. Heroy, Jan. 1st,	$25 00	
" " Apl. 1st,	25 00	
" " July 1st,	25 00	
" " Oct. 1st,	25 00	
Balance on hand,	25 00	
	$125 00	

Surrogate's Clerk.

By Balance Dec. 1st, 1889,		$ 250 00
By Appropriation for 1889,		1,000 00
		$1,250 00

Smith Heroy to Jan. 1st, '90,	$250 00
J. M. Dorland to April 1st, '90,	250 00
" " to July 1st,	250 00
C. P. Dorland to Oct. 1st,	167 66 } 83 33 }
Balance on hand,	249 01

$1,250 00

By balance on hand Dec. 1st, 1889,	$ 150 00
By Appropriation for 1890,	1,600 00

$1,750 00

Rent of Armory to Feb. 1st, '90,	$375 00
" " " May 1st,	375 00
" " " Aug. 1st,	375 00
Balance on hand,	625 00

$1,750 00

Armorer of Separate Companies.

By Balance on hand December 1st, 1889,	$ 66 74
By Appropriation for 1890,	400 00

$466 74

To J. M. Corcoran, Sal'y to Dec. 1,				$33 33
" " " " to Jan. 1,				33 33
" " " " to Feb.,				33 37
" " " " to Mch.,				33 33
" " " " to April,				33 33
" " " " to May,				33 33
" " " " to June,				33 33
" " " " to July,				33 33

To J. M. Corcoran, Sal'y to Aug.   33 33
"   "   "   "   to Sept.   33 33
"   "   "   "   to Oct.   33 33
"   "   "   "   to Nov.   33 33
To Balance on hand,   66 74
                                    _____
                                    $466 74

Keeper Drake's Draw Bridge.

By Balance Dec. 1st, 1889, $87 50
By Balance overdrawn,   262 50
                                             _____
                                             $350 00

To P. H. Brower to Dec. 1st, $87 50
"   "   " to Mch. 1st,   87 50
"   "   " to June 1st,   87 50
"   "   " to Sept.,   87 50
                                _____
                                $350 00

Jail Physician.

By Appropriation for 1890, $100 00
Dr. J. P. Wilson Sal'y to April 1st, $25 00
"   "   "   " to July 1st,   25 00
"   "   "   " to Oct. 1st,   25 00
Balance on hand,   25 00
                                       _____
                                       $100 00

Fish and Game Protection.

By Balance Dec. 1st, 1889, $25 00
By Fine of Tanner and Brown,   8 23
"   "   of Harry Day,   25 00
"   "   of Curtis and Tompkins,   10 00
"   "   of Noble, Marsh, Baxter, Leonard
Zeph, et al.,   30 00
By Fine of Gilbert Hunt,   10 00
"   "   of Ira Van Vliet,   30 00

                                                  $138 23

To Frank Akerly, $25 00
To Frank J. Decker,   8 50
To Matthew Kennedy,   15 00
"   "   "   5 00
"   "   "   15 00
To State Treasurer,   69 73

                                   $138 23

Credit Balances.

RECAPITULATION.

General Fund, $4,839 44
Poor Fund,   774 24
Funded Debt,   1,173 50
Hudson River State Hospital,   1,607 06
Binghamton State Hospital,   78 50
Utica State Hospital,   146 89
Home of Good Shepherd,   100 00
Brunswick Home,   297 76

Albany Penitentiary,	48	30
Willard State Hospital,	2,851	65
Auburn Asylum for Insane Criminals,	14	13
N. Y. State Institution for the Blind,	8	76
N. Y. Institute for Deaf and Dumb,	157	41
Middletown Homeopathic Asylum,	50	20
Separate Fund,	850	18
County Judge,	500	00
" Surrogate,	500	00
" District Attorney,	375	00
" Treasurer	312	50
" Superintendent of Poor,	425	00
Matron,	75	00
Chaplain,	25	00
Surrogate's Clerk,	249	01
Rent of Armory,	625	00
Armorer,	66	74
Jail Physician,	25	00
Repairs to Alms House		56
	$16,174	**83**

Debit Balance.

Court and Jury,	$576	92	
Po'keepsie Orphan Home,	672	82	
Colored Orphan Asylum,	11	57	
St. Joseph's Institute,	330	00	
Keeper Drake's Draw Bridge,	262	50	
Balance,	14,321	02	$16,174 83

Bonded Indebtedness.

Amount of debt divided as follows:

Deficiency Loan,	$38,000 00
Refunded 1890,	20,000 00
	$58,000 00

Amount maturing 1891, $20,000 00

Surplus and Deficiency.

	SURPLUS.	DEFICIENCY.
Amenia,	$	$120 76
Beekman,		42 36
Clinton,		3 42
Dover,		54 36
East Fishkill,		20 34
Fishkill,		421 41
Hyde Park,		21 65
Lagrange,	14	
Milan,		11 65
North East,	2 40	
Pawling,	72 51	
Pine Plains,		13 57
Pleasant Valley,		27 12
Po'keepsie,		119 68
Po'keepsie City,		142 29
Red Hook,	286 11	
Rhinebeck,		205 86
Stanford,		26 31
Union Vale,	186 85	
Wappinger,		25 95
Washington,	55 21	

Unsettled Tax Sales.

Sales 1883.

DOVER.

Owners.	Purchaser.	Surplus.
John Canton,—A. Tompkins,		$22 87

EAST FISHKILL.

E. Fishkill Peat W'ks,—I. VanVlack,		3 64

FISHKILL.

Elizabeth Rogers,—A Brill,		$13 25
James Burns,—A. Brill,		3 57
Mrs. J. B. Schenck,—M. A. Fowler,		70 56
Mrs. M. Wade,—M. A. Fowler,		156 40
" " " "		9S 00
		$342 18

MILAN.

H. Plattner,—E. M. Myers,		$16 91

NORTH EAST.

James Down,—N. Best,		
Mrs. N. Donovan,—Butts & Baker,		93

POUGHKEEPSIE.

A. Crapsey,—E. Crummey,		85
J. Gaffney,- J. H. Millard,		
J. McCafferty,—C. F. Cossum,		1 17
J. McManus.—J. W. Meadler,		3 36
M. Murray,—G. W. Churchill,		8 61
Mr. Doty,—F. T. Baldwin,		5 19
M. McCavara,—P. Flagler,		2 34
G. R. Williams,—P. Flagler,		2 62
G. T. Tripp,—P. Flagler,		2 64
		$26 78

STANFORD.

Est. Calvin Morse,—O. K. Smith, $13 81

Sales 1884.

FISHKILL.

J. B. Schenck, Heirs,—J. H. Millard,

"   "   "   —H. H. Hustis, $1 77

HYDE PARK.

—— Huested,—H. Warren, $3 41

NORTH EAST.

C. Irish,—G. W. Butts,   14

POUGHKEEPSIE.

J. V. W. Doty,—W. H. Lawson, $16 61

"   "   "   "   55

S. M. McNiel,—   "   "   4 26

J. Smith,—   "   "   20 51

John Styles,—J. D. Humphrey,   15 21

A. Scully,—   "   "   8 01

James Olliver,—W. H. Lawson,   76

                                    —— $65 91

Sales 1885.

EAST FISHKILL.

M. A. Emory,—O. N. Sprague, $4 78

D. Canary,

FISHKILL.

D. Canary,—H. A. Holmes, $1 05

J. Burns,—   "   "   1 41

                                    —— $2 46

POUGHKEEPSIE.

C. H. Fowler,—H. J. Bates,	$31 45
Chas. Cossum,—C. F. Cossum,	8 70
A. Stass,—H. A. Holmes,	1 30
P. Conroy,—H. A. Holmes,	2 01

Sales 1886.

HYDE PARK.

F. Peter's Estate,—H. Werner,	$3 67

POUGHKEEPSIE.

—Duncan, —J. S. Van Cleef,	1 95

Sales 1887.

FISHKILL.

Wm. McLaughlin,—J. Dearin,	3 83
Patrick Walsh,—M. A. Fowler,	51

POUGHKEEPSIE.

J. McCavary,—C. L. Odell,	25 11
W. H. Smith,—M. A. Fowler,	26 71

Sales 1888.

FISHKILL.

Michael McDermott,—J. J. Smith,	10

POUGHKEEPSIE.

Daniel Shields,—J. J. Smith,	5 79

Sales 1889.

CLINTON.

S. Hester,—S. Hester,	1 32
T. A.Cookingham,-Aug.Cookingham,	25 60

DOVER.

Seth Swift est.,—H. Roth,	40
Dover Marble Co.,—C. W. H. Arnold,	50 21
John Swift est.,—H. Roth,	3 70

Sales 1890.

AMENIA.

Levi Whitford,—D. C. Dakin,	8 95
S. & B. Howard,—R. McM. VanWyck,	55 92

CLINTON.

Chas. Kniffen, est.,—S. H. Brown,	6 81

DOVER.

Lucretia Marcey,est.,-Garw'd Marcey,	66 73

FISHKILL.

Nelson Goodfellow,—H. S. Brown,	16 88
Edward Quinn,—S. K. Phillips,	1 46
John Williams,—P. S. Bedell,	94
John McManus,— " "	46
James H. Post,— " "	1 83
Michael Mara,— " " ,	21 29

HYDE PARK.

Horatio Whitten,—T. E. Parker,	27 83

PAWLING.

Albert E. Nichol,—A. E. Nichol,	2 99

Recapitulation.

Sales of 1883, Surplus,		$426 94
" " 1884,	"	71 23
" " 1885,	"	50 70
" " 1886,	"	5 62
" " 1887,	"	56 21
" " 1888,	"	5 89
" " 1889,	"	81 23
" " 1890,	"	212 19
		$910 01

Mr. Vail moved that the sum of $2,517.35 be levied and assessed upon the Town of Pleasant Valley, for Town Allowances.

Motion carried.

Mr. Bartlett moved that the sum of $3,607.18 be levied and assessed upon the Town of Amenia, for Town Allowances.

Motion carried.

Mr. Gray moved that the sum of $2,592.06 be levied and assessed upon the Town of Poughkeepsie for Town Allowances.

Motion carried.   .

Mr. E. Herrick moved that the sum of $661.79 be levied and assessed upon the Town of Clinton, for Town Allowances.

Motion carried.

Mr. Sturgess moved that the sum of two hundred and fifty dollars ($250) be levied and assessed upon the Town

of Red Hook, for Roads and Bridges, and the same be made payable to the Commissioners of Highways.
Motion carried.

Mr. Howatt offered the following :

Resolved, That the sum of $877.30 be levied and assessed upon the Town of Hyde Park for new Bridges, and the same be made payable to the Commissioners of Highways.

Resolution adopted.

Mr. Germond moved that the sum of ($6) six dollars be levied and assessed upon the Town of Washington, and the same be made payable to John S. Wing, for services as Excise Commissioner of said town.
Motion carried.

Mr. Gray offered the following:

Resolved, That the sum of seventeen hundred and forty dollars ($1,740) be levied and assessed against the Town of Poughkeepsie for the payment of principal and interest on Bridge Bonds, and that the same be made payable to the Supervisor.

Resolution adopted.

Mr. Howatt offered the following:

Resolved, That the clerk be instructed to request the proper authorities of the " Hudson River State Hospital " to explain to this board, either by representative or in writing, the various items composing charges for clothing furnished inmates from this county during the past year, and why such charges are so largely in excess of all previous accounts for clothing.

Resolution adopted.

Mr. Germond moved that the sum of $50 be levied and assessed upon the Town of Washington, for Poor Fund, and the same made payable to Supervisor of said town.
Motion carried.

Mr. Humphrey offered the following :

Resolved, That the Clerk of the Board be directed to advertise for bids for printing and binding *six hundred* copies of the Proceedings of this Board—*four hundred* copies to be in paper, and *two hundred* copies in cloth, the bids to be for an amount per page, the Work of the same style and quality as last year; all bids to be in by Dec. 8th, 2 o'clock p. m. And also for printing Court Calenders for the ensuing year, to be of the usual quality and number. That the County Treasurer be directed to pay the bills for printing the same, upon certificate of the Clerk, that the work has been done according to contract.

Resolution adopted.

Mr. Andrews moved that the sum of three dollars ($3) be levied and assessed upon the Town of Beekman, and the same made payable to Andrew Tray for services as Excise Commissioner for the year 1890.

Motion carried.

Mr. Wood offered the following:

Resolved, that the sum of $3,167.93 be levied and assessed against the Town of Wappinger, and that the additional sum of $333.59 be levied and assessed against said town, exclusive of the Village of Wappingers Falls.

Resolution adopted.

Mr. E. Herrick offered the following:

Resolved, That a committee of two be appointed to confer with livery-men and make arrangements for the Transportation of Lunatics during the year 1891, from the City of Poughkeepsie to the Hudson River State Hospital.

Resolution adoption.

The Chair named as such Committee Messrs E. Herrick and Able.

Mr. Germond called up Resolution for allowance to Wood & Morschauser, and moved its adoption.

Ayes and nays called.

All members present voting in favor thereof.

Ayes 19.

Resolution adopted.

On motion of Mr. Pugsley the Board adjourned.

———

TUESDAY, December 2d, 1890.

1:30 P. M.

Board met.

Quorum present.

Mr. Austin in the Chair.

Mr. J. A. Herrick presented the following which was read and laid over under the Rule :

To the Honorable, the Board of Supervisors of Dutchess County :

Your Committee on Justices' Accounts would respectfully report that they have examined the following bills and recommend they be levied and assessed upon the County.

NAME AND TOWN.	ASKED.	ALLOWED.	COUNTY. CHARGE.
1. E. Knickerbocker, Stanford............$ 9 05		$ 9 05	$ 9 05
2. Thos. A. Gurney, Po'keepsie Town. 10 50		10 50	10 50
3. Martin Croak, " " . 11 35		11 35	11 35
4. John H. Ollivett, " " . 16 40		16 40	16 40
5. C. V. Coon, " " . 2 00		2 00	2 00
6. Edmund Tanner, Wappinger........ 3 75		3 75	3 75
7. A. B. Smith, Payable to the City... 80 43		80 43	80 43

J. A. HERRICK,
JOHN C. MILROY,
K. ANDREWS,
Committee on Justices' Accounts.

Mr. Bartlett presented the claim of I. P. Conklin for excessive tax, which was on his motion, referred to the Committee on Excessive taxation.

Mr. Milroy moved that the sum of $130 be levied and assessed upon the town of Rhinebeck for insurance upon the Town Hall, and the same be made payable to the Supervisor of said Town.

Motion carried.

Mr. Morehouse moved that the sum of $2.20 be levied and assessed upon the Town of Milan, and the same be made payable to A. L. Husted of said Town.

Motion carried.

Mr. E. Herrick moved that the sum of $4 be allowed C. H. Tripp and the same amount to Solomon Smith for services as health officers, and the same be levied and assessed upon the Town of Clinton.

Motion carried.

Mr. Sturgess called up resolution for appropriation of $234.00 upon the County to meet deficiency arising from the assessment of the Cheney Towing Co., in Town of Red Hook, and moved its adoption.

Ayes and nays called.

All members present voting in favor thereof.

Ayes 19.

Resolution adopted.

Mr. Mylod offered the following resolution : That the sum of $50 be levied and assessed upon each Town of the County, and the same be made payable to the Supervisor

118 *Proceedings of the*

of said Towns to be used by them to erect sign boards on the highways as required by law, in their respective Towns.

On motion of Mr. E. Herrick, the above resolution was referred to the Committee on Roads and Bridges.

Mr. Pugsley moved that the Board adjourn.

Ayes and nays called.

Ayes—Messrs. E. Herrick, Howatt, Morehouse, Rogers, Sturgess and Swift—6.

Nays—Messrs. Able, Genung, Germond, Lee, Mylod, Pugsley, Scutt, Vail, Williams, and Wing—10.

Ayes, 6 ; nays, 10.

Motion lost.

On motion of Mr. Pugsley the Board adjourned.

WEDNESDAY, December 3d, 1890.
10:30 A. M.

Board met.

Quorum present.

Mr. Austin in the Chair.

Mr. Germond, from the Committee on School Commissioners accounts, presented the following, which were read and accepted.

To the Honorable, the Board of Supervisors of the County of Dutchess ;

GENTLEMEN :—Pursuant to a resolution adopted by the Board of Supervisors of 1869, I have the honor to transmit herewith my third annual report, touching the Educational interests of the First Assembly District of Dutchess County, for the year ending November 30, 1890.

In each of my former reports, with added comments and varied suggestions, I endeavored to submit a full and detailed account of the condition of our Public Schools.

Subject to the modifications of demonstrated experience, the work accomplished during the past year has been in accordance with the views expressed in my previous communications.

In this report, therefore, I will make as little intrusion as possible upon your valuable time by giving you a brief summary of our Educational status. This School Commissioner District, which is one of the largest of the State, embraces the territory of thirteen towns, comprises one hundred and forty School Districts, and includes nearly two-thirds of the schools of the County.

Of the one hundred and forty School Districts, seven have their school houses in the adjoining Counties of Columbia and Putnam. The year has been another of educational activity and progress. Encouraging results have been attained.

The work of improving the condition of our school houses has gone steadily forward.

At Fishkill-on-Hudson, Pawling, Green Haven, Clove and Webotuck, new school houses that are highly creditable to their respective districts, are in the process of erection.

Many of the old school buildings have been thoroughly repaired, newly painted, and reseated with new furniture.

Though we do not propose to ask or demand anything unfair or unreasonable relative to the improvement of our school houses, yet we remain unconvinced of the wisdom or soundness of any policy that will tolerate old and indecent school buildings to such an extent that the health, comfort, and educational advancement of the children will be engendered thereby.

Generally speaking, I am happy to say that the people are manifesting zealous pride in the maintenance of good schools.

As Commissioner, I feel justly proud of our teachers. Relative to requisite qualifications, I believe that they will compare very favorably with the teachers of any other Commissioner District in the State.

As a body, they deserve to be complimented upon their faithful and efficient labor.

As a class, our trustees deserve to be thanked for performing their duties with energy and ability.

Our Teachers' Institute held at Matteawan last April, was a pronounced success.

Prof. Isaac H. Stout, our conductor, gave excellent satisfaction.

He was ably assisted by teachers from Normal Schools.

Arbor Day was very generally observed, with gratifying results.

The uniform examinations for testing the educational qualifications of the teachers, seem to meet with popular favor.

Eight examinations have been held during the year.

I have examined one hundred and sixty different candidates, and have granted one hundred and thirty-eight certificates, ten first grades, fifty-nine second grades, and sixty-nine third grades.

Some of the candidates of the second and third grades have attained certificates of higher grades at subsequent examinations.

Of the one hundred and sixty applicants examined, fifty-one failed to pass the examinations required.

Our voluminous clerical duties have been dispatched with all possible celerity.

I have made about one hundred and thirty-five official visits during the year.

In making my school inspections, I have endeavored to do my official duty in carefully observing the methods of the teachers and closely watching the progress of the pupils.

Upon the whole, I can say with confidence, that the year just closed may properly be recorded in the educational history of this Commissioner District as one of fruitful accomplishment in bringing our Public Schools to that high standard of usefulness whereby they will be able to continu. ally send for the students, properly prepared, for the responsibilities and obligations of true American Citizenship.

I am, very respectfully yours,

WILLIAM R. ANDERSON,

Commissioner.

MILLBROOK, N. Y., December 1, 1890.

To the Honorable, the Board of Supervisors of Dutchess County:

In compliance with custom. I respectfully submit the following report of the condition of the educational status of this district.

DESCRIPTIVE.

This Commissioner District consists of seventy-one School Districts, all of which with one exception, have their school houses within the county.

VISITS.

I have made during the school year one hundred and forty-six visits to the different schools ; and, as many schools consist of several departments, the total number of visits is much greater. From a survey of the whole field I am able to report an improved condition of the schools.

IMPROVED METHODS OF TEACHING.

The greatest improvement, however, is in the line of methods of teaching. Especially has great advancement been made in the teaching of reading. The " Alphabetical Method," is scarcely known, and while the application of the improved methods in teaching is as yet quite crude in some schools, our annual institute, combined with the excellent instruction given in our many educational journals, will gradually overcome the defect.

SCHOOL BUILDINGS AND SCHOOL FURNITURE.

While no new buildings have been erected during the year, a few have been renovated and refurnished. There are a few more, however, which need renovation and new furniture. I trust that the inhabitants of these districts will awaken to the fact that a pleasant school room is quite as essential as a pleasant home, and that some action will be taken the coming year to have a better condition of things.

While economy is an excellent virtue to practice, yet, when it is indulged in at the expense of public education, its reaction upon a community is unfavorable to the interests of good morals and intelligent citizenship.

The law clothes the School Commissioner with the power to condemn and to order repairs, including new seats, to the value of $200.

The exercise of this power seems arbitrary at best and ought to be considered an insult to the intelligence of a community.

I trust that there shall be no occasion for any action on my part.

TEACHERS' INSTITUTE.

Our District Institute was held Oct. 25–29. It was a success both as regards attendance and the interest manifested.

ARBOR DAY.

Arbor Day was observed in nearly all the districts.

The interest manifested by teachers, pupils and patrons in planting trees, vines, etc·, far surpassad my expectations.

Arbor Day bids fair to be a popular one with the children.

I am of the opinion that our school library system should be abolished, and the money devoted to that purpose be diverted into some other channel. In most districts, it is used for the payment of teacher's wages instead of the purchasing of books to be placed in the district library.

Respectfully yours,

JOHN A. VANDERWATER,

School Commissioner,

2nd Dist., Dutchess Co.

Dated at New Hamburgh, Dec. 3, '90.

Mr. Williams offered the following :

Resolved, That the Clerk of this Board, in extending and apportioning the State taxes against the property of this County, be directed to omit the capital stock assessment of the Poughkeepsie Gas Light Company, the Poughkeepsie Transportation Company, the Poughkeepsie City Railroad Company. and the Poughkeepsie Electric Light and Power Company of Poughkeepsie, assessed upon the City tax book for 1890, at $95,000, as the State tax upon that amount paid to the State Comptroller.

Laid over for further action.

Mr. Pugsley moved to adjourn.

Ayes and nays called.

Ayes—Messrs. Able, Andrews, Bartlett, Dudley, E. Herrick, J. A. Herrick, Kreiger, Lee, Milroy, Morehouse, Mylod, Pugsley, Swift, Wing—13.

Nays—Germond, Genung, Vail, Williams, and Wing.

Ayes, 13 ; nays, 5.

Motion carried.

WEDNESDAY, Dec. 3, 1890.

1.30 P. M.

Board met.

Quorum present.

Mr. Austin, from the Special Committee on Public Buildings, outside of the City, of 1889, presented the following, which was read and laid over under the Rule.

To the Board of Supervisors of Dutchess County:

GENTLEMEN :—

The Special Committee appointed by the Board of 1889, upon public buildings outside of the city, would respectfully report that they have caused repairs to be made to the poor house and buildings, and have expended for said repairs the sum of $985.18, which exceeds the appropriation of last year, viz.: $500 ; leaving a deficiency of $485.18, which we would recommend that the same be levied and assessed upon the county, exclusive of the city, and credited to the Poor Fund.

The following are the vouchers for payments by said Committee :

JULY 21st, 1890.

REPAIRS TO DUTCHESS COUNTY POOR HOUSE.

BILLS PAID by COUNTY TREASURER.

James Reardon	$ 71 22
Wm. E. Smith	51 84
Beers & Trafford	159 80
Mead & Murdock	71 66
Wm. H. Austin	79 27
Frank Shay	38 25
Stanford & McDonagh	20 00
R. H. Andrews	7 40
	$499 44

JULY 22d, 1890.

REPAIRS TO DUTCHESS COUNTY POOR HOUSE.

BILLS PAID FROM POOR FUND.

Merritt & Colvill...$	21. 90
A. B. Smith...	15
Swift Bros.	14 96
Wm. H. Austin	105 51
A. S. Coffin	13 88
R. T. Monfort..	8 20
W. G. Cowee......	16 20
Swift Bros.	64 85
S. M. Davidson...	22 53
A. S. Coffin	7 05
Frank Shay	27 54
Devine & Tompkins..	168 12

$485 74

The above amount is due the Poor Fund account.

All of which is respectfully submitted.

WM. H. AUSTIN,

LEWIS D. GERMOND,

W. H. BARTLETT,

Committee.

Mr. Milroy moved that the personal assessment against Wm. Pink in the assessment roll of the Town of Rhinebeck, be stricken from said roll, the same being recommended by a majority of the Assessors of said town.

Mr. Milroy asked for unanimous consent to present the same, which was granted and the motion carried.

Mr. Lee moved that the sum of $10 be levied and assessed upon the Town of Pawling, and the same be made payable to the Pawling Cemetery.

Motion carried.

Mr. Mylod moved that a committee from Supervisors outside of the city, of three be appointed by the Chair to audit the City Supervisors' accounts.

Motion carried.

The Chair named as such committee, Messrs. Howatt, Sturgess and Rogers.

Mr. Howatt moved that the Chair appoint a committee of three from the City Supervisors to audit the bills of the Supervisors outside of the city.

Motion carried.

The Chair named as such committee, Messrs. Mylod, Kreiger and Pugsley.

On motion of Mr. Pugsley, the rules were suspended to hear Dr. Gallaudet.

Dr. Gallaudet addressed the Board, asking for an appropriation for Gallaudet Home.

Rules resumed.

Mr. Pugsley moved that the thanks of the Board be extended to Dr. Gallaudet for information, etc.

Motion carried.

Mr. Genung moved that the sum of $5.15 be levied on and assessed upon the Town of East Fishkill and the same be made payable to John L. Hall for services as Constable.

Motion carried.

On motion of Mr. Pugsley the Board adjourned.

FRIDAY, Dec. 5, 1890.

Board met.

Quorum present.

Mr. Austin in the Chair.

Journal read and approved.

Mr. Able offered the following :

Resolved, That the sum of $6 be assessed and levied upon the Town of Union Vale, and the same made payable to Michael M. Vincent for services rendered as Commissioner of Excise.

Resolution adopted.

Mr. Able in the Chair.

Mr. Austin called up the Report of the Special Committee of 1889 on Public Buildings, outside of the City, and moved its adoption.

Ayes and nayes called.

All members present voting in favor thereof.

Ayes, 17.

Report adopted.

Mr. J. A. Herrick called up the Report of the Committee on accounts of Justices, and moved its adoption.

Ayes and nays called.

All members present voting in favor thereof.

Ayes, 17.

Report adopted.

Mr. Austin, at the request of Mr. Humphrey, called up the Report of P. A. M. Van Wyck, Superintendent of Drake Draw Bridge, and the Resolution for disbursements of said Superintendent and the appointment of keeper and fixing Salary for the same, and moved the adoption of the same.

Ayes and nayes called.

All members present voting in favor thereof.

Ayes 17.

Report adopted.

Mr. Williams called up the Resolution in regard to incorporations which pay their State Tax to the Comptroller.

Mr. Germond moved this matter be made a Special Order for Tuesday, December 9, at 11 A. M.

On motion of Mr. Bartlett the Board adjourned to meet Monday, December 8, 1890, at 2 P. M.

———

MONDAY, Dec. 8, 1890.

Board met.

Quorum present.

Mr. Austin in the Chair.

Minutes read and approved.

Mr. Vail, from the Committee on Miscellaneous Bills, presented the following, which was read and laid over under the rule :

GENTLEMEN :—Your Committee on Miscellaneous Bills respectfully report that they have examined the Bills referred to them, and recommend that they be paid as allowed.

NAME.	ASKED.	ALLOWED.
J. Benjamin & Son	$ 15 00	$ 15 00
J. Benjamin & Son	33 00	33 00
Barnes Brothers	67 62	67 62
D. H. Stringham	7 00	7 00
W. H. Sheldon	255 00	255 00
W. R. Farrington	18 30	18 30
Reynolds & Spink	104 50	104 50
M. S. Reynolds & Co	200 50	200 50
John J. Herley	7 00	7 00
Moore's House Furnishing	8 50	8 50
Wetzel Bros	33 00	33 00
Chas. Joseph	6 55	6 55
Wm. E. Scott & Co	12 00	12 00
John Eley	29 15	29 15
Levi Melhado, assignee	10 00	10 00
Wood & Tittamer	11 32	11 32
Perkins & Brother	120 54	120 54
Timmins	2 25	2 25
Drossy & Co	8 25	8 25
W. C. Little & Co	18 00	18 00
Court B. Cunley	3 60	3 60
Franklin Germond	4 00	4 00
Walter D. Hicks	4 00	4 00
John H. Cox	4 00	4 00
J. P. Ambler	27 70	27 70
Schou & Phillips	61 47	61 47
Elsworth & Dudley	5 05	5 05
Otto Faust	39 00	39 00
Geo. Dunwoody	7 00	7 00
Myers, the Jeweller	8 00	8 00
Henry Stibbs	5 37	5 37
D. C. Foster & Sons	202 00	202 00
Jerome Paper Co	9 00	9 00
S. S. Peloubet	17 50	17 50
Luckey, Platt & Co	156 31	156 31
	$1,521 48	$1,521 48

E. WRIGHT VAIL,
G. F. LEE.
GUILFORD DUDLEY.

Mr. Rogers offered the following:

Resolved, That the sum of $13,058.46 be levied and assessed upon the Town of Fishkill for Town Allowances.

Resolved, That the sum of $472 be levied and assessed upon the Town of Fishkill, exclusive of that portion of said Town within the corporate limits of the villages of Fishkill Landing and Matteawan for Town Allowances.

Resolved, That the sum of $4000 as fixed by the Commissioners of Highways and the Town Auditors, pursuant to Chapter 395 of the Laws of 1873 and the several acts amendatory thereof, be levied and assessed upon the Town of Fishkill, exclusive of that portion thereof, included within the corporate limits of the villages of Matteawan and Fishkill Landing, and that the same be made payable to the Commissioners of Highways of said Town.

Resolution adopted.

Mr. Mylod offered the following:

Resolved, That the salary of the County Treasurer from and after January 1st, 1891, shall be $1250 per year, and the Treasurer shall not thereafter be allowed to retain any part of the compensation allowed for receiving and paying State taxes, nor shall he retain any of the commissions received by him on account of the Trust Funds, but the same shall be credited to the County as required by law.

JOHN J. MYLOD.

Resolution adopted.

Mr. Gray moved that John Hoolehan be allowed $13.75, and the same be levied and assessed upon the Town of Poughkeepsie.

Motion carried.

Mr. Williams called up Resolution for assessment of Incorporations in City of Poughkeepsie, &c., and moved its adoption

Ayes and nays called.

Ayes—Messrs. Able, Andrews, Bartlett, Dudley, Gray, E Herrick, J. A. Herrick, Howatt, Lee, Morehouse, Mylod, Pugsley, Rogers, Swift, Vail, and Wood—16.

Nays—Mr. Germond—1.

Ayes 16.

Nays 1.

Resolution adopted.

The Clerk presented the following bids for printing proceedings of the Board and Court Calendars.

POUGHKEEPSIE, N. Y., Dec. 8, 1890.

Board of Supervisors :

GENTLEMEN :—We will print Court Calendars for 28 cents per page.

POUGHKEEPSIE NEWS COMPANY.

December 8, 1890.

To Board of Supervisors, S. Heroy, Clerk.

GENTLEMEN ;—We will print Court Calendars, under the usual specifications, for twenty-four cents per page.

Yours truly,

COOKINGHAM & CO.,

Stanfordville, N. Y.

POUGHKEEPSIE, N. Y., December 8, 1890.

To the Board of Supervisors of Dutchess County, N. Y. :

We will make Court Calendars for the ensuing year, same style and quality as last year, for 24 cents per page, per 100 copies.

LANSING, VAN KEUREN & BROWN.

Dec. 8th, 1890.

TO THE BOARD OF SUPERVISORS, }
S. HEROY, CLERK. }

GENTLEMEN :—We will print 600 copies of the proceedings of the

Board of Supervisors—400 copies to be bound in paper, and 200 copies bound in cloth—paper, style and quality of work to be the same as last year, at seventy-eight cents per page.

Yours truly,

COOKINGHAM & CO.,

Printers,

Stanfordville, N. Y.

OFFICE OF THE }
ENTERPRISE PUBLISHING HOUSE. }

POKEEPSIE, N. Y., Dec. 8, 1890.

To the Board of Supervisors, Dutchess County :

We will make 600 copies of the Proceedings of the Board of Supervisors for 1890, 200 copies to be bound in cloth, and 400 copies to be bound in paper, to be the same style and quality as last year for seventy-eight cents per page.

LANSING, VAN KEUREN & BROWN.

Mr. J. A. Herrick moved that the Contract for Printing the Proceedings of the Board and the Court Calendars be awarded to Lansing, VanKeuren & Brown.

Motion carried.

Mr. Rogers offered the following :

We hereby certify that the Commander and Relief Committee of Howland Post, No. 48, Grand Army of the Republic, have delivered to us a statement whereby they fix and determine the amount of money required for the relief of the Poor and Indigent Soldiers and their Families for the ensuing year at two hundred dollars ($200.)

C. O. OSBORNE,

CHARLES ROTHERY,

W. H. PEATTIE,

Auditors of the Town of Fishkill, N. Y.

Resolved, That the sum of $200 be levied and assessed upon the Town of Fishkill for the relief of the Poor and Indigent Soldiers and their Families under the supervision of the Relief Committee of Howland Post, No. 48, Grand Army of the Republic, and the same be made payable to the Supervisor.

Resolution adopted.

Mr. J. A. Herrick offered following :

Resolved, That the Clerk be allowed the usual sum of $75 for the preparation and distribution of the Proceedings of the Board, and the same be paid from the Contingent Fund.

Laid over under the Rule.

Mr. Williams offered the following :

Resolved, That the Chairman and Clerk of this Board be authorized to extend the contract with the Albany Penitentiary for the maintainance of prisoners made in 1888, according to the privilege therein granted.

Resolution adopted.

On motion of Mr. Pugsley, the Board adjourned.

———

TUESDAY, Dec. 9th, 1890.

Board met.

Quorum present.

Minutes read and approved.

Mr. Sturgess from Committee on District Attorney's Accounts, presented the following which was read and laid over under the Rule :

To the Honorable, the Board of Supervisors of Dutchess County :

GENTLEMEN :—Your Committee on District Atterney's Accounts would report that they have examined the bills presented to them, and would recommend that the same be allowed, as stated below, and the same be levied and assessed upon the county.

	ASKED.	ALLOWED.
William F. Germain......	$ 73 00	$ 55 00
Chas. W. Vincent	53 00	43 00
Martin Heermance.....................	139 57	139 57
		$237 57

All of which is respectfully submitted.

EDWARD STURGESS,

EDWARD HERRICK,

KROMALINE ANDREWS.

Committee.

To the Honorable, the Board of Supervisors of Dutchess County :

I respectfully submit my annual report as follows :

In the case of the People against William Wilcox, indicted for larceny, the defendant failed to appear for trial, and his bail bond was declared forfeited. The amount thereof, two hundred dollars ($200) was received by me and paid to Isaac W. Sherrill, Esq , County Treasurer. No other County funds have come into my hands. All fines imposed by the Court, in criminal cases, having been paid to the Dutchess County Clerk, will appear in his report. I have expended, for necessary disbursements, in the discharge of my official duties, the sum of one hundred and thirty-nine dollars and fifty-seven cents ($139.57), which I ask to have repaid to me.

MARTIN HEERMANCE,

District Attorney.

DUTCHESS COUNTY, S S. :

MARTIN HEERMANCE, being duly sworn, says that the

foregoing report is true to the best of his knowledge and belief.

MARTIN HEERMANCE.

Sworn to, before me, this }
26th day of Nov., 1890, }

F. W. PUGSLEY,
Notary Public.

Mr. Kreiger from Committee on Military Affairs presented the following which was read and laid over under the Rule:

To the Honorable, the Board of Supervisors of the County of Dutchess:

GENTLEMEN :—Your Committee on Military Affairs would respectfully report having examined the following bills and find them correct and recommend the payment of the same:

	ASKED.	ALLOWED.	COUNTY CHARGE.
Charles Kirchner	$33 50	$33 50	$33 50
Daniel Sullivan	15 00	15 00	15 00
H. Haubennestel	19 60	19 60	19 60
W. Haubennestel	150 00	150 00	150 00
	$218 10	$218 10	$218 10

WM. H. KREIGER,
JOHN J. MYLOD,
F. W. PUGSLEY,
Committee.

Mr. Krieger also offered the following:

Resolved, That the Committee on Public Buildings in the City of Po'keepsie be directed to pay all Bills direct to parties holding them, by draft on the County Treasurer, with vouchers attached, the same as last year.

Resolution adopted.

Mr. Rogers moved that the sum of $25 be levied and assessed upon the Town of Fishkill, and the same be made payable to Hackett & Williams for services rendered.

Motion carried.

Mr. Mylod offered the following :

Resolved, That Mark Dubois, of the News-Press, Geeorge W. Davids, of the Eagle, Derrick Brown, of the Enterprise, and Burnett Ackert of Star, be allowed $30 each, and the same be paid from the Contingent Fund.

Laid over under the Rule.

Mr. Williams moved that a Committee of two be appointed to make a Contract with the Albany Penitentiary and that the Chairman of this Board be named as one of said Committee.

Motion carried.

Chair named as an additional member of Committee. Mr. Williams.

Mr. Mylod moved that the Resolution adopted by this Board, viz.: That no allowance or charge or grant be made by this Board, to any persons or corporations, except those authorized by Law, be reconsidered.

Ayes and nays called.

Ayes—Messrs. Bartlett, Dudley, Genung, Gray, J. A.

Herrick, Kreiger, Milroy, Mylod, Pugsley, Rogers, Swift, and Williams.—12.

Nays—Messrs. Able, Andrews, Germond, E. Herrick, Howatt, Lee, Morehouse, Sturgess, Vail, Wing, and Chairman—11.

Ayes 12.

Nays 11.

Motion carried.

Mr. Howatt moved that the sum of ten dollars ($10) be levied and assessed on the Town of Hyde Park, for veterinary inspection of horses, &c., and the same made payable to John Faust, V. S.

Motion carried.

Mr. Mylod moved that the rules be suspended to hear D. Porter Lord in regard to bill of H. R. S. H.

Motion carried.

Mr. Lord addressed the Board.

Rules resumed.

Mr. Vail called up the Report of the Committee on Miscellaneous Bills and moved its adoption.

Ayes and nays called.

All members present voting in favor thereof.

Ayes 20.

Report adopted.

On motion of Mr. Pugsley, the Board adjourned.

TUESDAY, December 9th, 1890.

1:30 P. M.

Board met.

Quorum present.

Mr. Austin in the Chair.

Mr. Germond from the Committee on Superintendent of the Poor's accounts presented the following which was read and laid over :

To the Honorable Board of Supervisors of Dutchess County :

GENTLEMEN :—Your Committee on Accounts of the Superintendent of the Poor, respectfully report that they have examined the books and vouchers presented by him and find them correct.

Below we submit a general statement of receipts and disbursements which show the cost of maintaining the institution.

Total amount of receipts	$829 82
Appropriation	8,000 00
Surplus on hand Nov. 1, 1889	3,078 07
	$11,907 89
Total disbursements to Nov. 1,1890, as per schedule annexed.	$10,389 14
Surplus Nov. 1, 1890	$1,518 75

Your committee would recommend that the sum of $8,000 to be appropriated for the Poor Fund for the ensuing year and the same be levied and assessed upon the county, exclusive of the city.

All of which is respectfully submitted.

'LEWIS D. GERMOND,
SHELDEN WING,
E. WRIGHT VAIL,
GEORGE WOOD,
W. H. BARTLETT,
Committee.

Receipts.		Expenditures to Nov. 1st, 1890.	
Cows and Calves.	$116 50	Physician and Drugs	$ 578 49
Beef and Pork.	105 92	Reprs., Freight and Labor	805 10
Hams and Shoulders.	123 64	Potatoes and Pork	1,736 27
Potatoes	103 44	Beef	1,689 18
Bastardy	160 00	Flour	410 80
Pigs	104 00	Groceries	1,380 90
Lard	16 32	Clothing and Dry Goods.	784 96
Board	50 00	Boots and Shoes	157 92
Rye	30 00	Cows	203 50
Hay	20 00	Feed and Straw	430 03
		Coal and Wood	1,009 40
	$829 82	Counsel Fees	225 00
		Bastardy	227 80
		Temporary Relief	282 82
		Insurance	130 00
		Board of Children	83 50
		Incidental Expenses.	253 47

	$10,389 14
Receipts	829 82
	$9,559 32

RECAPITULATION.

Surplus on hand Nov. 1st, 1889	$ 3,078 07
Appropriation	8,000 00
	$11,078 07
Expended	9,559 32
On hand Nov. 1st, 1890	$1,518 75

Number of Paupers received and on hand and discharged at the Dutchess County Poor House, for Nov. 1, 1889, to Nov. 1, 1890 :

TOWN.	Received.	Discharged.	Years.	Months.	Days.
At Large-Tramps.	128	128			567
Amenia	7	4	3	8	61
Beekman.	8	2	5	15	42
County	3		3		
Clinton	3	3		11	31
Dover.	6	4	1	16	85
East Fishkill	12	4	7	22	31
Fishkill	24	15	9	52	107
Hyde Park	7	4	2	16	78
La Grange	2	1		5	12
Milan.	3	1	2	4	3
North East	7	4	3	10	48
Pawling	2	1	1	3	17
Pine Plains.	3	1	1	9	41
Pleasant Valley	2		1	1	19
Poughkeepsie	13	8	1	33	239
Red Hook.	14	8	4	44	142
Rhinebeck	7	4	1	30	62
Stanford	10	5	6	7	85
Union Vale	19	13	3	42	153
Washington.	9	8		27	102
Wappinger.	2	1	1	7	11
Total	291	219	54	362	1936

Paupers, Weeks 4643 5-7
Superintendent's Family, six Persons 312
Keeper's Family and Matron, three Persons 156

5111 5-7
Average Number for the Year 98
No. Paupers Nov. 1, 1890 72
Cost of Keeping Paupers per Week.. .... 1.87

Mr. Vail presented the following :

To the Honorable, the Board of Supervisors of Dutchess County :

GENTLEMEN :—We, the undersigned members of the Farmers' Club of this County, do hereby respectfully request that your Honorable Board grant to the said Club the use of the room known as the Supervisor's Room, to be used for its sessions of one day each during the year 1891, which may be held monthly, said meetings not to interfere in any way or at any time with the present uses of the said Supervisor's Room, and we, your humble petitioners, will forever pray, &c.

WALTER F. TABER,
A. M. UHL,
TIMOTHY HERRICK,
R. M. BROWN,
C. H. POWELL,
JOHN COOKINGHAM,
SMITH KNAPP,
SAMUEL C. BARIGHT,
PHINEAS R. WING,
WM. H. HART,
JOHN S. WING,
GEORGE S. HALSTED,
WILSON HAM,
THOMAS S. WING,
JOEL S. WINANS,
D. S. HALSTED,
GEO. LAMOREE,
E. WRIGHT VAIL.

The following gentlemen are appointed Committee to present the foregoing to the Honorable Board of Supervisors :

WALTER F. TABER, President.
A. M. UHL,
TIMOTHY HERRICK,
SMITH KNAPP.

Mr. Vail moved that petition be granted.

Motion carried.

Mr. Williams moved that the Resolution adopted by this Board in regard to the assessment of incorporated companies in the City of Poughkeepsie, be reconsidered.

Ayes and nays called.

Ayes.—Able, Dudley, Genung, E. Herrick, Howatt, Krieger, Milroy, Mylod, Pugsley, Sturgess, Vail and Williams.—12.

Nays.—Andrews, Bartlett, Germond, Gray, J. A. Herrick, Lee, Morehouse and Wing.—8.

Ayes 12.

Nays 8.

Motion carried.

Mr. Williams withdrew the resolution.

Mr. Howatt moved that the Resolution reconsidered this A. M., be made Special Order for Wednesday, 11 A. M.

Motion carried.

Mr. Mylod offered the following:

Whereas, The State Comptroller collects the State taxes upon the capital stock of the Poughkeepsie Gaslight Company, the Poughkeepsie Transportation Company, the Poughkeepsie City Railroad Company and the Poughkeepsie Electric Light and Power Co., of the City of Po'keepsie, the personal assessment of which companies is $95,000. Therefore;

Resolved, That in apportioning the State taxes to be collected in this county among the towns and city, the Clerk of this Boark first deduct $95,000, the amount of the personal assessments of said companies from the total equalized valuation of said city and then apportion said taxes upon all the remaining property, as equalized in this county, including said city.

Ayes and nays called.

All members present voting in favor thereof.

Ayes 21.

Resolution adopted.

Mr. Rogers offered the following :

Resolved, That the sum of $26 be levied and assessed upon the Town of Fishkill, and the same be made payable to George G. Judson for services as Commissioner of Highways of said Town. Also

Resolved, That the sum of $28 be levied and assessed upon the Town of Fishkill, exclusive of that portion of said Town within the corporate limits of the Villages of Fishkill Landing and Matteawan, and that the same be made payable to George G. Judson for services as Commissioner of Highways of said Town.

Resolutions adopted.

Mr. Germond moved that the Rules be suspended to hear Myron Smith in regard to Repairs to Alms House.

Motion carried.

Mr. Smith addressed the Board.

Rules resumed.

John A. Herrick called up the Resolution for appropriation for Clerk, and moved its adoption

Ayes and nays called.

Ayes—Messrs. Bartlett, Dudley, Genung, Germond, Gray, E. Herrick, J. A. Herrick, Krieger, Lee, Milroy, Morehouse, Mylod, Pugsley, Rogers, Sturgess, Swift, Vail, and Wing—18.

Nays—Able, and Andrews—2.

Ayes 18.

Nays 2.

Resolution adopted.

Mr. Mylod offered the following :

Resolved, That the system heretofore adopted of issuing warrants for all payments ordered by the Board, which are county charges, signed by the Clerk and countersigned by the Chairman, be continued by this Board. Also

Resolved, That⁀the Clerk be, and hereby is, directed to draw such warrants, which shall specify the name of the payee, the amount of the payment, the name of the fund drawn upon, and the date of the Resolution ordering the payment, and date when payable. Such warrants when signed by the Clerk, and countersigned by the Chairman, to be payable at their face value by the County Treasurer, and may be cashed by the Town Collectors and City Treasurer, out of county funds in their hands. Also

Resolved, That the Clerk be, and hereby is, directed to have these Resolutions printed, and a copy thereof pasted in each tax book.

Resolution adopted.

On motion of Mr. Pugsley the Board adjourned.

WEDNESDAY, Dec. 10, 1890.

Board met.

Quorum present.

Mr. Austin in the Chair.

Minutes read and approved.

Mr. Wing, from Committee on Sheriffs' Accounts, presented the following, which was read and laid over :

RECAPITULATION.

Board of Prisoners 1,113 weeks at $3.50	$3,895 50
Receiving and Discharging Prisoners	538 50
Subpœnaes	1,239 69
Warrants	455 79
Court Account	1,322 00
Jail Account	938 25
Surrogate's Supplies	180 50
Sundries (Court House and Jail Supplies)	68 31
Penitentiary Receipts	32 00
	$8,670 54

We recommend that the above named sum be allowed and levied and assessed upon the County.

> SHELDEN WING,
> WM. KRIEGER,
> JOHN U. ABLE,
>   Committee.

Dutchess County, ss.:

J. W. Van Tassell, of the Town of E. Fishkill, being duly sworn, says that the above account is correct, and that such services or disbursements have been made or rendered. and that no part thereof has been paid or satisfied.

> J. W. VAN TASSELL.

Sworn to before me, this 24th day }
     of November, 1890.   }

> C. S. HOWLAND,
>   Notary Public.

Mr. Lee offered the following :

Resolved, That Ordinance No. 4 passed by the Board of Supervisors of 1877 imposing a Tax upon Dogs within the several Towns of Dutchess, be and is hereby re-enacted, and made authority for the taxing and collecting of tax on Dogs to create a Fund to pay for injuries upon Sheep occasioned by Dogs in and for the County of Dutchess, and further

Resolved, That said Ordinance shall take effect immediately.

Resolution adopted.

Mr. Germond offered the following :

Resolved, That L. K. Strouse & Co. be allowed the sum of ($21.85) twenty-one dollars and eighty-five cents. for Law Books ordered by Judge Guernsey, as authorized by this Board, and the same be levied and assessed upon the County.

Laid over under the Rule.

Mr. Wing offered the following :

WHEREAS, A majority of the voters in the Town of Dover at the Town Election held in March last, voted to change the working of highways of said Town to the new system. Therefore,

Resolved, That the said system be so changed as directed by said voters.

Resolution adopted.

Mr. Germond offered the following :

Resolved, That the County Treasurer be directed to transfer from the Separate Fund Account any balance in his hands to the Poor Fund.

Resolution adopted.

Mr. E. Herrick moved that the sum of $12.50 be levied and assessed upon the Town of Clifton, and the same be made payable to Wilson Sitzer, for damage to horse falling through a bridge.

Motion carried.

Mr. Milroy moved that the sum of $12.50 be levied and assessed upon the Town of Rhinebeck, and the same be made payable to Wilson Sitzer.

Motion carried.

Mr. Williams offered the following :

Resolved, That the Committee on Legislative Enactments be requested to prepare an Ordinance for the Protection of Game and Fish, and to submit the same to the Board.

Resolution adopted.

Mr. Mylod called up Resolution for appropriation to Reporters, and moved its adoption.

All members present voting in favor thereof.

Ayes 24.

Resolution adopted.

The hour for the Special Order having arrived, that

being action upon the resolution reconsidered yesterday, Mr. Howatt moved the adoption of the Resolution.

Mr. Mylod moved that the resolution be laid upon the table indefinitely.

Ayes and nays called.

Ayes.—Messrs. Bartlett, Dudley, Genung, J. A. Herrick, Krieger, Mylod, Pugsley, Rogers, Swift and Wood —10.

Nays.—Messrs. Able, Andrews, Germond, Gray, E. Herrick, Howatt, Lee, Milroy, Morehouse, Scutt, Sturgess, Vail, Williams and Wing—14.

Ayes 10.

Nays 14.

Motion carried.

Mr. Howatt called for ayes and nays upon the adoption of the original resolution.

Ayes.—Messrs. Able, Andrews, Germond, Gray, E. Herrick, Howatt, Lee, Milroy, Morehouse, Scutt, Sturgess, Vail and Wing—13.

Nays.—Messrs. Bartlett, Dudley, Genung, J. A. Herrick, Krieger, Mylod, Pugsley, Rogers, Swift, Williams and Wood—11.

Ayes 13.

Nays 11.

Resolution adopted.

Mr. Sturgess called up the Report of the Committee on District Attorney's Accounts, and moved its adoption.

Ayes and nays called.

All members present voting in favor thereof.

Ayes 24.

Report adopted.

Mr. Krieger called up the Report of the Committee on Military Affairs and moved its adoption.

Ayes and nays called.

All members present voting in favor thereof.

Ayes 24.

Report adopted.

On motion of Mr. Pugsley, the Board adjourned.

———

WEDNESDAY, December 10th, 1890.

Board met.

Quorum present.

The Clerk presented Justices' Report.

Read and filed.

Also the following :

POUGHKEEPSIE, N. Y., Dec. 10th 1890.

To the Honorable, the Board of Supervisors of Dutchess County :

GENTLEMEN :—You are respectfully invited to visit and inspect the Poor House at any date convenient to your Honorable Body so to do,

Yours very respectfully,

MYRON SMITH,

Superintendent of the Poor.

Invitation accepted with thanks.

Mr. Bartlett moved that a committee of two be ap pointed by the Chair to make arrangements for said visi and to fix the date for the same.

Motion carried.

The Chair named Messrs. Bartlett and Wing as such committee.

Mr. Able offered the following :

WHEREAS, A majority of the voters in the Town of Union Vale, at the town election held in March, last voted to change the system of working the highways of said town, therefore

Resolved, That the said system be so changed, as directed by voters of said Town.

Resolution adopted.

Mr. Milroy moved that the sum of six dollars be levied and assessed upon the Town of Rhinebeck, and the same be made payable to Rickert Bros.

Motion carried.

Mr. Germond called up the Report of the Committee on Superintendent of the Poor's Account and moved its adoption.

Ayes and nays called.

All members present voting in favor thereof.

Ayes 19.

Report adopted.

Mr. Germond also presented the following.

DEPARTMENT OF PUBLIC INSTRUCTION,
ALBANY, N. Y., Dec. 8, 1890.

LEWIS D. GERMOND, ESQ., POUGHKEEPSIE, N. Y.,

SIR:—My attention has been called to the fact that one of the school commissioner districts in the County of Dutchess is much larger than the other, there being seven towns in one district and thirteen in the other. The Board of Supervisors of the County, of which I am told you are a member and the Chairman of the Committee on School Commissioner's Accounts, has authority to re-arrange the Commissioner Districts, and I write this letter to call the matter up for your consideration. It would seem that if the towns of North East, Pine Plains and Stanford were added to the northern commissioner districts, there would then be ten towns in each commission district, and one commissioner district would have 104 school districts, while the other would have 99, making them very nearly equal in extent. The best educational interests would seem to depend upon equalizing the size of school commissioner districts so far as may be practicable. Of course, other matters are to be taken into consideration than the mere number of towns or the mere number of school districts. Your Committee and the Board will fully understand that much better than I. I am not prepared to unqualifiedly urge the re-arrangement of commissioner districts, for I have not been able to give the matter very much examination or consideration, but from what I have learned touching it, it seems to me that there might be a re-arrangement with advantage to the educational interests of Dutchess County, and I therefore call the matter to your attention for consideration, and such action as may, under all the circumstances seem advisable. I am, yours respectfully,

A. S. DRAPER,

Superintendent.

Mr. Howatt moved that the communication be laid upon the table.

Motion carried.

On motion of Mr. Pugsley the Board adjourned.

THURSDAY, December 11th, 1890.

10:30 A. M.

Board met.

Quorum present.

Mr. Austin in the Chair.

Minutes read and approved.

Mr. Mylod presented the following, which was read and referred to Committee on Excessive Taxation :

PO'KEEPSIE, December 10, 1890.

To the Board of Supervisors of the County of Dutchess, N Y. :

Your petitioner, Homer E. Briggs, of the City of Po'keepsie, N. Y., respectfully represents :

First.—That on the 2nd day of October, 1889, he attended the sale made by the County Treasurer of Dutchess County of premises sold for unpaid taxes, and the parcel assessed to Dover Marble Co., owner Dover Marble Co., described as Marble Quary and Saw Mill, bounded north by lands of Thos. Wheeler estate, south by lands of E. A. Preston, east by lands of Huron Allis, west by lands of Perry Wheeler. Saw Mill bounded south by lands of E. A. Preston, north and east by highway, west by Ten-Mile River, taxes thereon returned unpaid by collector in 1889, $15.60. Amount due at time of sale, $19.79, was struck off to one C. W. H. Arnold for the sum of seventy dollars, which sum, as your petitioner is informed and believes, was immediately paid to the County Treasurer by said C. W. H. Arnold, who took his certificate. That subsequently for full value the said certificate was assigned by the said C. W. H. Arnold to your petitioner, and your petitioner is now the owner of such certificate.

Second.—That prior to the assessment above set forth made by the assessors of the Town of Dover, as your petitioner is informed and believes, the Dover Marble Co. sold and conveyed all its right, title and interest in and to the above described premises to one Jacob J. Mattern, of the City of New York, and was not the owner of the premises at the date of such assessment.

Wherefore, your petitioner respectfully asks that said County Treasurer may be directed to refund to him the sum of seventy dollars paid by him as aforesaid.

HOMER E. BRIGGS.

Dutchess County, ss.:

Homer E. Briggs, being duly sworn, says that he has read the foregoing petition and knows the contents thereof ; that the same is true of his own knowledge, except as to the matters therein stated to be alleged upon information and belief, and that as to those matters he believes it to be true.

HOMER E. BRIGGS.

Subscribed and sworn to before me }
this 10th day of Dec., 1890. }

S. H. BROWN,

Notary Public.

Mr: Lee, from the Committee on Legislative Enactments presented the following:

AN ORDINANCE providing for the Protection of Trout in the County of Dutchess.

The Board of Supervisors of Dutchess County do ordain as follows :

SECTION 1. No person shall take, catch, kill or expose for sale or have in his or her possession after the same has been taken, killed or caught, any speckled trout or brook trout, in the County of Dutchess, between the 1st day of August and the 1st day of April in any year.

§ 2. Any person or persons violating the above section or any part thereof, shall be deemed guilty of a misdemeanor, and shall in addition thereto, be liable to a penalty of twenty-five dollars for each violation one-half of which penalty shall be paid to the complainant.

§ 3. The penalties imposed by this Ordinance may be recovered and execution enforced in the manner provided by Chapter 534, of the Laws of 1879, and the acts amendatory thereof.

§ 4. All Acts or Ordinances or parts of the same heretofore passed by the Board of Supervisors of the County of Dutchess, which are inconsistent with this Ordinance, are hereby repealed.

§ 5. This Ordinance shall take effect immediately.

Ayes and nays called.

Ayes—Messrs. Able, Andrews, Bartlett, Dudley, Genung, Germond, Gray, E. Herrick, Howatt, Lee, Milroy, Morehouse, Rogers, Scutt, Sturgess, Vail and Wing.—17.

Nays—J. A. Herrick, Mylod and Swift.—3.

Ayes 17.

Nays 3.

Ordinance adopted.

Mr. Dudley, from Committee on Officers of the Board Accounts presented the following which was read and laid over under the Rule.

To the Honorable, the Board of Supervisors of Dutchess County :

GENTLEMEN :—Your Committee would respectfully report that they have examined the following bills, and recommend that the parties be allowed the amounts named below, and that the same be levied and assessed on the County.

NAME AND TOWN.	ASKED.	ALLOWED.	COUNTY CHARGE.
John P. Ambler, City	$346 05	$346 05	$346 05
Smith Heroy, "	810 00	810 00	810 00
	$1,156 05	$1,156 05	$1,156 05

All of which is respectfully submitted.

GUILFORD DUDLEY,
EDWARD STURGESS,
JOHN C. MILROY,
Committee.

Mr. Gray, from the Committee on Town Auditors' Accounts presented the following :

To the Honorable, the Board of Supervisors of Dutchess County :

Your Committee on Town Auditors' Accounts would respectfully report that they have examined the bills presented to them, and would recommend that the persons named be allowed the amounts named below and the same levied and assessed as follows :

TOWN OF FISHKILL.

	ASKED.	ALLOWED.
Eustus Horton	$46 00	$46 00
Charles Rothery	46 00	46 00
C. O. Osborne	36 00	36 00
Wm. H. Peattie	46 00	46 00

TOWN OF LA GRANGE.

	ASKED.	ALLOWED.
John S. Landon	$4 00	$4 00
Elias Van Benschoten	4 00	4 00
Jay Howard	4 00	4 00

AUGUSTUS B. GRAY,
JOHN U. ABEL,
E. WRIGHT VAIL.

Committee.

Report accepted.

Mr. Germond offered the following :

Resolved, That the sum of $3 be levied and assessed upon the Town of Washington and same be made payable to George Sackett.

Resolution adopted.

Mr. Mylod moved that a committee of three be appointed to audit the Asylum bills for the ensuing year.

Motion carried.

The Chair named as such committee, Mylod, Krieger and Wood.

Mr. Pugsley moved to adjourn.

Ayes and nays called.

Ayes.—Mr. Wing.—1.

Nays.—Messrs. Able, Andrews, Bartlett, Genung, Germond, Gray, E. Herrick, Lee, Milroy, Morehouse, Mylod, Rogers, Scutt, Sturgess, Vail and Williams.—18.

Ayes, 1.

Nays, 18.

Motion lost.

Mr. E. Herrick moved that the Rules be suspended to hear Capt. Haubennestel.

Motion carried.

Captain Haubennestel addressed the Board.

Rules resumed.

Mr. Mylod offered the following:

Resolved, That the Committee on Military affairs be authorized to rent the armory at such times as will not conflict with the Military, and that the Committee have power to take such action as may be proper to have any military order changed which may be in conflict with the spirit of this Resolution.

Resolution adopted.

On motion of Mr. Pugsley the Board adjourned.

THURSDAY, December 11, 1890.
1:30 P. M.

Board met.

Quorum present.

Mr. Scutt, from the Committee on Constables' Accounts, presented Report of Committee, which was read and laid over under the Rule.

To the Honorable Board of Supervisors:

GENTLEMEN :—Your Committee on Constables Accounts would respectfully report that they have examined the following bills, and find them
correct, and recommend the same be levied and assessed upon the
County.

JOHN SCUTT.
S. B. ROGERS.

	NAME.	TOWN.	Asked.	Allowed.	County Charge.	Town Charge.
1	F. J. Decker	City	$1,074 20	$1,074 20	$1,074 20	
2	Hugh Morgan	City	969 90	969 90	969 90	
3	Eli Mastin	P. Valley	6 85	6 85	6 85	
4	A. J. Thayer	Dover	26 00	26 00	26 00	
5	S. L. Buckley	Amenia	131 43	131 43	131 43	
6	J. J. Dowd	City	21 20	21 20	21 20	
7	F. R. Cromwell	Union Vale	4 00	4 00	4 00	
8	A. P. Abel	Union Vale	183 10	183 10	183 10	
9	Geo. W. Slocum	Pawling	15 20	15 20	15 20	
10	Chas. W. Stone	T. of Po'keepsie	17 55	17 55	17 55	
11	Isaac Kilmer	Milan	10 25	10 25	10 25	
12	J. C Ferguson,	City	6 00	6 00	6 00	
13	J. H. Malloy	Red Hook	9 80	9 80	9 80	
14	C. P. Wheeler	Rhinebeck	7 30	7 30	7 30	
15	Wm. Sleight	"	17 75	17 75	17 75	
16	F. A. Ross	Red Hook	10 25	10 25	10 25	
17	Chas. Shumaker	Hyde Park	17 95	17 95	17 95	
18	M. Knickerbocker	Stanford	5 80	5 80	5 80	
19	S. H. Williams	Stanford	9 50	9 50	9 50	
20	J. St. George	Po'keepsie	5 65	5 65	5 65	
21	Hilend Rose	Po'keepsie	26 40	26 40	26 40	
22	Thos. Mahar	Wappinger	57 65	57 65	57 65	
23	Thos. Fitzpatrick	Wappinger	153 75	153 75	153 75	
24	U. Wallace	Wappinger	7 55	7 55	7 55	
27	M. E. Rikert	Clinton	16 50	14 00	14 00	2 50
28	Chas. Corey	North East	34 35	12 35	12 35	22 00
29	John Hollahan	Po'keepsie	72 25	72 25	72 25	
30	Willis Vanburen	Fishkill	24 85	24 85	24 85	
31	Theodore Moith	Fishkill	35 25	35 25	35 25	
32	Joseph Kelley	Matteawan	6 65	6 65	6 65	
33	John Heeb	Rhinebeck	9 25	9 25	9 25	
34	Thos. Fitzpatrick	Wappinger	35 85		17 40	18 45

Mr. Able presented the following which was accepted and adopted :

To the Honorable, the Board of Supervisors of the County of Dutchess :

Your Special Committee appointed to contract for the transportation of Lunatics from the City of Poughkeepsie to the Hudson River State Hospital would respectfully submit the following :

Article of agreement made this 11th day of December, 1890, between the Board of Supervisors of the County of Dutchess, of the first part, and Morris G. Lloyd & Son, of the City of Poughkeepsie, of the second part.

WITNESSETH, In consideration of the sum of one dollar to us in hand paid by the party of the first part, the receipt whereof is hereby acknowledged, doth agree to furnish the requisite means for, and convey any and all Lunatics from any part of the City of Poughkeepsie as soon as may be, after receiving the certificate of committal of any Lunatic, for the sum of two dollars for each and every Lunatic so conveyed to the Hudson River State Hospital, for the term of one year, commencing Jan. 1st, 1891. Payments for the same made quarterly upon application to the County Treasurer.

Witness our hands this 11th day }
of December, 1890.   }

M. G. LLOYD & SON.

EDWARD HERRICK,
JOHN U. ABLE,
Committee.

Mr. J. A. Herrick presented the following, which was read and laid over under the Rule.

To the Honorable, the Board of Supervisors of Dutchess County :

GENTLEMEN :—Your Committee on Printers' Bills respectfully report that they have examined the following bills and recommend that the following amounts allowed be assessed on the County :

NAME AND TOWN.	ASKED.	ALLOWED.	COUNTY CHARGE.	COUNTY EXCLUSIVE OF CITY CHARGE.
Po'keepsie News Co., City..........$1,472 00		$1,297 00	$1,291 16	$ 5 84
Sunday Courier, City...............	134 00	59 00	56 50	2 50
Platt & Platt, City..................	1,231 69	1,127 01	1,123 52	3 49
Lansing, Van Keuren & Brown, City	236 53	145 80	142 78	3 02
Po'keepsie Publishing Co, City..	32 85	32 85	32 85	
Amenia Times, Amenia.............	30 50	30 50	30 50	
Fishkill Printing Ass'n, Fishkill.	20 50	20 50	20 50	
" Standard, Fishkill........	30 50	30 50	30 50	
" Journal, Fishkill.........	24 00	24 00	24 00	
Pine Plains Herald, Pine Plains.	31 00	31 00	31 00	
" Register, Pine Plains	29 00	29 00	29 00	
Pawling Journal, Pawling........	31 00	31 00	31 00	
Rhinebeck News, assigned to James Hogan, Rhinebeck...	13 00	13 00	13 00	
Rhinebeck Gazette, assigned to James Hogan, Rhinebeck...	26 50	26 50	26 50	
Red Hook Journal, Red Hook..	29 00	29 00	29 00	
Wappinger's Chronicle, Wappinger's Falls...	21 00	21 00	21 00	
Pine Plains Register, Pine Plains	3 00	3 00	3 00	
Millerton Telegram, Millerton...	21 00	21 00	21 00	
Pine Plains Herald, Pine Plains.	4 00	4 00	4 00	

The Committee recommend that the compensation to be paid the two papers publishing the Session Laws be fixed at twenty cents per folio.

The Committee further recommend that all the papers published in the County may advertise in one issue of their paper proclamations of Sheriff at one dollar each, notices of Jury Drawing at one dollar each, and jury lists at two dollars each.

J, A. HERRICK,
C. W. SWIFT,
GEO. F. LEE,
Committee.

Mr. Vail offered the following :

WHEREAS, under the Registry Law relating to rural election districts, the Board of Registry in each district is required to be in session three days, such Board consisting of five members, possibly of six.

And whereas, the registration this year has shown that at two of the sessions of the said Boards, but little work was to be performed.

And whereas, in most cases members of said Boards were allowed, under construction of law, pay for two days for each of said sessions.

And whereas, more than one member of the Boards of Election have claimed and received pay for taking election returns, stubs and unused ballots to the County Clerk.

And whereas, by reason thereof an unnecessary expense of several thousand dollars has been laid upon the taxpayers of the county.

And whereas,we believe the registration may be made as effective and much more economical.

First.—By making it the duty of the Town Clerk of each Town to copy all names from the poll lists of the last preceding election, for each election district in his town, in the required number of Registry books and to add thereto the names of all qualified voters who may request to have their names inserted in such Registry. Such additions to be made by the Town Clerk up to the day of session of Board of Registry.

Second.—By limiting the session of the Board of Registry to one day, at which they shall review the Registry books as prepared by the Town Clerk, add names of known voters, erase names known not entitled to vote, and add names of all personally appearing.

Third.—By the Inspectors designating some one person in each election district to take the election returns, stubs and unused ballots to the County Clerk.

Fourth.—By fixing a fair compensation to the Town Clerk,at say three cents per name, all copies to be counted as making but one name.

Fifth.—By fixing pay for members of Board of Registry at three dollars each for the session. Board to serve without Clerk.

Therefore, be it Resolved, that the Members of Assembly from this County be and hereby are requested to use their influence to secure amendments to the Registration and Election Laws in accordance with the foregoing suggestions.

Resolution adopted.

Mr. Vail also moved that the Chairman and Clerk of this Board be appointed a committee to present a copy of the above Resolution to the Senator from this District and the Members of Assembly from this County.

Motion carried.

Mr. Bartlett in the Chair.

Mr. Howatt offered the following :

Resolved, That a committee of three be appointed, of which the Chairman shall be one, to visit each of the Towns of this County during the ensuing year. And accompanied by the Supervisor of the Town, being visited, they shall have possession of the Tax Book of each Town and that they shall spend from one to two days in each Town visiting property, with a view to enable them to make up a report to the best of their ability, as to the value of property as assessed and equalized by the Board of 1890. Said report to be presented to the Board of 1891 during the first week of their session. This committee to be allowed per diem salary, railroad mileage and hack hire, with no other compensation.

Mr. Pugsley moved as an amendment that the Resolution be made a Special Order for Tuesday, Dec. 16th, 1890, at 11 A. M.

Ayes and nays called.

Ayes—Messrs. Able, Dudley, Pugsley, Scutt, Swift, Williams and Wood—7.

Nays—Messrs. Andrews, Genung, Germond, Gray, E. Herrick, J. A. Herrick, Howatt, Lee, Miloy, Morehouse, Mylod, Sturgess, Vail and Wing—13.

Ayes 7.

Nays 13.

Amendment lost.

Mr. Howatt moved the adoption of the original Resolution.

Mr. Williams objected.

Ayes and nays called.

Ayes—Messrs. Andrews, Genung, Gray, E. Herrick, Howatt, Lee, Morehouse, Scutt, Sturgess, Vail and Wing —13.

Nays—Messrs. Able, Dudley, Germond, J. A. Herrick, Mylod, Pugsley, Swift, Williams and Wood—9.

Ayes 13.

Nays 9.

The Chair declared the Resolution lost, it not having received a majority of two-thirds of the members present, as required by Rule 10.

Mr. Pugsley moved that the matter be made a Special Order at 11 A. M., Tuesday, Dec. 16th, 1890.

Motion carried.

Mr. Mylod offered the following:

NINETEENTH SEPARATE COMPANY,
POUGHKEEPSIE, N. Y., Dec. 11, 1890.

To the Honorable Board of Supervisors, Dutchess County :

GENTLEMEN :—You are most respectfully invited to visit and inspect the Armory, Tuesday evening, December 16th, 1890, at 8 o'clock, and also witness a drill by the 15th and 19th Separate Companies.

Very respectfully,

Your Obedient Servant,

WM. HAUBENNESTEL,

Captain.

Mr. Wing moved that the Invitation be accepted.

Motion carried.

Mr. E. Herrick offered the following :

Resolved, That on and after Jan. 1, 1891, all Patients that are charge-able to this County, committed to the Hudson River State Hospital, from this City, shall be placed in the hands of Morris G. Lloyd & Son for delivery to said Hospital, by the committing officer.

Resolution adopted.

Mr. Able offered the following :

Resolved, That the County Treasurer is hereby authorized and in-structed to pay Morris G. Lloyd & Son quarterly from the Contingent Fund, as per agreement made for the conveyance of Lunatics from the City of Poughkeepsie to the Hudson River State Hospital.

Mr. J. A. Herrick moved that the sum of $10.65 be levied and assessed upon the Town of Union Vale, and the same be made payable to Judson A. Denton, Justice of the Peace.

Motion carried.

Mr. Wing, from Committee on Sheriff's Accounts, called up the Report of the Committee and moved its adoption.

Ayes and nays called.

All members present voting in favor thereof.

Ayes 21.

Report adopted.

Mr. Vail offered the following :

WHEREAS, That on the 25th of November, 1889, Justice Wolven, of Pleasant Valley, paid to the County Treasurer, fines amounting to $20 (twenty dollars) which amount should—as per a former resolution of this Board—be paid to the Supervisor to be used for Town expenses ; now, therefore, be it

Resolved, That the County Treasurer be and is hereby directed to pay the Supervisor of Pleasant Valley, twenty dollars (20), and charge the same to the General Fund.

Resolution adopted.

Mr. Pugsley offered the following :

Resolved, That on account of the number of Standing Committees who are yet to report, and the large amount of work still to be done by this Board, it is inexpedient for this Board to visit the County Poor House this year, and that the Clerk of the Board send our regrets to Superintendent Smith.

Resolution adopted.

On motion of Mr. Pugsley the Board adjourned.

———

FRIDAY, Dec. 12, 1890.

Board met.

Quorum present.

Mr. Austin in the Chair.

Minutes read and approved.

Mr. Herrick, from Committee on Printers' Bills, called up Report of said Committee and moved its adoption.

Ayes and nays called.

All members present voting in favor thereof.

Ayes 17.

Report adopted.

On motion of Mr. Pugsley the Board adjourned.

———

MONDAY, December 15th, 1890.
2 P. M.

Board met.

Quorum present.

Mr. Austin in the Chair.

Minutes read and approved.

Mr. Swift from Committee on Surrogate's Accounts, presented the following, which was read and laid over under the Rule.

To the Honorable Board of Supervisors of Dutchess County:

Your Committee on Surrogate's Accounts would respectfully report that they have examined the accompanying bills and find the same correct, and they recommend that the amount thereof be levied and assessed upon the County,

NAME.	TOWN.	ASKED.	ALLOWED.	COUNTY. CHARGE.
John P. Ambler,	Pokeepsie City...........	$294 54	$294 54	$294 54
Myron H. Barlow,	" "	17 50	17 50	17 50
H. Alonzo Brown.	" "	8 00	8 00	8 00

CHARLES H. HUMPHREY.
C. W. SWIFT,
EDWARD STURGESS.

Dec. 4th, 1890.

Mr. Mylod, from Committee on Public Buildings and Accounts of County Treasurer, presented the Reports of said Committee, which were read and laid over under the Rule.

To the Honorable, the Board of Supervisors of the County of Dutchess:

GENTLEMEN :—Your Committee on Public Buildings respectfully report that it has carefully examined the following bills referred to it and recommend the payment of the same.

NAME AND TOWN,	ASKED.	ALLOWED.	COUNTY CHARGE.
P. H. Ward, Po'keepsie City.	$ 63 15	$63 15	$63 15
Frank Shay, Millbrook.	75 25	75 25	75 25
" " "	59 42	59 42	59 42
Andrew Bilyou, Po'keepsie City.	227 64	227 64	227 64
Shurter & Briggs, " "	156 33	156 33	156 33
Geo. Hughes & Son, " "	104 10	104 10	104 10
Wm. Gibson, " "	15 00	15 00	15 00
L. B. Stanton, " "	15 65	15 65	15 65
Owen Cook, Agent, " "	8 35	8 35	8 35
The Diossy Law Book Co., New York City	20 25	20 25	20 25
Po'keepsie Gas Light Co., Po'keepsie City.	32 80	32 80	32 80
James Maher, " " .	12 35	12 35	12 35
Geo. Worrall, " " .	15 00	15 00	15 00
	$805 29	$805 29	$805 29

JOHN J. MYLOD,

D. E. HOWATT,

AUG. B. GRAY,

Committee.

To the Honorable, the Board of Supervisors of Dutchess County :

GENTLEMEN :—Your Committee appointed to examine the books and accounts of Isaac W. Sherrill, Treasurer, respectfully report that they have examined the items of receipts and disbursements of said Treasurer, and find them correct.

The Report of the Treasurer shows the total receipts to be $335,570 54

Total Payments.. 321,249 42

Balance on hand .... $ 14,321 12

Your Committee would recommend the following appropriations for the ensuing year :

General Fund............ .... $10,500 00

Court and Jury Fund........ .... 7,000 00

County Judge Salary........................ .... 2,000 00

Surrogate's Salary... 2,000 00

Clerk's Salary	1,000 00
County Treasurer	1,250 00
District Attorney	1,500 00
Rent of Armory	1,600 00
Armorer	400 00
Bonds	20,000 00
Interest on Bonds	2,560 00
Supervisors' Pay Roll	2,500 00
State Tax	1C9,987 94
Justices of the Supreme Court and Stenographers	2,014 55
Note, City National Bank	7,000 00
	$171,342 49

Supt. of Poor, County Charge exclusive of the City	$1,700 00
Matron of Poor House " "	300 00
Chaplain " "	100 00
	$2,100 00

Your Committee would also report that they have examined the following bills and recommend the payment of the same :

Isaac W. Sherrill	$200 00
John P. Ambler	40 58
N. Ball	2 00
	$242 58

All of which is respectfully submitted,
JOHN J. MYLOD,
G. F. LEE,
GUILFORD DUDLEY,
Committee on County Treasurer's Accounts.

Mr. E. Herrick, from Committee on Coroners' and Physicians' Account, presented the following, which was read and laid over under the Rule :

GENTLEMEN :—Your Committee on Coroners' and Physicians' Bills respectfully report that they have examined the Bills referred to them, and recommend that they be paid and levied according to the following statement :

NAME AND TOWN.		ASKED.	ALLOWED.
John T. Wilson,	City	$275 00	$155 00
S. D. McIntosh,	"	20 00	20 00
J. P. Wilson,	"	60 00	55 00
J. F. Lamb,	"	130 00	105 00
J. G. Porteous,	"	50 00	40 00
Robt. K. Tuthill,	"	60 00	45 00
H. R. Powell,	"	165 00	120 00
A. Hasbrouck,	"	20 00	10 00
Po'keepsie Cemetery,	"	24 00	24 00
C. E. Seeger,	"	5 00	5 00
J. Marill,	"	325 00	165 00
J. W. Poucher,	"	50 00	30 00
F. A. Faust,	"	115 00	65 00
Wm. Cramer,	"	270 00	140 00
E. H. Parker,	"	20 00	10 00
J. C. Payne,	"	30 00	15 00
J. E. Sadlier,	"	30 00	20 00
Reed & Forman,	"	8 00	
E. A. Wood,	"	8 00	5 00
Michael Farren, assigned			
E. V. Vincent,	City	5 00	5 00
W. R. Case,	"	10 00	10 00
C. E. Lane,	"	10 00	10 00
A. B. Lewis,	"	44 00	
Van Dyne & Mellady,	"	70 00	70 00
J. C. Otis,	"	10 00	5 00
J. P. Ambler,	"	26 35	26 35
W. G. Stevenson Est.,	"	15 00	
R. C. Van Wyck,	"	50 00	35 00
W. J. Bogardus,	Fishkill	30 00	30 00
J P. Schenck,	"	10 00	10 00
H. B. Rosa,	"	5 50	5 50
E Moith,	"	130 00	110 00
J. H. Doughty,	"	170 00	165 00
Wm. J. Conklin,	"	100 00	100 00
E. Feller & Son, Red Hook		3 00	3 00
R. J. Carroll,	"	20 00	20 00
H. L. Cookingham,	"	140 80	119 80

Wm. R. Lown, Red Hook,		10 00	10 00
T. J. Barton,	"	30 00	20 00
Alexander Near,	"	5 00	5 00
Peter Feroe,	"	25 00	25 00
J. E. Losee,	"	5 00	5 00
P. H. Potts,	"	5 00	5 00
A. Lee Wager,	"	25 00	15 00
B. N. Baker,	"	5 00	5 00
C. S. Van Etten,	"	45 00	45 00
H. C. Wilbur, Pine Plains,		106 69	90 83
Geo. L. Johnson,	"	10 00	10 00
Eggleston Bros., Amenia		18 00	18 00
G. H. Codding,	"	42 00	32 00
Robert Lawson, Pok. Town		5 00	5 00
Wm. E. Traver,	"	5 00	5 00
John G. Harris,	"	4 00	
Judson A. Denton,	"	27 25	27 25
Duane Odell,	"	7 60	5 00
C. L. Fletcher,	Dover	10 00	10 00
Thos. Hammond,	"	20 00	10 00
F. Tallman,		3 00	3 00
M. H. Angell, Pls'nt Valley		40 00	15 00
H. T. Fink, M.D., La Grange		20 00	10 00
C. H. Tripp,	Clinton	10 00	5 00
H. Pearce,	Pawling	10 00	10 00
M. C. Northrop, Stanford		10 00	5 00
D. H. Knapp,	Union Vale	30 00	20 00
L. C. Wood,	Wappinger	70 00	55 00
I. M. Cornell,	"	10 00	10 00
Wm. Baxter,	"	10 00	10 00
G. H. Van Wagner, "		70 00	30 00
T. K. Cruse,	"	30 00	15 00
J. H. Goodale,	Rhinebeck	20 00	10 00
D B. Ward,	City	45 00	25 00
S. K. Phillips,	Fishkill	15 00	15 00
D. M. Sheedy,	City	90 00	70 00
J. R. Strong,	Fishkill	10 00	5 00
D. O. K. Strong,	"	10 00	10 00
J. S. Bird,	Hyde Park	10 00	5 00

Samuel Rogers,	Fishkill		48 00	48 00
J. G. Frost, assigned				
To August Doughty		38 50		
A. B. Lewis		140 00		
P. B. Hayt		300 00		
J. P. Heath		193 51		
Reed & Forman		212 00	884 06	884 06
W. J. Conklin,	Fishkill		2 00	2 00
W. J. Conklin,	"		883 45	883 45
W. S. Watson, assigned to D. M. Ormsbee			10 00	5 00
C. H. Hoysradt,	Fishkill		134 00	134 00
St. Joachim Church,	"		30 00	30 00
D. Nickerson			10 00	10 00
J. H. Redfield,	Wappinger		20 00	20 00
M. T. Pultz,	Stanford		20 00	10 00
G. M. Wellman,	Dover		10 00	5 00
E. S. Hoyt,	Clinton		5 00	5 00
J. Morschauser, Po'keepsie City			8 00	8 00
R. E. Knapp, Coal, assigned J. Beynolds			33 00	33 00
S. Philipps,	Fishkill		4 65	4 65
J. Flanery,	"		52 00	52 00
F. T. Hopkins,	"		35 00	35 00
F. Luther,	"		5 00	5 00

To the Honorable, the Board of Supervisors of Dutchess County:

PO'KEEPSIE, November, 1890.

GENTLEMEN :—I hereby certify that the following named gentlemen are entitled to the sum set opposite their respective names, for services as jurymen on inquisitions held before me, as per table annexed:

JOSEPH G. FROST,

Coroner.

John Trowbridge	$25 00
Samuel J. Farnum	29 00
John A. Bayly	27 00
Frederick Boos	25 00
Philip Lampert	26 00
Wilson Hicks	22 00
Edwin V. Vincent	26 00

Robert W Frost.. 29 00
Joseph H. Titus................................ ... . 35 00
James H. Ward.. 24 00
Stephen A. Perkins.......... .... 33 00
Denton C. Anderson.......................... .... 37 00
Edgar A. Adriance.............................. .... 27 00
George R. Fitchett.. .. .. 13 00
Charles E. Butts,   Salt Point...... .... 6 00
James I. Marshall, ... 6 00
Emanuel Briggs, ... 6 00
William Lary, ... 6 00
John D. Odell, ... 6 00
William Sheldon, ... 6 00
William Bedell, Clinton Corners... 6 00
Isaac Hewlett, Pleasant Valley...................................... .... 6 00
Silas Downing, ... 6 00
Frank G. Traver, ... 6 00
George W. Doty, ... 6 00
John J. Harris,   New Hamburgh.. 2 00
William E. Powell, ... 2 00
Lewis J. Hewes, ... 2 00
John S. Myers, ... 2 00
John R. Matthews, ... 2 00
C. M. Clark, ... 2 00
Frank Frost, 618 Dean Street, Brooklyn 2 00
Patrick Fahey, 509 8th Avenue, South Brooklyn, assigned to John
    G. Harris............... .. .. 2 00

FISHKILL, N. Y., Dec. 2d, 1890.

List of persons who served on Juries at the request of William J. Conklin, one of the Coroners in and for the County of Dutchess, and the number of days such persons served.

TOWN OF FISHKILL.

	DAYS.
William R. Brown	5
Sherwood Phillips	33
William Brown	3
Howard C. Ormsbee	4

170 *Proceedings of the*

Joseph C. Sawyer...
George Wilson..
Levi Ellis..
Charles H. Hoysradt..
Samuel Rogers..
John T. Smith..
Wm. H. Aldridge.............-..
John C. Bassett..
Charles E. Martin..
William H. Rogers..
Benjamin Hammond..
John B. Whitson..
Conrad B. Bevier...
Edmund S. Phillips...
Benjamin Sullivan..
John Clifton...
Addison G. Ormsbee..
Leveritt L. Inman..
Samuel Leith...
John L. Hall...
William H. Miller..
Weldon F. Weston..
Albert W. Underhill..
Daniel M. Ormsbee...
Theodore Moith..
John Flannery..
Thomas I. McGlasson..
David E. Colwell...
Alfred Kemp..
Frank D. Spaight...
S. H. Tillmann...
Henry B. Schenck...
James E. Shurter...
Charles H. Ticehurst...

EAST FISHKILL.

Edward Lasher..
George F. Horton..
Charles E. Knapp..
Andrew Riker..

John C. Dockerty 1
Charles Underhill 1

FISHKILL.

Moses C. Sandford 5
Albert Townsend 4
L. W. Perrine 4
Samuel K. Phillips 4
William H. Gifford 1
Charles Reeves 1
Benjamin F. Treen 6
John F. Mase 1
Roswell S. Judson 1
John F. Gerow 1
Benjamin J. Hubbell 1
Herman Greene 2
Greenwood Ammerman 2
Edward J. Kelly 2
Henry B. Bevier 2
George Harris 2

TOWN OF POUGHKEEPSIE.

John G. Harris 2
Robert Lawson 2
John Auberson 2
George Auberson 2
William G. Ferris 2
Cyrus Baker 2
Frank Myers 2

WAPPINGER.

J. A. Redfield 2
Charles Whitman 2

FISHKILL.

Edgar G. Greene 2
George M. Harding, ... 5
Nathaniel W. Purdy 5
James E. Dean 2
DeWitt C. Smith 2
Charles W. Cary 2

W. F. Wakeman 2
Willett Pierce 2
L. D. Bogardus 2
Peter Russell 2
C. Ed. Taylor 3
William H. Southard 6
B. Frank Greene 3
William H. Burlingame 2
C. E. Jaynes 2
W. J. Pralatowski 2

I hereby certify that the above services were rendered at my request between the first day of November, 1889, and the first day of November, 1890 ; also that there is still due Edmund S. Phillips,Fishkill, for one day, and Frank Luther, Fishkill, for three days' services performed during the year, Jan. 1st, 1889 to Nov. 1st, 1889, the same having been omitted from the list presented November, 1889.

WILLIAM J. CONKLIN,
Coroner.

I hereby certify that the following named gentlemen are entitled to the sums set opposite their respective names for services as Jurymen at at Inquests held by me :

William Sadler, Pine Plains $1 00
Amos Bryan, ... 1 00
William Husler, ... 1 00
J. S. Bowman, ... 1 00
P. S. Wolven, ... 1 00
Geo. T. Rickets, ... 1 00
Walter Van Benschoten, ... 1 00
Hoffman Hoysradt, ... 1 00
Fred. Bostwick, ... 1 00
Chas. M. Benjamin, Amenia 1 00
David Rundall, ... 1 00
Geo. F. Dennis, ... 1 00
Geo. H. Sutherlands, ... 1 00
John M. Haskin, ... 1 00
Geo. Middlebrook, ... 1 00
Paul A. Barr, ... 1 00

Jerry Pierce, Pawling,	....	2 00
Wm. R. Lee,	....	2 00
Geo. F. Lee,	....	2 00
Geo. W. Chase,	....	2 00
Thomas Elliot,	....	2 00
Jno. J. Arnold,	....	2 00
Samuel J. Barber,	....	2 00
Peter Govey,	....	2 00

HENRY C. WILBER,
Coroner.

Pine Plains, Nov. 15th, 1890.

The following named gentlemen are entitled to pay as Jurors for the time set opposite their respective names :

DAYS.

William Carroll, Rhinebeck	....	2
R. C. Worden,	....	2
George Saltford,	....	2
C. Rikert,	....	2
John P. Hermance,	....	2
Sylvester Holt, Red Hook	....	4
Horatio E. Moore,	....	2
S. R. Burnett,	....	2
A. J. Howland,	....	2
John Morgan,	....	2
F. G. Fraleigh,	....	2
A. J. Gedney,	....	2
E. B. Pells,	....	4
Alfred Folmsbee,	....	2
Wm. G. Donaldson,	....	2
Peter Troy,	....	2
Silas W. Coon,	....	2
J. A. Stoutenburg,	....	2
Robt. A. Coon,	....	2
Wm. R. Lown,	....	2
Walter Sheldon. Madalin	....	2
Fred. A. Ross,	....	2
Wilbur Rockefeller,	....	2
George Coon,	....	2

174 *Proceedings of the*

Peter Feroe, Madalin,	....	2
Frank Potts,	....	2
Zachariah Minkler,	....	2

Mr. Mylod presented the following:

To the Honorable, the Board of Supervisors of the County of Dutchess:

Your Committee appointed to burn the Bonds and Coupons paid by the County Treasurer during the past year, have received from said officer the following number of Bonds and Coupons amounting to Twenty-three thousand three hundred and sixty dollars ($23,360).

40 Canal and Deficiency Loan Bonds, Nos. 121 to 160 inclusive, $500 each......	$20,000 00
116 Coupons, due March 1st, 1890, Nos. 121 to 236 inclusive..	2,030 00
76 Coupons, due September, 1890, Nos. 161 to 236 inclusive...	1,330 00
	$23,360 00

They would respectfully report that all the above Bonds and Coupons have been burned and destroyed.

All of which is respectfully submitted.

JOHN J. MYLOD,
LEWIS D. GERMOND,
S. B. ROGERS,
Committee.

Report accepted and Committee discharged.

Mr. Sturgess presented the following:

AN ORDINANCE to enable the electors of the Town of Red Hook, Dutchess County, New York, to vote by District for Town Officers, passed pursuant to Chapter two hundred and eighty-five of the laws of eighteen hundred and seventy-eight, on the 15th day of December, 1890.

The Board of Supervisors of the County or Dutchess. do hereby enact as follows:

SECTION 1. The Town of Red Hook shall be divided into election districts for the election of all Town Officers required by law to be elected by ballot, and said districts shall correspond in number and boundaries to the election districts into which such Town may now or hereafter be divided for the purposes of voting at the general State election, and shall hold its election at such place in said district as may be designated by the Supervisor, Town Clerk and Assessors of said Town as now divided by law.

§ 2. The Supervisor, Assessors and Town Clerks of the Town of Red Hook, shall meet at the Office of the Town Clerk, in said Town, on the first Monday in February in each year, at ten o'clock in the forenoon, and in case a majority of said Officers for any cause do not attend on that day, it shall be the duty of those who do attend to adjourn to some future day, not exceeding five days, and they shall immediately thereupon give notice in writing to those who do not attend at the time of such adjournment, and it shall be the duty of said officers to attend on said adjourned day, and to proceed in the same manner as though a majority had attended on the day appointed by law. They shall designate the house in each of the election districts at which elections shall be held during the year, and they shall thereupon give notice, written or printed, of the annual town election in said district, together with a list of such town officers as are to be elected at such election, to be posted in at least four public places in each district, at least eight days before the holding of such annual town election, which election shall be on the same day as that on which the annual town meeting is or shall be hereafter held in other towns in the county.

§ 3. The Supervisor and Justices of the Peace in said Town shall compose the boards of the annual town meeting, and shall meet at the Town Clerk's Office on the day succeeding each annual town election, at ten o'clock in the forenoon, and proceed to complete the canvass and declare the result as herein provided for annual town elections.

§ 4. If a special election shall be called to fill a vacancy in any town office, the town clerk shall give the like notice as provided in section second, together with a list of such town officers as are to be elected at such election, and the justices of the peace, in said town, shall meet at the town clerk's office on the day following such election, and proceed in the same manner as at the annual town meeting.

§ 5. The inspectors of election chosen at the annual town election in and for said town as inspectors of election for the general election, are hereby authorized and required to serve as inspectors at the annual town election next ensuing, and they shall have all the powers and be subject to the same duties and liabilities, and receive the same compensation as is now or may hereafter be provided by law for inspectors of general election. The inspectors, or a majority of them, shall appoint a clerk, to be called clerk of the poll, who shall take the constitutional oath of office, which shall be administered to him by the chairman of the board, and shall keep a poll list and make such other minutes as shall be required. As soon as the polls of an election shall have been finally closed, the inspectors in their several districts shall proceed to canvass the votes. Such canvass shall be public, and shall not be adjourned or postponed until it shall have been finally completed. When the canvass shall have been completed and the result ascertained, a statement of all the votes for each candidate shall be made in writing, certified and signed by the inspectors of such district, with one ballot of each kind found to have been given for the officers to be chosen at such election, securely attached to such statement. The inspectors in each district shall designate one of their number who shall deliver such statement so made and certified to the board of the annual town meeting, which shall be held on the succeeding day, on or before ten o'clock in the forenoon of the said day. The board of such annual town meeting shall then proceed to complete the canvass, by adding all the statements from the several districts together and declare the result the same as though such votes had been polled at such annual town meeting, and the persons having the greatest number of votes shall be declared elected to the office for which they have been designated respectively.

§ 6. All such business as is now usually done at the annual town meetings, other than that provided for specially in and by this act, shall hereafter be done by the said board of the annual town meeting at their meeting on the day succeeding the annual town election immediately after completing the canvass of the votes as herein provided. Such business shall be done in the presence of and under the direction of the said board of the annual town meeting. It shall be done in public, and every elector of said town who shall be present shall be entitled to vote on all questions there decided.

§ 7. This ordinance shall take effect immediately.

At the regular annual Town Meeting held in and for the Town of Red Hook on the 4th day of March, 1890, a vote was taken by ballot for the purpose of submitting the question of the division of the Town into election districts, the ballots were endorsed " For Division into Election Districts," and " Against Division into Election Districts."

The following was the result : the whole number of votes cast was 649. In favor of dividing said Town 601 ; against, 48.

DUTCHESS COUNTY, SS. :

I, Campbell W. Hicks, Town Clerk of the Town of Red Hook, in said County, do hereby certify that the above is a true copy of the result of said vote as recorded and filed in this office.

CAMPBELL W. HICKS,

Town Clerk.

RED HOOK, December 13th, 1890.

Ayes and nays called.

All members present voting in favor thereof.

Ayes, 17.

Ordinance adopted.

Mr. Mylod offered the following :

Whereas, During the year 1888, the County Treasurer sold for unpaid taxes a vacant lot returned as belonging to one Patrick Walsh, of the Town of Fishkill, N. Y., to J. J. Smith, of this city, for the sum of $3.33, and

Whereas, That on the 30th of October, 1890, the County Treasurer gave the said J. J. Smith a deed for the above property, and since that time said Smith cannot find the lot, Now, therefore be it

Resolved, That the County Treasurer be and hereby is directed to refund the said J. J. Smith the amount paid in pursuance to Chapter 263 of the Laws of 1883.

Resolution adopted.

Mr. Smith moved that the Po'keepsie News Co. be allowed the sum of $68.20, for printing County Treasurer's Report and court calendars, and the same levied and assessed upon the County.

Laid over under the Rule.

Mr. Able offered the following :

Resolved, That the sum of $4.77 be refunded from the Highway Fund of the Town of Union Vale, for excessive tax against the estate of C. H. Colwell.

Resolution adopted.

Mr. Mylod presented the following bids for lighting the County Buildings for the ensuing year :

PO'KEEPSIE, N. Y., Dec. 13, 1890.

To the Honorable, the Board of Supervisors of Dutchess County :

The Po'keepsie Gas Light Co. will light the Public Buildings, now using electricity, from January 1, 1891, to January 1, 1892, for the sum of $325 (three hundred and twenty-five dollars.)

JOHN TRACY,

Agent Po'keepsie Gas Co.

PO'KEEPSIE ELECTRIC LIGHT & POWER CO., }
PO'KEEPSIE, N. Y., Dec. 15, 1890.   }

Mr. Mylod, Chairman Committee on Public Property :

DEAR SIR,—This Company will light the Court House, Jail and Surrogate's Office with Incandescent Lights, also furnish whatever gas may be required in its absence, for the year 1891, for the sum of four hundred and thirty-two dollars ($432), payments to made monthly.

Yours truly,

JOHN N. CANDEE,

Manager.

Laid over under the Rule.

Mr. Germond called up Resolution for appropriation to L. K. Strouse & Co., and moved its adoption.

Ayes and nayes called.

All members present voting in favor thereof.

Ayes 18.

Resolution adopted.

Mr. Dudley called up the Report of the Committee on Officers of the Board Accounts, and moved the adoption of the same.

Ayes and nays called.

All members present voting in favor thereof.

Ayes 19.

Report adopted.

On motion of Mr. Howatt the Board adjourned.

————

Tuesday, Dec. 16th, 1890.
10:30 A. M.

Board met.

Quorum present.

Mr. Austin in the Chair.

Minutes read and approved.

Mr. Genung, from the Committee on County Clerk's Accounts, presented the following which was read and laid over.

180   *Proceedings of the*

To the Honorable Board of Supervisors of Dutchess County:

Your Committee on County Clerk's Accounts, respectfully report that they have examined all bills presented to them and recommend that they be allowed and assessed on the County as follows:

ISAAC S. GENUNG,
JOHN C. MILROY,
GEORGE WOOD.

NAME AND TOWN.	ASKED.	ALLOWED.	COUNTY CHARGE.	COUNTY EXCLUSIVE OF CITY CHARGE.
A. V. Haight, Po'keeepsie City	$1,448 37	$1,448 37	$1,245 87	$202 50
H. S. Acker, "	76 00	76 00	76 00	
W. Wallace Smith, "	111 50	111 50	111 50	
Richard E. Lusk & Son,"	260 00	260 00	260 00	
Banks & Brothers, Albany	11 60	11 60	11 60	
J. P. Ambler, Po'keepsie City	248 26	248 26	248 26	
Theo. A. Hoffman, "	1,952 09	1,952 09	1,952 09	
" "	522 00	522 00	522 00	

A. V. HAIGHT.

Total bill for printing tickets.. $1,545 00

270,000 tickets outside of City, seven inches long, of which five and one-half inches were used for the regular County ticket exclusive of School Commissioners, and one and a half inches were used for School Commissioners, not voted in City... • $945 00

Five and a half sevenths of this is for the County, including the City... 742 50

One and a half sevenths of this is for the County, exclusive of the City... 202 50

$945 00

120,000 tickets in City seventeen inches long, of which five and a half inches were used for the regular County ticket, exclusive of the City ticket, and eleven and a half inches were used for the City ticket alone $600 00

Five and one-half seventeenths of this is for the County, including the City............................ 194 12

Eleven and one-half seventeenths of this is for the City alone..... .... 405 88

$600 00

Mr. Mylod, from Special Committee on Supervisor's Accounts, outside of the City, presented the following, which was read and laid over under the Rule.

Report of Committee on Supervisors' Accounts, Exclusive of the City:

GENTLEMEN :—Your Committee on Supervisors' Accounts, exclusive of the City, respectfully report that they have examined the several bills presented to them, and recommend that they be allowed and assessed as below :

NAME.	TOWN.	Asked.	Allowed.	County Charge.	Exclusive of the City Charge.
Henry Bostwick,	Union Vale............	$46 00	$46 00	$46 00	
James H. Russell,	Beekman..............	42 00	42 00	42 00	
David E. Howatt,	Hyde Park............	17 50	17 50	17 50	
C. J. Rockefeller,	Red Hook..............	36 00	36 00	36 00	
Wm. H. Bartlett,	Amenia................	9 84	9 84		9 84
Wm. H. Austin,	La Grange............	9 68	9 68		9 68
Lewis D. Germond,	Washington......... ...	9 00	9 00		9 00
George Wood,	Wappinger.............	18 20	18 20	18 20	
		$188 22	$188 22	$159 70	$28 52

County Charge $159 70
Exclusive of the City......... 28 52

JOHN J. MYLOD,
F. W. PUGSLEY.

Mr. Howatt, from Special Committee on City Supervisors' Accounts, presented the following :

To the Honorable, the Board of Supervisors, Dutchess County :

GENTLEMEN :—Your Committee appointed to audit the accounts of the City Supervisors, present the following bills and recommend their payment:

Wm. Krieger... $30 00
J. J. Mylod.. 135 00

D. E. HOWATT,

S. B. ROGERS,

EDWARD STURGESS.

Committee.

Laid over under the Rule.

Mr. Germond offered the following :

Resolved, That the sum of five hundred dollars ($500) be levied and assessed upon the County exclusive of the City, for necessary repairs to the Poor House during the year 1891.

Laid over under the Rule.

Mr. Swift called up the Report of the Committee on Constables' Accounts, and moved its adoption.

Ayes and nays called.

All members present voting in favor thereof.

Ayes 19.

Report adopted.

Mr. Mylod called up Report of the Committee on County Treasurers' Accounts, and moved its adoption.

Ayes and nays called.

All members present voting in favor thereof.

Ayes 19.

Report adopted.

Mr. Swift called up Resolution for appropriation for printing County Treasurer's Report and Court Calendars, and moved its adoption.

Ayes and nays called.

All members present voting in favor thereof.

Ayes 19.

Report adopted.

Mr. Swift also called Report of the Committee on Surrogate's Accounts, and moved its adoption.

All members present voting in the affirmative.

Ayes 19.

Resolution adopted.

The hour having arrived for the Special Order, that being the consideration of the Resolution for appointing Committee to visit Towns, &c.

Mr. Howatt withdrew the Resolution.

On motion of Mr. Pugsley the Board adjourned.

TUESDAY, Dec. 16, 1890.

1:30 P. M.

Board met.

Quorum present.

Mr. Austin in the Chair.

Mr. Howatt, from the Committee on Equalization,

presented the following, which was read, and on his motion was ordered printed and made a Special Order for Thursday, December 18, 11 A. M.

To the Honorable Board of Supervisors, Dutchess County :

GENTLEMEN :—Your Committee on Equalization present the following for consideration :

TOWNS.	ACRES.	REAL ASSESSED.	PERSONAL.	REAL EQUALIZED.	TOTAL EQUALIZED.
Amenia.......	25,846	1,258,448	241,100	1,312,329	1,553,429
Beekman...	17,580	710,610	38,900	730,778	769,678
Clinton.......	23,797	941,847	107,900	853,374	961,274
Dover.........	31,087	982,429	176,200	1,019,941	1,196,141
E. Fishkill..	33,047	1,202,834	96,625	1,179,957	1,276,582
Fishkill.......	17,091	3,805,738	537,440	4,362,064	4,899,504
Hyde Park..	23,145	2,233,560	140,350	2,008,937	2,149,287
LaGrange ..	25,814	956,439	99,650	1,042,507	1,142,157
Milan.........	22,583	529,089	46,900	551,995	598,895
North East.	25,860	962,137	111,050	1,443,068	1,554,118
Pawling......	27,151	1,334,401	298,900	1,230,788	1,529,688
Pine Plains	18,273	841,174	156,015	688,403	844,418
P. Valley...	19,774	909,551	210,893	885,665	1,096,558
Po'keepsie..	17,302	1,707,929	150,000	2,604,871	2,754,871
City......	1,587	9,718,890	3,813,850	9,780,530	13,594,380
Red Hook .	22,272	2,999,015	640,350	2,423,015	3,063,365
Rhinebeck..	21,199	3,027,168	354,760	2,407,928	2,762,688
Stanford....	31,573	1,403,498	132,400	1,250,124	1,382,524
Union Vale.	23,198	580,406	32,650	611,821	644,471
Wappinger..	16,037	2,167,204	137,800	1,812,567	1,950,367
Washington.	36,656	1,366,555	141,350	1,438,260	1,579,610
Total.......	480,872	39,638,922	7,665,083	39,638,922	$47,304,005

D. E. HOWATT,
L. D. GERMOND,
SHELDON WING,
S. B. ROGERS,
J. A. HERRICK,
F. W. PUGSLEY,
Committee.

Mr. Rogers offered the following:

Resolved, That the sum of five hundred dollars ($500) be levied and assessed upon the County, and the same be made payable to the Treasurer of Highland Hospital, at Matteawan, N. Y.

Laid over under the Rule.

Mr. Rogers also moved that the above matter be made a Special Order for Wednesday, Dec. 16th, at 2 P. M.

Motion carried.

Mr. Mylod moved that the contract for lighting the Court House, Jail and Surrogate's Office be awarded to the Po'keepsie Gas Light Co., said company being the lowest bidder,

Motion carried.

Mr. Howatt moved that C. S. Howland be allowed the sum of ten dollars ($10) for services rendered to Committee on Equalization, and the same be paid from the General Fund.

Laid over under the Rule.

Mr. Mylod called up the Report of the Committee on Public Buildings and moved its adoption.

Ayes and nays called.

Ayes 19.

Report adopted.

On motion of Mr. Bartlett, the Board adjourned.

WEDNESDAY, Dec. 17, 1890.

10:30 A. M.

Board met.

Quorum present.

Mr. Austin in the Chair.

Minutes read and approved.

The Chairman presented the following :

At a Special Term of the Supreme Court, held at the Court House, in the City of Poughkeepsie, on the 17th day of December, 1890.

Present.—Hon. JOSEPH F. BARNARD, Justice :

The People of the State of New York on the Relation of John I. Platt and James B. Platt.

AGAINST

The Board of Supervisors of Dutchess County.

On reading and filing the affidavit of John I. Platt, whereby it appears that the said relators are entitled to the relief they seek, and that their bill against the Board of Supervisors, of the County of Dutchess, set forth and described in said affidavit as a lawful charge against said County, and, on motion of Robert F. Wilkinson of counsel for the relators.

It is ordered that the defendant, the Board of Supervisors of Dutchess County, show cause at a Special Term of this Court, to be held in the Court House, in the City of Poughkeepsie, on the 20th day of December, 1890, at 9 o'clock A. M., or as soon thereafter as counsel can be heard, why a peremptory writ of mandamus should not issue out of and under the seal of this Court, directed to the said Board of Supervisors, requiring them to audit and allow the bill of Platt & Platt, referred to, and described in the affidavit aforesaid, and cause the same to be assessed and levied upon and collected from the County of Dutchess. in like manner as other legal charges against said county, are assessed, levied and collected.

Let this order be served upon the Chairman of the said Board of Supervisors of Dutchess County, on or before noon of the 18th day of December, 1890, sufficient reasons appearing therefor, and such service shall be sufficient notice of the application for the said writ.

J. F. BARNARD.

Justice Supreme Court.

DUTCHESS COUNTY, SS.:

John I. Platt, being sworn, deposes and says,that he is a member of the firm of Platt & Platt,editors and publishers of the Po'keepsie Daily Eagle, a daily newspaper published in the City of Po'keepsie and aforesaid County ; that deponent's firm was employed by the County Clerk, of the County of Duchess, pursuant to Sec. 10, Chapter 262, of the New York Session Laws of 1890, to publish in said newspaper, a list of all nominations to office, certified under the provisions of that Act, together with the name and residence, and the street number of residence, and the place of business, and the party or other designation of each candidate. That deponent's firm published the said list of nominations, as ordered by said County Clerk, accordingly ; that the same contained thirty-three and one-half folios ; that said publication was repeated seven times in the said Po'keepsie Daily Eagle, before the day of the last general election, to wit, November 4, 1890 ; that at the legal rate for legal advertising, the amount of the bill of deponent's firm for such publication was one hundred and twenty-five dollars and sixty-two cents, which amount is a fair and just compensation for the services so performed by deponent's firm, on the employment of said County Clerk as aforesaid ; that deponent's firm duly presented its bill for said services, which was by law a charge upon the County of Duchess, to the Board of Supervisors of the said County, and demanded payment thereof ; but that the said Board of Supervisors has hitherto refused, and now refuses to audit and allow the said bill of deponent's firm, or to cause the amount thereof to be levied and collected in like manner as in case of other lawful charges against said County.

JNO. I. PLATT.

Subscribed and sworn to before me)
this 16th day of December, 1890.)

JNO. E. ACKERMAN,
Notary Public.

Mr. Pugsley moved that the Chairman and Clerk be authorized to make a return to the Supreme Court.

Motion carried.

Mr. Herrick moved that the Committee on Printers Bills be authorized to employ necessary Counsel to defend the same.

Motion carried.

Mr. Bartlett offered the following:

Resolved, That the thanks of this Board are due and hereby tendered to the 19th and 15th Separate Companies, for the Exhibition drill witnessed last evening, and for the more substantial entertainment furnished, and that the Clerk of the Board be directed to send to each of said Companies a bound copy of the Proceedings.

Resolution adopted unanimously.

Mr. Able presented the following :

To the Honorable, the Board of Supervisors of the County of Dutchess :

Yonr Committee on Excessive Taxation having examined the various items submitted to them would respectfully report as follows :

That the sum of $2.63 be assessed upon the Town of Dover, and paid to the Wm. B. Newton estate.

That the sum of $6.36 be assessed upon the Town of Amenia and made payable to Isaac P. Conklin.

D. H. Post,   Fishkill, Town Charge.............................. $ 5 52
Lewis Tompkins,   "   "   " 44 00

JOHN U. ABLE.
WM. H. BARTLETT,
LEWIS D. GERMOND,
Committee.

Report adopted.

Mr. Milroy, from the Committee on Charitable Institutions and Asylums, presented the following which was
read and laid over under the Rule.

To the Honorable, the Board of Supervisors of Dutchess County:

Your Committee on Charitable Institutions and Asylums would respectfully report that they have examined the bills and estimates for
maintenance in the said Institutions of patients chargeable to the County
of Dutchess, for the ensuing year, and respectfully report that there will
be required to be levied and assessed upon the County the sum of
$42,044.14, to meet the bills that will come due, and recommend that said
amounts be levied and assessed upon the County as follows :

NAME.	ASKED.	COUNTY CHARGE
Willard State Hospital................................	$11,000 00	$11,000 00
Hudson River "	18,500 00	18,500 00
Binghamton State"	4,365 00	4,365 00
Albany Penitentiary................................	4,510 37	4,510 37
State Asylum for Criminals........................	585 00	585 00
State Homeopathic Asylum........................	225 00	225 00
New York Institute for Deaf and Dumb...........	187 50	187 50
Colored Orphan Asylum...........................	409 50	409 50
State Asylum, Utica..............................	260 00	260 00
New York Institute for Blind.....................	99 13	99 13
Asylum for Idiots................................	64 50	64 50
Home of the Friendless, County exclusive of City		1,300 00
Almshouse Commissioners.........................	196 14	196 14
H. T. Hufcut...................................	342 00	342 00

Your Committee would also report that they have examined the Communication from Chautauqua County referred to them, and would recommend that a Committee be appointed to represent this Board in the Meeting to be held (as stated in said communication) at Albany, in January, 1891.

We would also recommend that a resolution be adopted by this Board, requesting the Senator from this District, and the Members of Assembly from this County, to use their influence to repeal the act passed by the Legislature for the State care of the insane

> JOHN C. MILROY,
> WM. H. KRIEGER,
> EDWARD HERRICK,
> CHAS. WILLIAMS,
> CYRUS F. MOREHOUSE,
> Committee.

Mr Germond called up the resolution for appropriation for Repairs to Poor House, and moved its adoption.

Ayes and nays called.

All members present voting in favor thereof.

Ayes 17.

Resolution adopted.

Mr. Mylod called up the report of Committee on County Treasurer's Accounts, and moved its adoption.

Ayes and nays called.

All members present voting in favor thereof.

Ayes 19.

Report adopted.

Mr. Mylod also called up Report of Special Committee on Supervisor's Bills outside of the City, and moved its adoption.

Ayes and nays called.

All members present voting in favor thereof.

Ayes 19.

Report adopted.

Mr. Sturgess called up Report of the Special Committee on City Supervisors' Accounts, and moved its adoption.

Ayes and nays called.

All members present voting in favor thereof.

Ayes 19.

Report adopted.

Mr. Germond called up Resolution for appropriation for C. S. Howland and moved its adoption.

· Ayes and nays called.

All members present voting in favor thereof.

Ayes 19.

Resolution adopted.

Mr. E. Herrick called up the Report of the Committee on Coroners and Physicians Accounts, and moved its adoption.

Ayes and nays called.

All members present voting in favor thereof.

Ayes 18.

Report adopted.

On motion of Mr. Pugsley, the Board adjourned.

WEDNESDAY, Dec. 17, 1890.

Board met.

Quorum present.

Mr. Austin in the Chair.

Mr. Genung offered the following:

Resolved, That the sum of $405.88 be levied and assessed upon the City of Poughkeepsie, for printing election tickets, and the same made payable to A. V. Haight.

Resolution adopted.

Mr. Milroy offered the following :

Resolved, That the sum of $89 be transferred from the General Fund to the Poor Fund, for expenses of Supt. of the Poor.

Also the sum of $32 from the Home of the Friendless appropriation to the Poor Fund.

Resolution adopted.

Mr. Howatt offered the following :

Resolved, That the sum of $2.25 be paid Lansing, VanKeuren & Brown, for printing the Equalization Table, and that the same be paid from the Contingent Fund.

Laid over under the Rule.

On motion of Mr. Pugsley the Board adjourned.

———

THURSDAY, December 18th, 1890.

10:30 A. M.

Board met.

Quorum present.

Mr. Austin in the Chair.

Minutes read and approved.

Mr. Wing offered the following :

Resolved, That the County Treasurer be and is hereby directed to pay to the Supervisor of the Town of Dover, twenty dollars ($20), being the amount of a fine paid said Treasurer by Justice of the Peace, Mr. George W. Dutcher, on January 8th, 1889.

Resolution adopted.

Mr. J. A. Herrick offered the following :

Resolved, That the Po'keepsie News Co. be allowed the sum of $175. Platt & Platt, the sum of $94.68. A. G. Tobey, the sum of $75, and Lansing, Van Keuren & Brown the sum of $90.73, for printing list of nominations, and the same be levied and assessed upon the City of Poughkeepsie.

Resolution adopted.

Mr. Mylod offered the following :

Resolved, That the County Treasurer be and hereby is authorized to borrow on his note as County Treasurer, from time to time, such an amount as may be necessary to provide for the payments of claims against the County, until March 1st, 1891, to an amount not exceeding $15,000 (Fifteen Thousand dollars).

Resolution adopted.

Mr. Wing offered the following :

Resolved, That the sum of $15.97 be levied and assessed upon the Town of LaGrange, and the same be made payable to Wm. H. Austin. for disbursing school monies.

Resolution adopted.

Mr. Genung offered the following :

Resolved, That Edward Sturgess be allowed the sum of $25.69, for disbursing school monies, and the same be levied and assessed upon the Town of Red Hook.

Resolution adopted.

Mr. Pugsley presented the following :

To the Honorable Board of Supervisors of the County of Dutchess :

The undersigned, U. S. Loan Commissioner, in and for the County of Dutchess, does hereby submit this annual report for the year ending October 31st, 1890 :

On hand at date of last report :
Thomas and Susan Smith property bought in by State under foreclosure of No. 78 Mortgage. Town of East Fishkill.. $350 00
Now on hand as follows :
Said Smith property held by State........................... $350 00
Rent received therefrom since the date of my last report.. 18 00

$368 00 $350 00

Less insurance paid Briggs & Underhill, April 15th, 1890.. $5 00
Less horse hire paid to visit property........................ 3 00
Less ¼ per cent. commission on $350, 1889............... 2 62
Balance due me at date of last report not including my commissions............................ 1 00
Balance on hand... $3 76
Dated Dec. 1st. 1890.

STEPHEN G. GUERNSEY,
Commissioner.

Mr. Germond moved that the Rules be suspended to hear John W. Finley, Sec. of State Charities Aid Association.

Motion carried.

Mr. Finley addressed the Board.

Rules resumed.

Mr. Wing offered the following:

Resolved, That G. F. Lee be allowed the sum of ($14) fourteen dollars for disbursing school monies, and the same be levied and assessed upon the Town of Pawling.

Resolution adopted.

Mr. Howatt called up the Report of the Committee on Equalization, and moved its adoption.

Ayes and nays called.

Ayes—Messrs. Able, Andrews, Bartlett, Dudley, Genung, Germond, E. Herrick, J. A. Herrick, Howatt, Lee, Morehouse, Mylod, Pugsley, Rogers, Scutt, Sturgess, Vail, Wing and Wood—20.

Nays—Mr. Williams—1.

Ayes 20.

Nays 1.

Report adopted.

Mr. Rogers called up the Resolution for appropriation for Highland Hospital, and moved its adoption.

Mr. Howatt raised a point of Order that the above Resolution conflicts with a former Resolution adopted by this Board.

The Chair decided the point of Order well taken.

Mr. Mylod moved that the Rules be suspended.

Ayes and nays called.

Ayes.—Messrs. Able, Andrews, Bartlett, Dudley, Genung, J. A. Herrick, Lee, Morehouse, Pugsley, Rogers, Swift, Williams and Wood.—13.

Nays —Messrs. Germond, E. Herrick, Howatt, Morehouse, Scutt, Sturgess, Vail and Wing.—8.

Ayes 13.

Nays 8.

Motion carried.

On motion of Mr. Vail the Rules were suspended.

Mr. Wood appealed from the decision of the Chair.

The ayes and nays being called the following members voted to sustain the Chair:

Messrs. Germond, E. Herrick, Howatt, Morehouse, Scutt, Sturgess and Vail—7.

The following members voted against sustaining the Chair:

Messrs. Bartlett, Dudley, Genung, J. A. Herrick, Lee, Mylod, Pugsley, Rogers, Swift, Williams and Wood–11.

Messrs. Able and Andrews excused from voting.

Ayes 7.

Nays 11.

Appeal sustained.

Mr. Rogers called for the ayes and nays upon the adoption of the Resolution.

Ayes—Messrs. Able, Andrews, Bartlett, Dudley, Genung, Gray, J. A. Herrick, Lee, Mylod, Pugsley, Rogers, Scutt, Swift, Williams and Wood—15.

Nays—Messrs. Germond, E. Herrick, Howatt, Morehouse, Sturgess, Vail and Wing—7.

Resolution adopted.

Mr. Wood offered the following:

Resolved, That the sum of ($500) five hundred dollars, be levied and assessed upon the County of Dutchess, and the same be made payable to the Treasurer of the Gallaudet Home for the use and benefit of that Institution.

Laid over under the Rule.

On motion of Mr. Pugsley the Board adjourned.

———

THURSDAY, December 18th, 1890.
1.30 P. M.

Board met.

Quorum present.

Mr. Austin in the Chair.

Mr. Mylod presented the following :

NINETEENTH SEPARATE COMPANY,
POUGHKEEPSIE, N. Y., Dec. 18th. 1890.

To the Board of Supervisors of the County of Dutchess :

I have the honor to report that I have received and paid to the County Treasurer for the use of headquarter room at the armory since last report, as follows :

Knights of St. George	$8 00
Grocers' and Butchers' Association	36 00
	$44 00
Less 20 per cent. For Company	8 80
	$35 20

Very respectfully,

WM. HAUBENNESTEL,

Capt. 19th Sep. Co.

Report accepted and filed.

Mr Milroy called up the Report of the Committee on Charitable Institutions and Asylums, and moved that so much of the same as relates to assessments be adopted.

Ayes and nays called.

All members present voting in favor thereof.

Ayes 17.

Motion carried.

Mr. Mylod moved that so much of said Report as relates to an appointment of a Committee be adopted.

Motion carried.

Mr. Able moved that the remainder of the matter in said Report be expunged.

Motion carried.

Mr. Pugsley called up the Resolution for allowance for printing Equalization Table and moved its adoption.

Ayes and nays called.

All members present voting in favor thereof.

Ayes 19.

Resolution adopted.

Mr. Rogers moved that the Chair appoint a Committee, as recommended by a report of Committee on Charitable Institutions and Asylums.

Motion carried.

The Chair named as such Committee Messrs. Milroy, Howatt and Rogers.

The Chair presented the following:

At a Special Term of the Supreme Court held at the Court House, in the City of Poughkeepsie, on the 18th day of December, 1890.

Present—HON. J. F. BARNARD, Justice.

The People of the State of New York, on the relation of John P. Wilson,

against

The Board of Supervisors of the County of Dutchess.

On reading and filing the affidavit of John P. Wilson, dated the 18th day of December, 1890, and on motion of Hackett & Williams, Attorneys, for the relator, ordered that the Board of Supervisors of the County of Dutchess show cause at a Special Term of this Court to be held at the Court House in the City of Poughkeepsie, on the 19th day of December, 1890, at 10 o'clock in the forenoon why a pre-emptory mandamus should not issue against the Board of Supervisors requiring them to audit the claim of John P. Wilson as to the matters stated in said affidavit at the sum of $230 instead of the sum of $115, and why the relator should no have such other relief as to the Court may seem just. It is further or dered that this order may be served on the Board of Supervisors by de livering a copy thereof to the Chairman of said Board and showing him the original thereof, service to be made on this day, and that to be suf ficient service.

J. F. BARNARD,

Justice of the Supreme Court.

DUTCHESS COUNTY, SS :

John P. Wilson, being duly sworn, says he is a practicing physician re siding in the City of Poughkeepsie, and has so resided and practiced fo: the past ten years and upwards. That during the year 1889 and 1890 under order made by Myron H. Smith, Superintendent of the Poor, o the County of Dutchess, and of Daniel W. Guernsey, County Judge, o the County of Dutchess, also of Joseph G. Grost, one of the Coroners o the County of Dutchess, he examined and made post mortem examin ations under the statute relating to lunatics, the following person: who were adjudged lunatics and were committed to various insane asy lums as such lunatics, viz :

James Umplebee, Amelia Mitchell, James Scott, Theodore Bronson Edward Rogers, Robert McNulty, Michael Hoban, John D. Smith,Louis: Hyland, John McLean, William Hackett, Mary Helley, William Dryer John O. Sullivan, Richard Muldray, Julia Applebee, Chas. Aken,Thoma Farrell, each of which examinations in lunacy were made under order made by Hon. D. W. Guernsey, as County Judge of Dutchess County That on the order of Myron Smith, Superintendent of the Poor o Dutchess County, he examined Michael Skelly in lunacy, and on the or der of Joseph G. Frost, one of the Coroners of said County of Dutchess he made post mortem examinations upon the bodies of William Wickson William White and of John Lake. That each of said services was wortl the sum of ten dollars, which is a just and fair charge for such examina tions and post mortems. That heretofore and on the 17th day of Novem ber, 1890, deponent presented a bill for such services to the Board of Su pervisors of the County of Dutchess, duly verified. That said Board o: Supervisors on or about the 17th day of December, 1890, refused to audi said bill at $230, but did audit the same at the sum of $115. That said Board of Supervisors gave no reason for refusing to audit the said claim at the sum of $230, which is a just and fair compensation for said services.

No previous application has been made for an order herein and moved to adjourn sine die this day.

JOHN P. WILSON.

Sworn to before me this 18th day of December, 1890.

JOS. F. HORAN,

Com. of Deeds in and for the City of Poughkeepsie,

Mr. E. Herrick moved that the Chairman and Clerk be authorized to make a return to the Supreme Court.

Motion carried.

Mr. E. Herrick offered following :

Resolved, That the Committee on Coroners' and Physicians' Accounts be authorized to employ Counsel to defend the same.

Resolution adopted.

On motion of Mr. Pugsley the Board adjourned.

FRIDAY, Dec. 20, 1890.
10:30 A. M.

Board met.
Quorum present.
Mr. Austin in the Chair.
Minutes read and approved.

The Chairman presented the following :

SUPREME COURT.

Trial Desired in Dutchess County.

E. WRIGHT VAIL,
agst.
The Board of Supervisors of the County
of Dutchess.

To the above named Defendants :

You are hereby summoned to answer the complaint in this action, and to serve a copy of your answer on the plaintiff's attorney within twenty days after the service of this summons, exclusive of the day of service, and in case of your failure to appear, or answer, judgment will be taken against you by default, for the relief demanded in the complaint. Dated December 18th, 1890.

DAN'L W. GUERNSEY,
Plaintiff's Attorney.

Office and Post Office address, 275 Main street,
Poughkeepsie, New York.

SUPREME COURT—DUTCHESS COUNTY.

E. WRIGHT VAIL,
agst.
The Board of Supervisors of the County
of Dutchess.

The plaintiff, for his cause of action, respectfully shows to this Court :

I. That the defendant consists of a body or board of officers, acting and who have acted for and on behalf of the County of Dutchess, State of New York.

II. That this plaintiff is a resident and taxpayer in the Town of Pleasant Valley in said County of Dutchess; that his assessment in said Town and County amounts to exceed the sum of one thousand dollars, and that he is liable to pay taxes upon said assessment in and to the county aforesaid, and that he has paid taxes upon an assessment of to exceed the sum of one thousand dollars within one year previous to the commencement of this action.

III.   That the said defendant, without power or authority of law, acting for and in behalf of said County, as a Board of Supervisors thereof, passed a resolution as follows, viz.: "*Resolved*, That the sum of five " hundred dollars be levied and assessed upon the County, and the same " be made payable to the Treasurer of Highland Hospital at Matteawan, " N. Y."

IV.   That the allowing and paying of such sum of five hundred dollars, or providing for its payment, by said defendant, is illegal and unjust, and a waste of the public funds of said County, and an injury to this plaintiff and all taxpayers of the County, by adding to the burden of taxation thereof.

Wherefore, this plaintiff asks judgment, that said defendant be restrained and enjoined from levying and assessing the said sum of five hundred dollars upon the County of Dutchess.   That said Resolution be declared null and void ; or for such other and further order as may be meet and proper, and his costs of this action.

DANIEL W. GUERNSEY,
Attorney for Plaintiff.

STATE OF NEW YORK, } ss :
COUNTY OF DUTCHESS.

E. Wright Vail being duly sworn, deposes and says he is the plaintiff named in the foregoing complaint, that he has heard read the same and knows the contents thereof, that the same is true of his own knowledge except as to the matters therein stated to be alleged upon information and belief, and as to those matters he believes it to be true.

E. WRIGHT VAIL.

Sworn to before me this 18th day }
of December, 1890.   }

E. H. TRAVIS,

Com. of Deeds in and for Poughkeepsie, N. Y.

STATE OF NEW YORK, } ss :
COUNTY OF DUTCHESS }

Edward Sturgess, Cyrus Morehouse, Lewis Germond, and Edward Herrick, being severally sworn say, and each for himself says, he has heard the foregoing complaint read, and knows the facts therein stated, and that the same are true.

LEWIS D. GERMOND,
EDWARD HERRICK,
EDWARD STURGESS,
CYRUS MOREHOUSE.

Sworn to before me this 18th day of }
December, 1890.   }

E. H. TRAVIS,

Com'r of Deeds in and for Poughkeepsie, N. Y.

SUPREME COURT.

E. WRIGHT VAIL,

vs.

The Board of Supervisors of the County of Dutchess.

On reading the Complaint in this action, duly verified, also the affidavit of Edward Sturgess, Lewis Germond, Cyrus Morehouse and Edward Herrick, that the defendant is about to levy and assess upon the County of Dutchess, the sum of Five Hundred Dollars for the Highland Hospital at Matteawan, N. Y., and has authorized the same by Resolution.

It is ordered that the defendant The Board of Supervisors of the County of Dutchess, and its attorneys, counselors, agents and assistants be, and each and every of them is, under the penalties by law prescribed, enjoined and restrained until the further order of the Court in the premises, from levying or assessing the said sum for the purpose aforesaid, and that said defendant, the Board of Supervisors of the County of Dutchess, show cause before me at the Court House, in the City of Poughkeepsie, on the 19th day of December, 1890, at 11 A. M., why this injunction should not be continued in force.

J. F. BARNARD,

Justice Supreme Court.

Dated the 19th day of December, 1890.

SUPREME COURT.

E. WRIGHT VAIL.

agst.

The Board of Supervisors of the County of Dutchess.

The above named plaintiff having applied, or being about to apply for an injunction herein restraining the defendant from laying and assessing upon the County of Dutchess, the sum of five hundred dollars for the Highland Hospital at Matteawan, as therein particularly mentioned. Now, therefore, we, E. Wright Vail and Lewis Germond, Ed. Sturgess. Ed. Herrick, Cyrus Morehouse, all of Dutchess County, N. Y., all by occupation farmers, do hereby jointly and severally undertake, promise and agree to and with the said defendant, that the plaintiff will pay to the defendant enjoined, such damages, not exceeding the sum of two hundred and fifty dollars, as it may sustain by reason of such injunction, if the Court shall finally decide that the said plaintiff is not entitled thereto ; such damages to be ascertained by a reference, or in such other manner as the Court may direct.

Dated Dec. 18th. 1890.

E. WRIGHT VAIL, [L. S.]

LEWIS D. GERMOND, [L. S.]

EDWARD STURGESS, [L. S.]

CYRUS MOREHOUSE, [L. S.]

EDWARD HERRICK. [L. S.]

STATE ON NEW YORK }
COUNTY OF DUTCHESS.   } SS :

E. Wright Vail, one of the subscribers to the above undertaking, being duly sworn, says that he is a resident and one of the subscribers to the above undertaking, being duly sworn, says, that he is a resident and free holder within this State, and is worth the sum of five thousand dollars, over and above all debts and liabilities which he owes or has incurred, exclusive of property exempt by law from levy and sale under an execution.

E. WRIGHT VAIL.

Subscribed and sworn to before me, }
    this 18th day of Dec., 1890.   }

E. H. TRAVIS.

Com. of Deeds in and for Poughkeepsie, N. Y.

STATE OF NEW YORK, }
COUNTY OF DUTCHESS.   } SS :

Lewis Germond, one of the subscribers to the above undertaking, being duly sworn, says, that he is a resident and holder within this State, and is worth the sum of five thousand dollars, over and. above all debts and liabilities which he owes or has incurred, exclusive of property exempt by law from levy and sale under an execution.

LEWIS D. GERMOND.

Subscribed and sworn to before me, }
    this 18th day of Dec., 1890.   }   .

E. H. TRAVIS,

Com. of Deeds in and for Poughkeepsie, N. Y.

STATE OF NEW YORK. }
COUNTY OF DUTCHESS.   } SS :

On this 18th day of December, in the year one thousand eight hundred and ninty, before me, the subscriber, appeared E. Wright Vail, Ed· Sturgess, Cyrus Morehouse, L. Germond and E. Herrick, to me personally known to be the same persons described in and who executed the above undertaking. and they severally acknowledged that they executed the same.

EVERETT H. TRAVIS.

Com. of Deeds in and for Poughkeepsie, N. Y.

SUPREME COURT—DUTCHESS COUNTY.

E. WRIGHT VAIL.

vs.

The Board of Supervisors of the County
of Dutchess.

STATE OF NEW YORK,) ss :
COUNTY OF DUTCHESS,)

Daniel W. Guernsey, being duly sworn, says that he is attorney for
plaintiff ; that he has been informed by a number of the members of the
Board of Supervisors, that they would probably adjourn to-day until
such time as they meet to sign the tax books, and that the matter at issue
in this action should be determined at once.

DANIEL W. GUERNSEY.

Sworn to before me December)
19th, 1890. (

E. H. TRAVIS,
Com'r of Deeds in and for Po'keepsie, N. Y.

Mr. Mylod moved that the Chairman be authorized to
make a return to the Supreme Court, and that a Committee be appointed by the Chair, to employ Counsel to
defend the same.

Motion carried.

The Chair named Messrs. Mylod, Dudley, and Rogers
as such Committee.

Mr. Howatt offered the following :

Resolved, That the sum of four dollars be levied and assessed upon the
Town of Hyde Park, and the same be made payable to L. S. Wigg, for
services as Clerk of 2d district of said Town.

Resolution adopted.

Mr. Vail moved to reconsider the Resolution in regard

to the appointment of Dr. John P. Wilson as Jail Physician.

Ayes and nays called.

Ayes—Messrs. Able, Andrews, Dudley, Germond, Howatt, Milroy, Pugsley, Sturgess, Swift, Vail, and Wing—11.

Nays—Messrs. Gray and Krieger—2.

Ayes, 11.

Nays, 2.

Motion carried.

Mr. Vail moved to rescind the appointment of Dr. John P. Wilson as Jail Physician.

Ayes and nays called.

Ayes—Messrs. Able, Andrews, Bartlett, Dudley, Germond, Howatt, Milroy, Pugsley, Sturgess, Swift, Vail, and Wing—12.

Nays—Messrs. Gray, Krieger, Mylod and Wood—4.

Ayes, 12.

Nays, 4.

Motion carried.

Mr. Vail nominated Dr. E. H. Parker for Jail Physician.

Mr. Krieger nominated Dr. J. P. Wilson for Jail Physician.

Mr. Vail moved that the Board proceed to ballot for Jail Physician, and that the Chair appoint two Tellers.

Motion carried.

The Chair appointed Messrs. Howatt and Kreiger Tellers.

Whole number of votes cast 16, of which Dr. E. H. Parker received, 10; Dr. J. P. Wilson received, 4; blank received, 2.

Dr. E. H. Parker was declared elected as Jail Physician.

Mr. Rogers offered the following:

Resolved, That the sum of $9,818.77 be levied and assessed upon the Town of Fishkill, exclusive of that portion of said Town which was within the corporate limits of the Village of Fishkill Landing, May, 1885, and made payable to the Supervisor of said Town, for the purpose of satisfying certain judgments against said Town, viz : Clara Phillips *vs.* Town of Fishkill.

Resolution adopted.

Mr. Howatt moved that the Board adjourn to meet Monday, Dec. 29th, 1890, at 2 P. M.

Motion carried.

MONDAY, December 29th, 1890.

Board met.

Quorum present.

Mr. Austin in the Chair.

Minutes read and approved.

Mr. E. Herrick offered the following:

Resolved, That the sum of $10 be allowed C. B. Herrick as Counsel in the case of John I. Platt against the Board of Supervisors, also $20 as Counsel in the case of John P. Wilson against the Board of Supervisors; the same to be paid from the General Fund.

Resolved, That the sum of $?0 be allowed H. H. Hustis as Counsel in the case of John P. Wilson against the Board of Supervisors : the same to be paid from the General Fund.

Laid over under the Rule.

Mr. Pugsley offered the following :

WHEREAS, As the Taxpayers of this County gave the State of New York $64,000 to build the Hudson River State Hospital,

And as the State Board of Lunacy have the right under the act of the Legislature of 1890, and are excluding pay patients from said Hospital, and are compelling the friends of pay patients to send them out of the County and even out of the State to find an asylum, thus discriminating against the taxpayers. Therefore,

Resolved, That the Committee heretofore appointed to meet representatives from other parts of the State upon matters concerning the insane, use their best efforts to have this County exempted from the provisions of the Act of 189:), so as to permit the Hudson River State Hospital to receive pay patients from this County.

Resolution adopted.

Mr. Vail offered the following :

Resolved, That a special committee be appointed to confer with such charitable institutions, located in the County, as might care for such parties as properly would be chargable upon the County, and make such suitable arrangements therefore, as in their judgment would be to the benefit of the County, and that such committee are hereby authorized to act, in connection with the County Superintendent of the Poor, for such purpose.

Mr. Able moved as amendment that the Superintendent of the Poor be authorized to make said arrangement.

Mr. Vail accepted the Amendment.

Mr. Rogers moved the whole matter be laid over till to-morrow, a. m.

Motion carried.

Mr. Pugsley moved to suspend the Rules to hear Gen. A. B. Smith, who presented the Board with a Photograph of the monument in honor of the 150th Regiment at Gettysburgh.

Mr. Pugsley on behalf of the Board accepted the same.

Rules resumed.

Mr. Vail moved that the thanks of the Board be extended to General Smith and the Committee for the photograph presented to the Board, and for the Invitation received, and it be carried by a rising vote.

Motion unanimously carried.

Mr. Williams presented the following, which was read, and on motion of Mr. Rogers was made a Special Order for Tuesday, December 30th, 10:30 A. M.

To the Honorable Board of Supervisors, Dutchess County:

GENTLEMEN :—We, the undersigned physicians and surgeons residing and practicing in the City of Poughkeepsie, and Dutchess County, N. Y., believing the sum of ten dollars to be a just and fair charge for an examination of a dead body before a Coroner, and twenty-five dollars to be a like fair and just charge for an ordinary autopsical examination, and ten dollars to be a fair and likewise just charge for an ordinary examination in lunacy, do hereby agree not to perform the duties of Coroner's Physician or act as examiner in lunacy, for a less sum than above stated. And we would respectfully ask your Board to fix the above charges as legitimate rates for said services, and to recommend them to your successor in office.

We are forced to this action by the knowledge and belief that our services are misunderstood, and our labors underrated, that our professional qualifications are gauged by the standard of the day laborer and that often in the past no account has been taken of our skill and ability. nor of the dangers we are obliged to encounter. And we further agree that unless more definite action is taken by your Honorable Body whereby we may be assured of the full payment of our bills at the rates above stated, that we decline in the future to act in a professional capacity as Coroner's Physicians and Examiners in Lunacy for the County of Dutchess.

> Henry C. Miller, M. D., Pine Plains.
> George Huntington, M. D., LaGrange.
> John M. Julian, Moore's Mills.
> C. H. Tripp, M. D.
> Milton H. Angell, M. D., Salt Point.
> Austin T. Fink. Freedom Plains.
> I. D. LeRoy, M. D., Pleasant Valley.
> J. H. Traver, M. D., Pleasant Valley.
> Richard F. Duncan, M. D., Pleasant Valley.
> A. McClaury, Pleasant Valley.
> W. L. Pultz, M. D., Stanfordville.
> Mortimer C. Northrop, M. D., Bangall.
> Elmore Losee, M. D., Bangall.
> William Baxter, Wappingers Falls.
> Isaac M. Cornell,   "   "
> L. C. Wood,   "   "
> G. H. VanWagner,   "   "
> C. E. Seger, New Hackensack.
> John H. Doughty, M. D., Matteawan.
> John P. Schenck, M. D.,   "
> W. S. Watson,   "
> Edgar H. Ellis,   "
> Jacob R. Strong,   "
> Arthur R. Tiel,   "
> C. M. Kittridge, Fishkill Landing.
> J. E. Moith,   Fishkill-on-Hudson.
> D. O. K. Strong,   "   "
> W. Marchesseault,   "   "
> Frank T. Hopkins.   "   "
> I. Young,   "   "
> W. J. O'Rielly,   "   "
> Robert K. Tuthill,   Poughkeepsie.
> J. Wilson Poucher,   "
> John C. Payne,   "
> Alfred Hasbrouck,   "

F. A. Faust,	Poughkeepsie.
Walter R. Case.	"
J. E. Sadlier,	"
John S. Wilson,	"
Horace R. Powell,	"
C. E. Lane,	"
R. C. VanWyck,	"
G. Everett Coutant,	"
Joseph T. Lamb,	"
Daniel W. Sheedy.	"
John P. Wilson,	"
Yzen F. Bates,	"
H. W. Barnum,	"
S. H. Yunghaans,	"
William Cramer,	"
D. B. Ward,	"
W. W. Seeley.	"
J. Marill,	"
J. Haidlauf,	"
N. Borst,	"
A. E. VanDuser,	"

Mr. Pugsley moved that the Board proceed to sign the Tax Book.

Motion carried.

Mr. Wood offered the following :

Resolved, That the sum of $7.65 be allowed Thos. Fitzpatrick for services as constable, and the same be paid from the General Fund.

Laid over under the Rule.

On motion of Mr. Pugsley the Board adjourned.

TUESDAY, December 30th, 1890.

10 A. M.

Board met.

Quorum present.

Mr. Austin in the Chair.

Minutes read and approved.

Mr. Vail called up Resolution for allowance to Judge Guernsey for counsel fees, and moved its adoption.

Ayes and nays called.

All members present voting in favor thereof.

Ayes 17.

Resolution adopted.

Mr. Germond moved that the Rules be suspended.

Motion carried.

Mr. Wood called up Resolution for allowance to Thos. Fitzpatrick, and moved that the same be adopted.

Ayes and nays called.

All members present voting in favor thereof.

Ayes 18.

Resolution adopted.

Mr. E. Herrick called up Resolutions for Allowances to Herrick & Loscy and H. H. Hustis, for counsel fees, in mandamus of J. I Platt and J. P. Wilson, and moved the adoption of the same.

Ayes and nays called.

All members present voting in favor thereof.

Ayes 22.

Resolution adopted.

Mr. Vail presented the following and moved that the same be spread upon the Minutes of the Board :

Motion carried.

SUPREME COURT.

E. WRIGHT VAIL,
agst.
Board of Supervisors.

BARNARD, J. :

The papers show that the defendants passed a Resolution to raise by taxation and to pay the Highland Hospital the sum of five hundred dol. lars.

Highland Hospital is not an institution supported by the County, and if indigent persons are supported there they are not indigent persons chargable to the County.

A Board of Supervisors has no power of taxation except such as is given directly by law or is necessarily annexed to a grant of power to legislate upon particular subjects. The revised statutes define the powers of the Board as to poor persons and as to county charges therefor. County charges are by statute stated to be "The sums necessarily expended in each county in the support of County Poor Houses and of indigent persons whose support is chargable to the County."

Whenever the statute mentions a power to audit and appropriate for a specific purpose the intention of the legislature is always to be taken as referring to that class of persons who are by legal agencies brought within the class.

A poor house is a public poor house and a person chargable to the County, must be one who is a poor person under existing laws and by law chargable to the County. The Board has no power to arbitrarily raise by taxation outside of the strict statute limitation of county charges in respect to the poor.

The injunction should be granted.

STATE OF NEW YORK, } ss :
COUNTY OF DUTCHESS. }

I, Theodore A. Hoffman, Clerk of the County of Dutchess, and also

Clerk of the County Courts of said County, and of the Supreme Court of the State of New York, in and for said County, the same being Courts of Record, do hereby certify : that I have compared the preceding copy with the original decision of Justice Barnard, filed December 22, 1890, and remaining on file in my office, and that the same is a correct transcript therefrom and of the whole of such original.

In testimony whereof, I have hereunto subscribed my name, and affixed the seal of said Courts and County, the 7th day of January, 1891.

[L. S.]   THEO. A. HOFFMAN,

Clerk.

Mr. Mylod offered the following :

Resolved, That Frank B. Lown and Samuel K. Phillips each be allowed the sum of twenty dollars for counsel fees in Mandamus Case.

Ayes and nays called.

All members present voting in favor thereof.

Ayes 23.

Resolution adopted.

Mr. Germond offered the following :

Resolved, That this Board approves the action of Myron Smith, Superintendent of the Poor, in transferring Children from the Home for the Friendless and other Institutions of the County to the Children's Aid Society of New York City.

And it is further *Resolved*, That the County Treasurer be directed to pay expenses of the future transfers from the appropriation of the said Home for the Friendless.

Resolution adopted.

Mr. Able offered the following :

Resolved, That the Special Committee appointed by this Board for the Collection of Claims against Persons and Estates, &c., be authorized to pay traveling and necessary expenses from Collections made. And, also, for any Clerical services be paid by the Treasurer, upon the audit of said Committee at least once in three months.

Resolution adopted.

The hour having arrived for the Special Order, that being the matter of the Petition of the Physicians of the County.

Mr. Germond moved that the Petition be laid upon the table indefinitely.

Ayes and nays called.

Ayes—Messrs. Able, Andrews, Genung, Germond, E. Herrick, J. A. Herrick, Humphrey, Krieger, Lee, Morehouse, Pugsley, Rogers, Scutt, Sturgess, Swift, Vail, and Wing—17.

Nays—Messrs. Gray, Mylod, and Williams—3.

Messrs. Bartlett, Dudley, and Wood excused from voting.

Ayes 17.

Nays 3.

Motion carried.

The Chairman offered the following :

Resolved, That in accepting the gift of the Photograph of the Monument erected at Gettysburgh, in honor of the 150th Regiment N. Y. Volunteers. We do so with a just feeling of pride in all of the soldiers of our country, who volunteered to meet danger and death on the battle field, and that we are proud that our country was honored with the only County Regiment on that historic battle ground, the most distinguished of all the battle fields of the Rebellion; and, as the 150th Regiment was then a tower of strength to the Nation, and did its first duty nobly— emblematical of the County from which it went—

Resolved. That as the Regiment had its birth in the Board of Supervisors of Dutchess County, it is proper that this Picture should be carefully preserved among the Archives of the County, to be handed down from generation to generation as an honored heirloom of the County, an emblem to all of the cost of Union and Liberty, and as a sign and token that in all trials and emergencies, Dutchess County always does her *duty*.

Resolution unanimously adopted by a rising vote.

Mr. Pugsley, having completed seven years service in the Board, made an address reviewing his work, and stated that like Jacob of old he had waited seven years, and Rachel was not his yet; in other words, that he had done his duty by the County, but the County had not done its duty by him.

Mr. Germond moved that a vote of thanks be tendered to Mr. Pugsley for services rendered to the County.

Motion unanimously carried.

Mr. John A. Herrick, the oldest member of the Board of Supervisors, was presented with a handsome chair. Mr. Mylod made the presentation speech. When Mr. Herrick accepted the gift he was heartily applauded.

Mr. Pugsley offered the following :

Resolved, That we thank the reporters of the Poughkeepsie daily papers, for the careful manner in which they have reported the Proceedings of this Board.

Resolution adopted.

Mr. Dudley offered the following :   .

Resolved, That the thanks of the Board are due the Janitor, Mr. Kruger, for his efficient service during the session of the Board.

Resolution adopted.

Mr. Bartlett offered the following :

Resolved, That to our veteran clerk we tender our thanks for his faith-

ful and efficient work done for the Board and for his assistance to the
several committees. That we extend to him our best wishes for his success and welfare.

Resolution unanimously adopted.

Mr. Wood offered the following :

Resolved, That we tender our thanks to our Chairman, Mr. Austin,
for the kind and able manner in which he discharged his duties and for
his assistance in our deliberations, and wish him a happy and successful
life, and it is the unanimous hope of this Board that he may carry to his
home and ever cherish happy memories of the Board of 1890 and of the
friends that he has made while presiding over this Body.

MR. CHAIRMAN AND GENTLEMEN :—It gives me great pleasure to have
the privilege of offering this resolution, expressing as it does the senti-
ments of the individual members of this board. To discharge the duty
of presiding officer over this or any similar body to the satisfaction of the
public and to retain the good will and esteem of all its members is no
easy task, and he who accomplishes the feat is a fit subject for congratu-
lation, and this is what our presiding officer has accomplished. We
therefore congratulate him. After all, what kinder works can be said,
what greater need of praise can be bestowed on any man than to be
truly able to say of him : "He had a duty to perform and he has performed that duty well." Our Chairman owed a duty to the
people of this County ; so well has he discharged the trust
that his every act is above reproach. He owed the duty to each member
of the Board to treat him with fairness and with courtesy, and so well
has he performed that duty that he has made of each a personal friend.
He has been moderate, conservative and firm, and withal has been fair.
And this is his reward : that when he returns to his home and his friends
in LaGrange, he will carry with him the consciousness of having done
his duty well and the certain knowledge that throughout the County
there are men who will think well and speak well of him.

Mr. Pugsley seconded the Resolution of Thanks and in
doing so took occasion to present Chairman Austin with
an ebony gavel having a gold plate and inscription.

Mr. Wood's Resolution was unanimously adopted by a rising vote.

Mr. Austin was taken completely by surprise and was quite affected. The Resolution of Thanks was carried by a rising vote, when Chairman Austin in fitting words thanked the Board and remarked that he had tried to do his duty faithfully, and if he had erred it was not an error of the heart. In conclusion he wished the mem. bers of the Board a Happy New Year.

Rules resumed.

Minutes of this day's proceedings read and approved.

Mr. Pugsley moved that this Board adjourn *sine die.*

Motion carried.

APPENDIX.

TOWN ALLOWANCES.

AMENIA.

Statement of Accounts, Charges and Claims, payable by the Town of Amenia, in the County of Dutchess, audited and allowed by the Board of Town Auditors, at a meeting of said Board, held at the House of E. H. Gazely, in the Town of Amenia, on Thursday, the sixth day of November, in the year 1890.

Name of person.	Nature of the demand.	Asked.	Allowed.
Wm. H. Bartlett	Supervisor and extra election expenses	$127 48	$127 48
Isaac H. Conklin	Justice of the Peace	16 00	16 00
Milo F. Winchester.	" "	85 17	85 17
James S. Chaffee.	" "	21 10	21 10
Phillip H. Barrett	" "	30 05	30 05
William H. Tannor	Assessor	20 00	20 00
Henry Rundall.	"	28 00	28 00
Henry Mygatt	"	16 00	16 00
E. M. Kempton	Town Clerk	70 83	70 83
Walter B. Culver	Excise Commissioner	9 00	9 00
Daniel L. Thomas	" "	9 00	9 00
Frank VanHovenburg	" "	9 00	9 00
Wm. Blytheman	Overseer of the Poor	56 77	56 77
Robert R. Knight	Physician	17 25	11 25
I. N. Mead	"	14 25	14 25
G. H. Codding	"	37 50	37 50
L. E. Rockwell	Physician and Health Officer	82 10	82 10

AMENIA—Continued.

G. H. Gazely .... Use of House for Town Meeting and Election Dist. No. 2.	35 00	35 00
Henry Mygatt.............. Inspector of Election Dist. No. 1...........................	19 00	19 00
Clark D. Wheeler .... Inspector of Election Dist. No. 1...........................	12 00	12 00
F. D. Rundall .... Inspector of Election Dist. No. 1......	16 00	10 00
Henry N. Winchester.... Inspector of Election, Dist. No. 2.......	19 00	19 00
G. S. Cline................... Inspector of Election, Dist. No. 2...........................	12 00	12 00
Wm. H. Tanner.............. Inspector of Election,Dist. No. 2..........................	19 00	19 00
Milton K. Rodgers.......... Inspector of Election, Dist. No. 2...........................	12 00	12 00
M. K. Lewis .... Inspector of Election, Dist. No. 2........	10 00	10 00
J. O. Peters............ ...... Inspector of Election,Dist. No. 1.............	12 00	12 00
John R. Thompson .... Inspector of Election, Dist. No. 1...........................	10 00	10 00
E. M. Kempton .... Clerk of Election.............	4 00	4 00
Charles Walsh...... .... " "	4 00	4 00
E. E. Cline.................. Clerk of Election, Dist. No. 2...	4 00	4 00
F. W. Irish................... Clerk of Election, Dist. No. 2........	4 00	4 00
Leonard Decker. .... Ex-Overseer of the Poor..	22 00	22 00
William Blytheman....... Constable......................	23 50	23 50
Seymour L. Buckley....... Constable......................	50 05	50 05
John L. Melius.............. Constable.....	7 70	7 70
Walsh & Griffen. .... Printing.......................	3 50	3 50
Mead & Murdock............. Overseers order......	10 93	10 93

AMENIA—Continued.

William R. Lee	Counsel to the Assessors...	10 00	10 00
N. D. Buckley	Highway expenses	2,800 00	2,800 00

$3,713 18 $3,707 18

We certify the above to be correct.

WM. H. BARTLETT,
M. F. WINCHESTER,
JAMES L. CHAFFEE,
P. H. BARRETT,
E. M. KEMPTON,
Auditors.

BEEKMAN.

Statement of Accounts, Charges and Claims, payable by the Town of Beekman, in the County of Dutchess, audited and allowed by the Board of Town Auditors, at a meeting of said Board, held at the house of Charles A. Miller, in the Town of Beekman, on Thursday, the sixth day of November, in the year 1890.

Name of Person.	Nature of the demand.	Asked.	Allowed.
Kromline Andrews	Supervisor	$ 22 50	$ 22 50
Charles A. Miller	Election Booths	44 20	44 20
Charles A. Miller	Use of Rooms	20 00	20 00
Judson A. Denton	Justice	14 55	14 55
Frank St. John	Assessor	40 00	38 00
Geo. W. Toffey	Justice	6 00	6 00
D. C. Tripp	Physician	5 50	5 50

BEEKMAN—Continued.

Edgar A. Sweet.............Justice............................	14 00	14 00
James R. DeLong.........Justice...........................	12 00	12 00
Edgar A. Sweet.............Inspector of Election.......	10 00	10 00
W. B. Storm ....Poll Clerk......	4 00	2 00
Joseph Morey.................Inspector of Election......	12 00	10 00
Benjamin Haxton... ..... " "	18 28	16 28
Remsom Dodge............. " "	18 28	16 28
Jeremiah Austin............Lumber...............	123 22	123 22
Henry D. Cypher........ Inspector of Election......	16 44	16 44
Edwin Flagler...............Assessor..	38 00	38 00
C. F. Rapell...... ....Inspector of Election.......	10 00	10 00
Henry Weeks.............. " "	2 00	2 00
Hiram Slocum........ .....Lumber......................	2 00	2 00
James H. Rupell............Com'r of Highways	343 83	343 83
James H. Rupell............Ex-Supervisor.................	17 60	17 60
Thomas E. Peters.... .....Inspector of Election... ...	10 00	10 00
Martin Johnson.............Foxes, bounty................	6 00	6 00
Charles H. Slocum........Use of Rooms	10 28	10 28
C. M. Couch...................Poll Clerk.........	2 00	2 00
Charles Brill................,.....Inspector of Election.......	10 00	10 00
Geraw Brill............. .....Poll Clerk...............	2 00	2 00
F. D. Mitchell. ....Physician	36 25	12 25
Rowland Brill...............Inspector of Election.......	10 00	8 00
Charles A. Muller.........Town Clerk..................	46 26	46 26
Theodore Seaman.........Constable.....................	4 00	2 00
Andrew Skidmore.........Inspector of Election.......	10 00	10 00
Andrew Skidmore.........Assessor.	34 00	34 00
Charles A. Millard........Foxes, bounty...............	11 00	11 00

$1,486 19 $1,448 33

We certify the above to be correct.

KROMLINE ANDREWS,
CHARLES A. MULLER,
JAMES R. DE LONG,
GEO. W. TOFFEY,
JUDSON A. DENTON,
EDGAR A. SWEET,
Auditors.

CLINTON.

Statement of Accounts, Charges and Claims payable to the Town of Clinton, in the County of Dutchess, audited and allowed by the Board of Town Auditors, at a meeting of said Board, held at the store of George H. Gazley, in the Town of Clinton, on Thursday, the 6th day of November, 1890.

Name of Person.	Nature of the Demand.	Asked.	Allowed.
Willliam A. Coons........	Services as Town Clerk...	$ 41 90	$ 41 90
John G. Hendricks........	" " Overseer of the Poor, 1882 and 1883....	52 00	10 00
William H. Sleight.......	Use of hall and stationery	21 93	21 93
John V. Chase	Arresting prisoner and mileage........................	1 24	1 24
William Hermance........	Services as Assessor.........	32 00	32 00
LeGrand Graham........	" ex-Town Clerk	21 85	21 85
" "	" Clerk of Election, Dist. No. 1............	4 00	4 00
Edwin S. Hoyt............	For issuing burial permits and death certificates..	2 00	2 00
Stephen B. Alley............	Services as Inspector of Election, Dist. No. 2....	16 00	16 00
William F. Townsend...	Services as Inspector Election, delivering returns.	22 35	22 35
Edward Smith............	Services as Clerk of Election, Dist. No. 2............	4 00	4 00
William N. White	Services as Inspector of Election and delivering returns	18 00	18 00
Thaddeus Stoutenburgh.	Services as Inspector of Election and delivering returns......	22 44	22 44
Isaac A. Olivet	Services as Overseer of the Poor, Dist. No. 1..... ...	7 50	7 50
Julius M. Lown.....	Services as Inspector of Dist. No. 2.............	16 00	16 00

CLINTON—Continued.

George S. Van Vliet.......Services as Inspector of Election and delivering returns......	18 00	18 00
Lorenzo Shultz............Bounty for killing four foxes.........	4 00	4 00
Theodore Doughty ....Services as Inspector of Election, Dist. No. 2..	16 00	16 00
Edwin Barnes............Medical attend'nce on poor	15 50	15 50
L. L. Marquet............Bounty for killing four foxes......	4 00	4 00
Lewis Van Vliet ....Services as Justice of the Peace..,......	16 45	16 45
Theron M. Browning......Services as Justice of the Peace.........	12 25	12 25
Myron Traver..........Services as Clerk of Election, Dist. No. 2..........	4 00	4 00
Leonard I. Tripp.........Services as Inspector of Election, Dist. No. 1......	16 00	16 00
Edward F. Delaney.......Services as Officer at the Polls, Dist. No. 1..........	2 00	2 00
Henry W. Lattin..........Services as Inspector of Election, Dist. No. 1......	16 00	16 00
" ....For election booths. ballot boxes, etc................	46 50	46 50
Charles B. Doughty.......Services as Clerk of Election, Dist. No 1..........	4 00	4 00
John O'Neil...............Overseer of the Poor, Dist. No. 2......................	8 75	8 75
John W. Robinson.......Services as Inspector of Election and delivering returns	10 60	10 60
Harvey S. Van Dyne......Services as Justice of the Peace............	13 75	13 75
Alanson Pink...............Services as Assessor........	24 00	24 00
John W. Free...............Services as Commissioner of Highways............	74 00	74 00
Edward Herrick...........Services as Supervisor......	39 95	39 95

CLINTON—Continued.

Mandeville G. Burger......Assessor.	28 00	28 00
George H. Gazely..........Use of hall for election, town meeting, etc.........	30 83	30 83
Martin E. Rikert............Services as Inspector of Election, Dist. No. 1....	16 00	16 00
	$643 79	$601 79
	60 00	60 00
	$703 79	$661 79

We certify the above to be correct.

EDWARD HERRICK, Supervisor,
LEWIS VAN VLIET,
THERON M. BROWNING,
HARVEY S. VAN DYNE,
WILLIAM A. COONS, Town Clerk,
Auditors.

DOVER.

Statement of Accounts, Charges and Claims, payable by the Town of Dover, in the County of Dutchess, audited and allowed by the Board of Town Auditors, at a meeting of said Board, held at Wing's Station, in the Town of Dover, on Thursday, the 6th day of November, in the year 1890.

Name of Person.	Nature of the Demand.	Asked.	Allowed.
M. K. Lewis.................Locks and Keys Consigned to T. P. W...................		$ 1 15	$ 1 15

DOVER—Continued.

W. K. Butts	Inspector of Election	10 00	10 00
E. H. Deuell	Poor Order	7 00	7 00
Merritt Humeston	For Irons for Railing	1 50	1 50
" "	Overseer Poor and Orders	56 75	56 75
Frank P. Hoag	Inspector and Delivering Canvass	22 00	22 00
F. N. Cutler	Justice of Peace	2 00	2 00
W. G. Banks	Clerk of Board of Registry	4 00	4 00
Geo. Hufcut	Assessor and Dividing Dis.	50 00	50 00
Albert Fry	" " "	46 00	46 00
P. H. Feeny	Locks, Keys and Screws	1 90	1 90
B. Coyle	Ex-Com. and Inspector	15 50	15 50
Jas. McArthur	Election Officer	2 00	2 00
S. Wheeler	Justice and Vital Statistics	30 00	30 00
A. H. Dutcher	" " "	77 25	77 25
Geo. W. Dutcher	Inspector,Building Booths, Poor Orders and V. S.	69 70	69 70
C. E. Hodge	Juryman on Road	1 50	1 50
Cleveland Titus	" "	1 50	1 50
Rozelle Meade	Assessor 46, Inspector 10	56 00	56 00
Geo. H. Sheldon	Inspector of Election	10 00	10 00
Chas. W. Vincent	Clerk of Election	4 00	4 00
C. L. Fletcher, M. D.	Poor Order	25 50	25 50
Theo. F. Jones	Juryman	1 50	1 50
Homer Wheeler	Inspector	10 00	10 00
Wm. Record	For Lumber	43 42	43 42
Frank A. Denton	Inspector	10 00	10 00
J. M. Waldron	Poor Order and Attendance on Election	20 75	20 75
Wm. Pierce	Juryman and Clerk of Election	5 50	5 50
Geo. M. Wellman, M.D.	Poor and Vital Statistics	51 25	51 25
John Coyle, Jr	Ex-Collector, Discrepancy in Tax Book, 1889	59 91	59 91
E. W. Benson	Overseer of Poor	19 50	19 50
A. Brisett	Janitor	8 00	8 00
J. A. Hanna & Co	Poor Order	35 00	35 00

DOVER—Continued.

Theo. Buckingham........Lumber..........................	19 60	19 60
Rev. D. J. McCormick....For Marriages Assigned to T. P. Whalen...............	2 50	2 50
Wm. P. Humeston .... ..For Making Ballot Boxes.	8 00	8 00
A. E. Bangs...... ....Clerk of Election and Board of Health............	14 00	14 00
J. A. Hanna & Co ....Locks, Ink, &c...............	5 66	5 66
Hon. Isaac O. Mitchell..Constable......	3 80	3 80
Prof. S. D. Whalen.........Inspector and Delivering Canvass to Supervisor...	12 00	12 00
Perry Edmonds..........Poor Orders................	14 98	14 98
Thomas Hammond, M.D.Excise Com. Poor Bill and Vital Statistics.............	13 50	13 50
Chas. W. Belding........ Highway Com., Note with Interest and Meeting with Highway Com.......	295 75	295 75
J. A. Hanna........... ... For Town Hall...............	40 00	40 00
James Fry................,.... Poor Master..............	27 00	27 00
A. J. Thayer ....Constable......................	66 65	66 65
Eugene Fox................. "	105 40	105 40
Henry Buckley....... ...... "	12 15	12 15
Mary E. Brown............ .Poor Bill Consigned to Wm. Record.....	10 00	10 00
Theo. Buckingham........Paid for 2 Graves for Poor.	5 00	5 00
Frank Tallady...... ....Constable......................	82 35	72 35
Freeman Tallman.........For Digging 2 Graves - (Order Poor Master).......	6 00	6 00
J. S. Wing...................Stationery and Lamps......	2 15	2 15
Chas. C. Gardner..... .....Overseer of Poor, 1889......	30 00	30 00
Albert Tompkins............Building Bridge.......	5 80	5 80
Sheldon Wing............. .Supervisor.. ....;..	53 00	53 00
C. L. Fletcher.............Vital Statistics......	8 75	8 75
T. P. Whalen..............Town Clerk, 1889, $20 00 and 1890, $51 00............	71 00	71 00
T P. Whalen...............Inspector of Election and Returning Canvass to County Clerk......	21 20	21 20

12   *Town Allowances.*

DOVER—Continued.

T. P. Whalen.............Vital Statistics and Board			
	of Health, 1889 and 1890	35 75	35 75
Chas. Van Benthuysen &			
Son......................Printing Vital Statistics,			
	Expressage and Postage		
	(Consigned to T. P.		
	Whalen).................	8 00	8 00
Chas. Walsh............Printing................		2 00	2 00
		$1,742 07	$1,732 07

We certify the above to be correct.

SHELDON WING, Justice,
ALLEN H. DUTCHER, Justice,
GEO. W. DUTCHER, Justice,
T. P. WHALEN, Town Clerk,
S. WHEELER, Justice,
FRANCIS N. CUTLER, Justice,
Auditors.

EAST FISHKILL.

Statement of Accounts, Charges and Claims, payable by the Town of East Fishkill, in the County of Dutchess, audited and allowed by the Board of Town Auditors, at a meeting of said Board, held at the Hotel of H. J. Meyers in the Town of East Fishkill, on Thursday, the 6th day of November. in the year 1890.

Name of Person.	Nature of the Demand.	Asked.	Allowed.
Isaac S. Genung.........Supervisor,disbursing Pub-			
	lic moneys, &c............	$ 53 49	$ 53 49

EAST FISHKILL—Continued.

John Ogden................Inspector and Registrar of Election, Dist. No. 1......	22 44	22 44
Wm. B. Ashby..............Inspector and Registrar of Election Dist. No. 1......	18 00	18 00
Wm. J. Storm.. ....Inspector and Registrar of Election, Dist. No. 1......	18 00	18 00
James Adriance.............Inspector and Registrar of Election, Dist. No. 1......	19 44	19 44
Garrett Roach............Inspector and Registrar of Election, Dist. No. 1	16 00	16 00
Herbert G. Rynders.......Inspector and Registrar of Election, Dist. No. 2......	16 00	16 00
Isaac Berian.................Inspector and Registrar of Election, Dist. No. 2......	18 00	18 00
L. W. Rapelje.............Inspector and Registrar of Election, Dist. No. 2......	16 00	16 00
Gilbert C. Doughty........Inspector and Registrar of Election, Dist. No. 2.....	16 00	16 00
Albert D. Genung........Inspector and Registrar of Election, Dist. No. 2......	19 12	19 12
L. C. Rapelje...............Clerk of Election, Dist. No. 2.........	4 00	4 00
B. W. Bonney..............Clerk of Election, Dist. No. 2............................	4 00	4 00
H. C. Sprague..............Inspector and Registrar of Election, Dist. No. 3......	22 28	22 28
J. W. Richards...............Inspector and Registrar of Election, Dist. No. 3......	18 00	18 00
George H. Knapp.........Inspector and Registrar of Election, Dist. No. 3......	16 00	16 00
L. V. Pierce. ....Inspector and Registrar of Election, Dist. No. 3.....	19 28	19 28
Collins Way...............Clerk of Election, Dist. No. 3.........................	4 00	4 00
Frederick Genung.........Clerk of Election, Dist. No. 3........................	4 00	4 00

EAST FISHKILL—Continued.

Frank Fowler	Commissioner of Highways and Clerk of Election, Dist. No. 1	54 00	54 00
A. A. Bogardus	Commiss'r of Highways	80 00	80 00
Morgan L. Rynders	" "	81 00	81 00
Edward Lasher	Ex-Commiss'r of Highways	10 00	10 00
Isaac S. Genung	Supervisor, Contract price for Iron Bridge per Res.	621 50	621 50
R. H. Sloan, M. D.	Medical attendance of poor	5 00	5 00
R. C. Van Wyck, M.D.	Medical attendance of poor and Health Officer	99 50	99 50
L. A. Sutton, M. D.	Medical attendance of poor	94 50	94 50
Isaac Van Vlack	Assessor and Excise Commissioner	39 00	39 00
Adriance Bartow	Assessor	49 00	49 00
Isaac S. Genung	"	36 00	36 00
Wm. H. Griffin	Excise Commissioner	15 00	15 00
R. B. Kain	" "	15 00	15 00
Webster A. Tompkins	Overseer of Poor	24 50	24 50
Richard Ostrom	" "	26 62	26 62
Storm Emans	Justice of Peace, &c.	59 80	59 80
B. Hopkins	" "	50 88	50 b8
S. A. Doughty	" " and Bonding Commissioner	44 50	44 50
J. M Tompkins	Justice of Peace	30 00	30 00
A. S. Emans	Town Clerk, Board of Health, &c	176 88	176 88
John J. Carman	Ex-Town Clerk, assigned to Storm Emans	10 00	10 00
Webster A. Tompkins	Constable	6 60	6 60
Mrs. Perry Kelley	Services and Health Board	30 00	30 00
Geo. W. Owen	Printing	2 00	2 00
R. C. Horton	Use of building for Election, Dist. No. 3	25 00	10 00
Austin Lamont, M. D.	Use of building for Election, Dist. No. 1	5 00	5 00

EAST FISHKILL--Continued.

Young Men's Christ'n As. Use of building for Election, Dist. No. 2............	20 00	20 00
I. S. Genung.................Supervisor, returning Collector's Bond..............	7 68	7 68

We certify the above to be correct.

ISAAC S. GENUNG,
S. A. DOUGHTY,
JOHN M. TOMPKINS,
B. HOPKINS,
STORM EMANS,
A. S. EMANS,

Auditors.

A true copy,

A. S. EMANS, Town Clerk.

FISHKILL.

Statement of Accounts, Charges and Claims, payable by the Town of Fishkill, in the County of Dutchess, audited and allowed by the Board of Town Auditors, at a meeting of said Board, held at the Town Clerk's office, in the Town of Fishkill, on Thursday, the 6th day of November, in the year 1890.

Name of Person.	Nature of the Demand.	Asked.	Allowed.
Edgar G. Greene............Registrar and Inspector of Election, Dist. No. 6......		16 00	16 00
Wm. L. Judson.............Registrar and Inspector of Election, Dist. No. 6......		22 44	22 44

FISHKILL—Continued.

Wm. F. Heaney............Registrar and Inspector of Election, Dist. No. 6.........	18 00	18 00
Theo. Post................ ......Special officer at polls, Dist. No. 4, assigned to Joseph Sunderland.......	2 00	2 00
Wm. H. Miller............Registrar and Inspector of ‧ Election, Dist. No. 6......	24 44	24 44
Theo. Post................Registrar and Inspector of Election, Dist. No. 8, assigned to Jos. Sunderland	22 60	22 60
Fred. Van Voorhis.........Registrar and Inspector of Election, Dist. No. 3......	16 00	16 00
Wm. A. Rothery............Registrar and Inspector of Election, Dist. No. 7......	16 00	16 00
Joseph Sunderland........Registrar and Inspector of Election, Dist. No. 8......	20 00	20 00
L. D. Wymbs............Registrar, Inspector and Board Health, Dist. No.8	32 00	32 00
Edgar C. Bloomer.........Registrar and Inspector, Dist. No. 5...............	20 00	20 00
Waldon Jones............Registrar and Inspector, Dist. No. 8............	16 00	16 00
Geo. C. Conklin.............Clerk of Election, Dist. No. 6................	4 00	4 00
C. E. Bartow............Clerk of Election, Dist. No. 8................	8 00	8 00
Chas. H. Wood............Clerk of Election, Dist. No. 8................	4 00	4 00
Wm. A. Humphries.......Clerk of Election, Dist. No. 5................	4 00	4 00
Geo. W. Tuthill............Inspector of Election, Dist. No. 1................	6 00	6 00
C. O. Osborne,............Clerk of Election. Dist. No. 2................	4 00	4 00
Gregory Mullen............Special officer, Dist. No. 8	2 00	2 00
John P. Schenck............Health officer, 1 year's salary, assigned to C. W.		

FISHKILL—Continued.

	Brundage	150 00	150 00
Samuel McKee	Delivering booths and putting up same	23 00	23 00
Henry S. Chapman	Work and material on Town Hall	7 50	7 50
Wm. A. Mase	Clerk of Election, Dist. No. 7, assigned to E. S. Phillips	12 00	12 00
Wm. A. Mase	Clerk of Election, Dist. No. 7, assigned to E. S. Phillips	4 00	4 00
John |Thorne	Fitting up polls, Dist. No. 8	1 00	1 00
S. G. & J. T. Smith	Blankets of Lock-Up	3 90	3 90
John W. Brett	Material for and making 18 Ballot Boxes	36 00	36 00
Conrad B. Bevier	Inspector of Election, Dist. No. 2, assigned to E. S. Phillips	6 00	6 00
H. R. Scofield	Clerk of Election, Dist. No. 5	8 00	8 00
F. G. Rikert	Registrar and Inspector of Election, Dist. No. 5	16 00	16 00
E. B. Chase	Inspector of Election, Dist. No. 2	6 00	6 00
Fred L. Rosa	Clerk of Election, Dist. No. 9	4 00	4 00
G. D. B. Brinckerhoff	Registrar and Inspector, Dist. No. 1	18 00	18 00
Sylvanus Mosher	Registrar and Inspector, Dist. No. 4	16 00	16 00
Edward McManus	Clerk of Election, Dist. No. 3, assigned to Wm. H. Peattie	4 00	4 00
F. E. Hignell	Clerk of Election, Dist. No. 2	4 00	4 00
Wm. H. Peattie	Registrar and Inspector, Dist. No. 3	16 00	16 00

FISHKILL—Continued.

Frank S. Sewell. ....Registrar and Inspector, Dist. No. 3......	16 00	16 00
F. Pangman..................Special Officer, Dist. No. 9	2 00	2 00
Conrad B. Bevier.......... Inspector of Election, Dist. No. 5...........................	10 44	10 44
Sherwood Phillips... ....Clerk of Election, Dist. No. 2..........................	4 00	4 00
Levi Hadfield............... Special Officer, Dist. No. 5	2 00	2 00
Chas. E. Martin.............Registrar and Inspector, Dist. No. 2......	16 00	16 00
Preston Greene..............Registrar and Inspector of Election Dist, No. 3.......	22 28	22 28
Joseph E. Schofield........Registrar and Inspector of Election Dist. No. 9.......	28 84	28 84
S. S. Mapes..................Registrar and Inspector of Election Dist. No. 1.......	22 44	22 44
C. E. Hatch.................Registrar and Inspector of Election Dist. No. 7.......	14 44	14 44
Sherwood Phillips........Clerk of Election Dist. No. 5	16 00	16 00
E. B. Chase.................Registrar and Inspector of Election Dist No. 5..... .	22 44	22 44
I. J. Wood ....Registrar and Inspector of Election Dist. No. 9........	30 84	30 84
A. W. Lasher...............Registrar and Inspector of Election Dist. No. 7......	16 00	16 00
Geo. G. Judson.. ....Registrar and Inspector of Election Dist. No. 5.......	18 00	18 00
James Gilleyer...............Ex-Auditor.....................	10 00	10 00
Thos. W. Blauvelt........ Registrar and Inspector of Election Dist. No. 6.......	16 00	16 00
W. H. Wood..................Board of Health..	6 00	6 00
C. E. Bartow ....Supplies of Election Dist. No. 8......	21 56	21 56
M. R. Hines ....Commissioner of Excise...	33 00	33 00
S. D. Pierce..... ....Special Officer Dist. No. 1.	2 00	2 00
Willes Phelps .... Maps of Election Districts.	50 00	50 00

FISHKILL—Continued.

Preston Greene............	Member of Board of Health	16 00	16 00
J. C. Sawyer.............	Registrar of Election, Dist.		
	No. 5......................	12 00	12 00
John Mitchell............	Commissioner of Excise...	33 00	33 00
H. F. Walcott............	Justice of the Peace.......	26 00	26 00
Jas. E. Dean............	Registrar and Inspector,		
	Dist. No. 9..................	16 00	16 00
C. S. Myers............	Registrar and Inspector,		
	Dist. No. 2............	22 36	22 38
E. R. Weed............	Registrar and Inspector.		
	Dist. No. 7................	24 44	24 44
Wm. F. Thomson........	Registrar and Inspector.		
	Dist. No. 4................	16 00	16 00
A. S. Brinckerhoff... ...	Registrar and Inspector.		
	Dist. No. 1................	12 00	12 00
Eugene Haight...........	Clerk of Election. Dist No.		
	4...........................	4 00	4 00
Thos. G. Aldridge........	Registrar and Inspector,		
	Dist. No. 4................	18 00	18 00
R. J. Horton............	Supplies, assigned to S. K.		
	Phillips, Dist. No. 4.......	1 17	1 17
E. J. Slipperly............	Clerk of Election, Dist. No.		
	2...........................	4 00	4 00
Edward McManus........	Clerk of Election, Dist.		
	No. 1, assigned to Chas.		
	J. Pell......	32 00	32 00
E. E. Harris..............	Registrar and Inspector,		
	Dist. No. 3..............	22 28	22 28
Elijah Mosher............	Registrar and Inspector,		
	Dist. No. 4...............	16 00	16 00
Alonzo Covert...	Registrar and Inspector,		
	Dist. No. 4..............	22 44	22 44
Thos. McEvoy........	Registrar and Inspector,		
	Dist. No. 7, assigned to		
	F. G. Rykert..............	22 44	22 44
Thos. Bradley............	Clerk of Election, Dist.		
	No. 4......................	4 00	4 00

FISHKILL—Continued.

Geo. Constable	Special Officer, Dist. No. 4	2 00	2 00
John Creagan	Registrar and Inspector, Dist. No. 2	20 00	20 00
R. J. Horton	Use of house for Poll, assigned to S. K. Phillips.	25 00	25 00
R. L. Carpenter	Clerk of Election, Dist. No. 5, assigned to Ben Sullivan	4 00	4 00
Wm. Decker	Clerk of Election, Dist. No. 6	4 00	4 00
Geo. E. Harris	Special Officer, Dist. No. 4	2 00	2 00
Chas. Talbot	Use of house for Poll, Dist. No. 1	30 00	30 00
H. C. Johnston	One Jug	60	60
Samuel McKee	Building 54 Booths at $3.35 each, assigned to First National Bank, Fishkill Landing	180 90	180 90
John Thorne	Use of house of Poll, Dist. No. 8	40 00	35 00
Wm. H. Drew	Registrar and Inspector, Dist. No. 1	22 28	22 28
H. C. Johnston	Ex-Auditor	10 00	10 00
Hopper & Bogardus	Tables for Polls, Dist. No. 1, 2 and 3	12 00	12 00
Geo. B. Schofield	Ex-Auditor	10 00	10 (0
D. E. VanAmburgh	Member Board of Health.	18 00	18 00
D. E. VanAmburgh	Registrar and Inspector, Dist. No. 8	31 35	31 35
Fishkill & Matteawan Gas Co	Gas for Town Hall	10 16	10 16
R. J. Horton	Member Board of Health (assigned to S.K. Phillips)	14 00	14 00
W. R. Scofield	Registrar and Inspector Dist. 2	22 56	22 56
Geo. W. Owen	Printing	72 25	72 25
Fishkill Standard	"	80 50	80 50
Fishkill Times	"	37 25	37 25

FISHKILL—Continued.'

D. R. Weed	Stationery and Supplies for Booths	52 20	52 20
Richard S. White	Special Officer, Dist. No. 4	2 00	2 00
D. M Horton	Registrar and Inspector, Dist No. 9	25 00	25 00
H. H. Hustis	Registrar and Inspector, Dist. No. 3	22 28	22 28
Frank G. Rikert	Insurance on Town Hall	8 00	8 00
Geo. K. Brundage	Commissioner of Excise	33 00	33 00
D. C. Smith	Assessor, Supplies for Poll, Dist. No. 9	3 84	3 84
Eureka Engine Co	Use of House for Polls, Dist. No. 9	55 00	55 00
Geo. M. Knapp	Clerk of Election, Dist. No. 1	8 00	8 00
Willis Van Buren	Ex-Constable, assigned to John T. Smith	511 80	457 75
Daniel Leach	Registrar and Inspector of Election, Dist. No. 1	4 00	4 00
Amand Miller	Assessor	208 00	208 00
C. E. Bartow	"	208 00	208 00
D. C. Smith	"	198 00	198 00
Jas. T. Brett	Coal for Town Hall and Lock-Up	65 23	65 23
G. W. Bradshaw	Services and Expenses, New Ballot Law	48 00	48 00
H. B. Bevier	Supplies of Lock-Up	10 70	10 70
Mark Breerly	Special Officer at Polls, Dist. No. 8	2 00	2 00
Wm. Bruce	Fumigating in Case of Diphtheria	3 00	3 00
Thos. Connelly	Services as Member of Board of Health	14 00	14 00
S. E. Heath	Inspector of Election, Dist. No. 2	4 00	4 00
Wm. S. Mase	Clerk of Election, assigned S. K. Phillips	4 00	4 00

FISHKILL—Continued.

Thos. W. Blauvelt. ...... Inspector of Election, assigned to S. K. Phillips.	8 00	8 00
L. W. Robinson .... Special Officer, Dist. No. 7	2 00	2 00
R. L. Carpenter .... Clerk of Election, assigned to Ben Sullivan	4 00	4 00
D. C. Rogers .... Supplies for Stone Crusher	16 15	16 15
Geo. Ellis .... Door Springs for Town Hall	9 00	9 00
Abram R. Willsie.. .... Commissioner of Highways, Outside Fishkill Landing and Matteawan	238 00	238 00
Abram R. Willsie .... Commissioner of Bridges, Town Charge	18 00	18 00
C. D. Cooper .... Commissioner of Highways, Outside Fishkill Landing and Matteawan	234 00	234 00
C. D. Cooper .... Commissioner of Bridges, Town Charge	120 00	120 00
Chas. W. Carey .... Constable	37 85	31 85
Frank Pangman .... "	3 75	3 75
H. F. Walcott .... Justice of Peace	16 75	16 75
S. K. Phillips.. .. .. Services as Counsel..	30 00	30 00
John Sewell .... Use of house for Polls	42 25	27 25
Chas. VanVoorhis. .... Clerk of Election, Dist.No. 5	4 00	4 00
Howland Post.. .... Relief...	161 07	161 07
G. H. Thomson .... Clerk of Election	4 00	4 00
Judson & Hancock .... Material and Work on Crusher and Town Hall.	20 67	20 67
Ben. Sullivan... ... . Services as Member of Board of Health	14 00	14 00
Phillips & Phelps .... Insurance on Town Hall..	8 00	8 00
James Hart. .... Services as Member of Board of Health	10 00	10 00
John Baldwin .... Services as Member of Board of Health	4 00	4 00
Ashfort Rothery .... Clerk of Election, Dist.No. 7	4 00	4 00

FISHKILL—Continued.

James Rogers	Team for Board of Health, assigned to Lewis Ellis	5 00	5 00
D. C. Rogers	Supplies for Lock-up	1 85	1 85
A. & C. F. Brett	" "	4 90	4 90
John Clifton	Member of Board of Health	14 00	14 00
Village of Matteawan	Use of house for Polls, Dist. No. 6	35 00	35 00
B. T. Hall	Fitting up Polls, Dist. No. 6	16 05	14 05
John F. VanTine	Inspector of Election. Dist. No. 1	20 00	20 00
Samuel Rogers	Commissioner of Poor, one year's salary	500 00	500 00
Schlosser & Wood	Counsel fees	110 20	110 00
G. W. Bradshaw	Registrar of Vital Statistics	200 50	200 50
Chas. D. Sherwood	Ex-Auditor	10 00	10 00
Michael Coogin	Special Officer at Polls, Dist. No. 7	2 00	2 00
S. H. Sanford	Board of Registry, Dist. No. 7	12 00	12 00
Wm. H. Burlingame	Ex-Auditor	10 00	10 00
John L. Hall	Constable, assigned viz., C. F. Wanzer, $300 00 Robert R. Mead, 206 56 S. K. Phillips and Sam'l Rogers, 100 00 Lewis Chase. 48 00	1,285 40	1,162 10
Jeremiah Stevenson	Constable, assigned to Lewis Chase, 40 00	171 25	160 35
Theodore Moith	Constable	1,723 85	1,585 90
John Mana	"	229 50	219 40
Levi Ellis	" assigned viz., John Schofield, $100 00 Geo. H. Harding, 100 00 C. F. Wanzer. 100 00 Lewis Chase, 286 00 S. K. Phillips, 50 00	1,016 95	951 25

FISHKILL—Continued.

Westfall & Greene........	Desk and Map frames....	28 75	28 75
Judson & Hancock........	Material and Work on Crusher and Bridges......	33 02	33 02
Egbert Conklin............	Material and Painting Town Hall and Lock-up	30 50	30 50
B. F. Greene.................	Disinfectants and Supplies	24 50	24 50
James G. Meyer.............	Counsel to Auditors........	40 00	40 00
Charles Simpson............	Clerk of Election............	4 00	4 00
G. W. Bradshaw..........	Town Clerk and disbursements, assigned to C. F. Wanzer. $300 00 J. G. Myers. 55 00	796 80	796 80
S. K. Phillips.............	Services searching records Unpaid Tax.............	15 00	15 00
W. A. Meyers.............	Clerk of Election, Dist. No. 1................	4 00	4 00
S. K. Phillips	Counsel to Town Board..	124 33	124 33
P. H. Morray............	Inspector of Election, Dist. No. 1.................	27 35	27 35
R. T. Van Tine......,......	Stationery for polls, Dists. Nos. 1, 2 and 3............	5 40	5 40
S. B. Rogers............	Supervisor...............	75 72	75 72
S. B. Rogers................	Supervisor, disbursements	91 65	91 65
Robert Carver.............	Stationery...................	7 90	7 90
Charles W. Anderson....	Inspector of Election, Dist. No. 1....................	4 00	4 00
Samuel H. Sanford........	Ex-Supervisor, disbursements........................	105 08	105 08
John B. Whitson............	Justice of the Peace........	1,416 40	1,416 40
S. B. Rogers............	Justice of the Peace........	1,169 80	1,169 80
David E. Van Amburgh..	Justice of the Peace........	91 65	91 65
Wm. H. Peattie..........	Taking down and carting booths......................	6 00	6 00
T. Coldwell, G. M. Wanzer, agent................	Use of house for polls. Dist. No. 7..................	25 00	23 00

FISHKILL.—Continued.

C. VanBenthuysen & Son . Registry blank, assigned to G. W. Bradshaw...... .	28 10	28 10
John Hurley ....For inspecting boiler of stone crusher......	5 00	5 00
Rebecca Miller .... Excessive tax............-......	7 38	7 38

We hereby certify that the Commissioners of Highways have delivered to us, pursuant to Chapter 395, of the Laws of 1873, and the amendments thereto, a certificate whereby they fix and determine the amount of money to be raised by tax for the maintenance and repairs of the highways, exclusive of the villages of Fishkill Landing and Matteawan, for the ensuing year at four thousand dollars............. . $4,000 00 $4,000 00

We certify the above to be correct.

G. W. BRADSHAW, Town Clerk.
C. O. OSBORNE,
W. H. PEATTIE,
ERASTUS HORTON,
CHARLES ROTHERY,

Auditors.

HYDE PARK.

Statement of Accounts, Charges and Claims, payable by the Town of Hyde Park, in the County of Dutchess, audited and allowed by the Board of Town Auditors, at a meeting of said Board, held at the House of M. H. Horning, in the Town of Hyde Park, on Thursday, the sixth day of November, in the year 1890.

Name of Person.	Nature of the Demand.	Asked.	Allowed.
David E. Howatt............	Services as Supervisor and Disbursing Money, assigned to John Hopkins.	$ 88 56	$ 88 56
A. B. Schryver..............	Services as Town Clerk and Disbursment..........	193 55	193 55
Isaac D. C. Pritchard......	Justice of the Peace........	37 85	37 85
Thomas S. Kipp.............	Commiss'er of Highways..	30 00	30 00
Noble G. Marsh.............	" " ..	34 00	34 00
A. J. Briggs.................	" " ..	38 44	38 44
G. S. Halsted......	Justice of the Peace........	18 00	18 00
Myers Fitchett.............	Assessor........................ ..	62 00	62 00
Coster Degroff.............	"	62 00	62 00
James Cummings.........	"	62 00	62 00
Samuel M. Rider............	Ex-Overseer of Poor........	13 70	13 70
Charles Plain	Overseer of Poor, assigned to Thomas E. Parker....	13 00	13 00
William E. Welch.........	Overseer of the Poor........	13 45	13 45
Ezra Plain...................	Ex.-Overseer of the Poor, assigned to Coster Degroff	68 25	68 25
H. T. Doremus..............	Inspector of Election, Dist. No. 1........................	21 80	21 80
Wm. H Schryver............	Inspector of Election, Dist. No. 1...................... .	16 00	16 00
C. W. H. Arnold............	Inspector of Election, Dist. No. 1.......	16 00	16 00
George D. Cronk............	Inspector of Election, Dist. No. 1......................	16 00	16 00
Edward Schryver.........	Clerk of Board of Registration	12 00	12 00

HYDE PARK—Continued.

William R. Gowan........Inspector of Election, Dist.		
No. 1............................	18 80	18 80
John R. Clark................Clerk of Election, Dist.		
No. 1......	4 00	4 00
John F. Calahan............Inspector of Election, Dist.		
No. 2.....	21 56	21 56
H. Fremont Vandewater. Inspector of Election, Dist.		
No. 2......	16 00	16 00
Thomas F. Leonard.......Inspector of Election, Dist.		
No. 2............................	16 00	16 00
George H. Briggs..........Inspector of Election, Dist.		
No. 2............................	18 56	18 56
Albert J. Briggs.............Clerk of Election, Dist.		
No. 2........................ .	4 00	4 00
Frank J. Traver.............Inspector of Election, Dist.		
No. 2...........................	16 00	16 00
Lewis Wigg...................Clerk of Election, Dist.		
No. 2...........................	4 00	4 00
H. B. Sleight............ ...Inspector of Election, Dist.		
No. 3	21 56	21 56
James Van Wagner.......Inspector of Election, Dist.		
No. 3....................... ...	16 00	16 00
George E. Schryver.. .....Inspector of Election, Dist.		
No. 3, assigned to A. B.		
Schryver....................	16 00	16 00
John J. Germond.........Inspector of Election, Dist.		
No. 3.................	16 00	16 00
F. W. Holmes....... ......Inspector of Election, Dist.		
No. 3...........................	18 56	18 56
John G. Briggs...... ....Clerk of Election, Dist.		
No. 3.......................	4 00	4 00
A. B. Schryver..............Clerk of Election, Dist.		
No. 4............................	4 00	4 00
Coster DeGroff.............Money paid for Contract		
on 16 Booths...............	56 58	56 58
Coster Degroff...... ....Distributing Booths to		
Polling Place and return	9 00	9 00

HYDE PARK—Continued.

I. D. C. Pritchard .... Making Ballot Boxes and Guard Rail....................	20 79	20 79
B. D. Wigg.................... Room for Election Purposes	25 00	25 00
Edwin U. Lasher .... Room for Election Purposes and Storing Booths	26 00	26 00
David E. Howatt........... Trustee for Election Purposes........................	25 00	25 00
F. W. R. Hopper............. Town Sealer...................	5 00	5 00
Coster DeGroff............. Constable......................	6 40	6 40
J. S. Bird..................... Contract for Medical Attendance on Poor.........	150 00	150 00
H. W. Rowe............... Justice of the Peace.......	31 10	31 10
Dr. J. L. Pritchard........ Returning birth and death certificate..............	1 80	1 80
J. S. Bird..................... Returning birth and death certificates	17 00	17 00
Edmund Barnes, M.D...... Returning birth and death certificate	2 70	2 70
Dr. John Poucher......... Returning birth and death certificate	45	45
Dr. John Leroy.............. Returning birth and death certificate.................	30	30
Joseph G. Frost, Coroner. Returning birth and death certificate.................	45	45
C. S. Van Etten............. Returning birth and death certificate.................	30	30
Rev. Robert Knapp........ Returning 4 marriage certificates....................	1 00	1 00
Rev. John F. Shaw........ Returning 2 marriage certificates....................	50	50
Rev. Edgar Beckwith...... Returning 2 marriage certificates....................	50	50
Rev. P. N. D. Bleeker.... Returning 1 marriage certificate....................	25	25
Rev. R. Herbert Gesner.. Returning 3 marriage certificates....................	75	75

HYDE PARK—Continued.

Rev. George Seebury......Returning 1 marriage certificate......	25	25
Rev. A. B. Schryver.......Recorder births, deaths and marriages, assigned to John Hopkins.............	27 90	27 90
Rev. T. B. Foster............Meeting with Board of Health, 2 days..............	4 00	4 00
Mr. C. Horning...... ....Room for Excise Board...	10 00	10 00
M. H. Horning. Estate...Room for Town meeting, assigned to John Hopkins	20 00	20 00
Edward H. Lasher.......Room for Court purposes.	2 00	2 00
Henry Murray ....Excise Commissioner and Blanks............	6 64	6 64
L. Lincoln Marquet.......Killing 5 foxes.............	5 00	5 00
James G. VanWagner... " 1 "	1 00	1 00
Charles Terpening........ " 3 "	3 00	3 00
Charles H. Marshall...... " 4 "	4 00	4 00
Edward R. Hewlett........ " 1 "	1 00	1 00
Lewis Baker................. " 1 "	1 00	1 00
Levi Wood..................... " 1 "	1 00	1 00
Charles McNamee......... " 2 "	2 00	2 00
Murray Howard............. " 2 "	2 00	2 00
Charles Daly................. " 1 "	1 00	1 00
John F. Callahan..........Clerk of Town Meeting...	4 00	4 00

$1,507 50 $1,507 50

We certify the above to be correct.

DAVID E. HOWATT,

A. B. SCHRYVER,

GEORGE S. HALSTED,

I. D. C. PRITCHARD,

HERMAN W. ROWE,

Auditors.

LA GRANGE.

Statement of Accounts, Charges and Claims, payable by the Town of La Grange, in the County of Dutchess, audited and allowed by the Board of Town Auditors, at a meeting of said Board, held at the house of H. H. White, in the Town of La Grange, on Thursday, the 6th day of November, in the year 1890.

Name of Person.	Nature of the Demand.	Asked.	Allowed.
Wm. H. Austin	Services as Supervisor	18 00	18 00
" "	Services as one of Registry Board	12 00	12 00
" "	Paid for booths, preparing voting places, material, etc	32 09	32 09
I. F. Dunkin	Services as Justice of the Peace	10 00	10 00
" "	Registry and Poll Clerk, 2d Dist	16 00	16 00
L. W. Vincent	Services in Registry Board, ballot clerk, and work preparing voting room in 2d Dist	20 00	20 00
Wm. Bodden, Jr	For stove, pipe, zinc, and putting up the same	10 75	10 75
Wm. H. Austin	For killing one old fox	1 00	1 00
John Kidney	For carting booths and lumber, per order Supervisor	3 00	3 00
R. Decker	For killing one old fox	1 00	1 00
John E. Townsend	Inspector, Registry Board, returning canvass to County Clerk and mileage, Dist. No. 1	21 80	21 80
Edwin J. Velie	Services as Inspector, Dist. No. 1	16 00	16 00
H. H. White	For use of house for Town purposes	33 00	33 00

LA GRANGE—Continued.

Henry L. Giddings	As Marshal in Dist. No. 1	4 00	4 00
William A. Dutcher	As Poll Clerk, Dist. No. 1	4 00	4 00
Isaac Burnett	" " " " " "	4 00	4 00
Townsend Cole	As Justice of the Peace...	11 70	11 70
" "	Taking John Teator to Alms House	2 50	2 50
George M. Burnett	Services as Constable	11 30	11 30
" "	Services as Overseer of the Poor	6 75	6 75
Chas. L. Cole	Services as Inspector and returning canvass to Supervisor	18 00	18 00
Isaac Burnett	Services as Justice of the Peace	12 60	12 60
Chas. Hitchcock	For killing four foxes	4 00	4 00
Howard Meddaugh	As Marshal in Dist. No. 2	4 00	4 00
Samuel McCabe	For use of house for election purposes, Dist No. 2.	21 00	21 00
James H. Landon	Services as Assessor	32 00	32 00
Austin T. Fink	For medical services	20 00	20 00
Joseph V. Genung	Meeting with Board of Health	2 00	2 00
Geo. B. Houghtaling	For killing one fox	1 00	1 00
Wm. H. Brower	For Inspector, taking returns to Supervisor and carting Booths, 2nd Dist.	20 00	20 00
E. R. Schryver	For Services as Town Clerk	42 86	42 86
E. R. Schryver	Paid for books, blanks, election supplies and ballot boxes	18 59	18 59
E. R. Schryver	Registrar Board of Health	28 00	28 00
Clark Barmore	As Ballot Clerk and taking stubs to C. Clerk, Dist. No. 1.	9 80	9 80
Joel O. Holmes, 2nd	As Inspector of Election in Dist. No. 2.	16 00	16 00

LA GRANGE—Continued.

Joel O. Holmes	For killing one fox	1 00	1 00
R. C. Devine	For services as Assessor	30 00	30 00
David B. Van Wyck	As Inspector and Del'g returns to County Clerk, Dist. No. 2	21 32	21 32
James Howard	As Inspector and Del'g unvoted ballots to County Clerk, Dist. No. 2	21 32	21 32
Chas. U. Monfort	Services as Highway Com-Nov. 6, '89 to Feb. 25, '90.	66 00	66 00
Ernest Emans	For killing two foxes	2 00	2 00
Elias W. Berry	For Inspector and Reg. Board, Dist. No. 2	18 00	18 00
Daniel Genung	For killing one fox	1 00	1 00
James Ferris	For killing two foxes	2 00	2 00
Chas. W. Monfort	Services as Highway Commissioner, February 27, '90, to November 6, '90	156 00	156 00
Chas. Madden	Services as Overseer of the Poor	7 50	7 50
Chas. T. Van Benschoten	Services as Poll Clerk, Dist. No. 2	4 00	4 00
John Nugent	For killing four foxes	4 00	4 00
Chas. W. Monfort	Roads and Bridges	250 00	250 00
Wm. H. Austin	For approving and returning Collector's Bond and Postage	6 82	6 82
Chas. E. Davis	For order from Overseer of Poor for provisions	5 00	5 00
Robt. H. Smith	Assessor	32 00	32 00

$1,116 70 $1,116 70

We certify the above to be correct.

ELIAS VAN BENSCHOTEN,
JAY HOWARD,
JOHN S. LANDON,
Auditors.

MILAN.

Statement of Accounts, Charges and Claims, payable
by the Town of Milan. in the County of Dutchess, audited and allowed by the Board of Town Auditors, at
a meeting of said Board, held at the house of Clement
Sweet, in the Town of Milan, on Thursday, the 6th
day of November, in the year 1890.

Name of Person.	Nature of the Demand.	Asked.	Allowed.
Cole Bros.	Material for Booths.	$5 68	$5 68
Warren Teator.	Killing Foxes	5 00	5 00
Frankin Sweet	" "	2 00	2 00
Simon Fitzsimmons.	" "	2 00	2 00
Arthur Phillips.	" "	9 00	9 00
J. L. Herman.	" "	2 00	2 00
Walter A. Smith	" "	3 00	3 00
Clement Sweet.	" "	12 00	12 00
Dr. J. H. Cotter.	Medical Attendance.	18 00	18 00
" "	Reporting Births & Deaths	3 50	3 50
James Fitzsimmons.	Ex-Poormaster.	36 25	36 25
Franklin Sweet.	Poormaster.	13 25	13 25
H. D. Ostrom	Poor Order.	10 00	10 00
Benjamin Sherow.	" "	5 00	5 00
Harvey Levy.	Inspector Dist. No. 1	18 00	18 00
Egbert Thompson.	" "	18 00	18 00
John A. Cole.	" "	23 88	23 88
Warren Teator.	" "	16 00	16 00
William R. Cole.	" "	23 80	23 80
John VanBenschoten	Inspector Dist. No. 1, and Clerk Town Meeting	22 00	22 00
James Levy.	Clerk Dist. No. 1, and Excise Commissioner.	13 00	13 00
Henry D. Pink.	Inspector Dist. No. 2	18 00	18 00
Wilson Sitzer	" "	12 00	12 00
John Cotting	" "	23 00	23 00
Otis Bowman	" "	18 00	18 00
Lewis Wildey.	" "	16 00	16 00
Clark Cornelious	" "	23 00	23 00

MILAN—Continued.

William H. Lamoree......Assessor	30 00	30 00
Lawrence Cotter........... "	36 00	36 00
William H. Allendorf...Assessor and Building Booths.........................	42 00	42 00
Cyrus F. Morehouse.......Supervisor................ .	53 03	53 03
George Edelman............Iron and Work.............. .	3 99	3 99
Courtland Wright.........Ex-Com. of Highways....	2 00	2 00
Alfred Pells..................Commiss'r "	48 00	48 00
R. E. VanDeusen..........Legal Services..............	5 00	5 00
Garret W. Link. ....Excise Commissioner.......	9 00	9 00
Cole Bros...................Use of house for Election Dist. No. 1, and storing Booths.........................	15 00	15 00
B. F. Sherow...............Use of house for Election Dist. No. 2.............	10 00	10 00
Eben Shook..................Constable Bill................	1 50	1 50
William VanEtten....... " "	3 80	3 80
John W. Stickle.............Ex-Supervisor...............	8 00	8 00
Dr. Walter Herick........Medical Services & Death permits.......	12 12	12 12
Cyrus F. Morehouse.......Note $800 for Highway and Inst....................	836 00	836 00
John Fish............. .... Town Clerk, assigned to Cyrus F. Morehouse.......	76 50	76 50
Clement Sweet...............Use of house Town Meeting.....................	10 00	10 00
Uriah Teator...............Justice of the Peace........	18 25	18 25
Ezra L. Morshouse........ " "	4 25	4 25
Wm. R. Cole.............. " "	19 50	19 50
A. L. Husted............. " "	14 25	14 25
George E. Decker.........Killing old fox	2 00	2 00
Eben Shook..................Killing fox, assigned to C. Couse & Son................	2 00	2 00

We certify the above to be correct.

EZRA L. MOREHOUSE,
WILLIAM R. COLE,
URIAH TEATOR,
A. L. HUSTED,
CYRUS F. MOREHOUSE,
JOHN FISH, Town Clerk,
Auditors.

NORTH EAST.

Statement of Accounts, Charges and Claims, payable by the Town of North East, in the County of Dutchess, audited and allowed by the Board of Town Auditors, at a meeting of said Board, held at the Town Room, in the Town of North East, on Thursday, the sixth day of November, in the year 1890.

Name of Person.	Nature of the Demand.	Asked.	Allowed.
Henry D. Clark.	Assessor	$ 30 00	$ 30 00
George Barton	"	38 00	38 00
Henry D. Clark..	Appraising sheep killed by dogs	8 00	8 00
Michael Rowe	Excise Commissioner	9 00	9 00
Fred Dakin.	" "	9 00	9 00
Webster Deacon.	" "	9 00	9 00
Chester L. Hatch	Janitor of polling place	2 00	2 00
A. F. Hoag, M. D	Certificates of births and deaths	4 00	4 00
L. P. Hatch.	Registrar Board of Health	11 75	11 75
G. H. Codding, M. D	Certificates of births and deaths..	3 50	3 50
J. D. W. Du Mond	Certificates of births and deaths, and Health Office	10 50	10 50
Hiram Rogers.	Assessor	36 00	36 00
E. B. Manning	Highway Commissioner	28 00	28 00
Wm. H. Jinks	" "	28 00	28 00
L. L. Barton	" "	22 00	22 00
L. P. Hatch	Supplies for Booths and Registry Board.	2 80	2 80
J. D. W. Du Mond	Rent of polling place, 2d District	10 00	10 00
John Scutt	Supplies for polling booths and Town Board	145 90	145 90
George Barton	Appraising sheep.	2 00	2 00
L. L. Barton	" "	2 00	2 00
E. B. Manning	" "	6 00	6 00

NORTH EAST—Continued.

Wm. H. Paine...............	Clerk of Election in 1888..	4 00	4 00
Chester A. Biggs.............	Justice of the Peace........	15 20	15 20
Webster Deacon.	Rent for polling place......	20 00	20 00
Wm. H. Jenks......... ...	Apprasing sheep	4 00	4 00
John W. Pulver..............	Returning collector's bond	13 00	13 00
Wm. H. Hoysradt.........	Overseer of the Poor........	10 00	10 00
Wm. T. Eggleston.........	'' ''	18 00	18 00
Leonard A. Lake...........	'' ''	10 00	10 00
James E. Myres...	Constable.....	11 05	11 05
Chandler Dresser............	Constable and duties at Election, assigned to E. W. Simmons..............	15 11	15 11
Levi P. Hatch.	Town Clerk...................	114 95	114 95
John N. Conklin............	Justice of the Peace........	10 00	10 00
George Kipp.....	'' ''	6 00	6 00
E. B. Rugg..................	'' ''	12 00	12 00
Geo. Bayley.................	Excessive taxation...........	1 00	1 00
James R. Paine..............	Excessive taxation...........	3 00	3 00
Israel Sabin...................	Police duty at Election...	4 00	4 00
W. H. Jenks...........	'' '' ''	4 00	4 00
Andrew Pulver.............	Clerk of Election.............	4 00	4 00
Rennus Hicks...............	Overseer of the Poor.......	14 25	14 25
D. S. Chapman.............	Clerk of Election and Town meeting......................	8 00	8 00
Millerton Telegram........	Printing	5 25	5 25
Theodore H. Hoysradt...	Clerk of Election............	4 00	4 00
E. Darwin Morse............	Inspector and Ballot Clerk	24 50	24 50
E. W. Simmons.	Inspector and Registrar..	26 52	26 52
John W. Clark..............	'' '' ..	18 00	18 00
Allen Thompson......	'' '' ..	16 00	16 00
Collins Barton..............	Inspector and Ballot Clerk	16 00	16 00
Darwin Beers...............	'' '' ''	18 00	18 00
Chas. P. Scutt......	'' '' ''	26 00	26 00
George Rogers	Registrar Clerk..............	18 00	18 00
Calvin Card..................	Inspector and Registrar...	18 00	18 00
Hoffman Sweet.............	'' '' ...	16 00	16 00
Orrin Wakeman.............	'' '' ...	16 00	16 00

NORTH EAST—Continued.

S. W. Patterson............Ex-Town Clerk............		**37 98**
	$979 26	$979 26
Deduct..	400 00	400 00
	$579 26	$579 26

We certify the above to be correct.
JOHN SCUTT, Supervisor,
LEVI P. HATCH, Town Clerk,
E. B. RUGG, Justice of the Peace,
JOHN W. CONKLIN, Justice of the Peace,
GEORGE KIPP, Justice of the Peace,
Auditors.

PAWLING.

Statement of Accounts, Charges and Claims, payable by the Town of Pawling, in the County of Dutchess, audited and allowed by the Board of Town Auditors, at a meeting of said Board, held at the Town Room, in the Town of Pawling, on Thursday, the 6th day of November, in the year 1890.

Name of Person.	Nature of the Demand.	Asked.	Allowed.
Albert Wooden..............Assessor,......................		$ 40 00	$ 40 00
Jerry S. Pearce............. "		38 00	38 00
Charles Townsend......... "		38 00	38 00
Geo. F. Lee..................Supervisor. For election booths.		55 00	55 00
Geo. A. Daniels..............Town Clerk..................		65 21	65 21

PAWLING—Continued.

Jas. S. Pearce	Ex-Town Clerk	16 00	16 00
Wm. R. Lee	For legal services	10 00	10 00
Chas. E. Baker	Ex-Com. of Highways	87 90	87 90
" " "	"	194 00	194 00
" " "	Com. of Highways, Money paid out and interest	2,459 00	2,459 00
Elmore Ferris	Services as Town Sealer	23 98	23 98
A. W. Corbin	Ex-Supervisor for approving and returning to County Clerk, collector's Bond	12 84	12 84
Geo. F. Lee	Supervisor	34 00	34 00
Dr. H. Pearce	For attendance to poor	42 50	42 50
Dr. H. Pearce & Co	For medicine for poor	14 73	14 73
Jas. S. Pearce	For Burying town pauper	20 00	20 00
Mal. P. Baker	For town poor	8 77	8 77
Merwin & Holmes	For town poor	2 75	2 75
Alvin W. Devine	Overseer of Poor	4 00	4 00
Patrick Burns	Overseer of the Poor	32 70	25 00
Albert J. Wooden	Election Clerk, Dist. No. 1	4 00	4 00
Wm. J. Carey	Election Clerk, Dist. No. 1	4 00	4 00
Robt. Cass	Election Clerk, Dist. No. 2	4 00	4 00
Herrick Thomas	Election Clerk, Dist. No. 2	4 00	4 00
Mal. P. Baker	Inspector of Election	10 00	10 00
Chas. Townsend	Inspector of Election	10 00	10 00
Philip H. Smith	Inspector of Election and printing	11 50	11 50
Geo. H. Vanderburgh	Inspector of Election, Dist. No. 2	10 00	10 00
Wilbur F. Dye	Inspector of Election, Dist. No. 1	10 00	10 00
Hiram S. Haviland	Inspector of Election, Dist. No. 1	10 00	10 00
Seward T. Green	Inspector of Election, Dist. No. 1, and making returns	17 00	17 00

PAWLING—Continued.

Jay Hurd	Inspector of Election, Dist. No. 2, and making returns	17 00	17 00
B. F. Burr	Inspector of Election, Dist. No. 1. and making returns	17 00	17 00
Geo. S. Norton	Inspector of Election, Dist. No. 1, and making returns.	10 00	10 00
John Gregory	Appointed Constable to attend Election, Dist. No. 1	2 00	2 00
Timothy Murphy	Appointed Constable to attend Election, Dist, No. 1	2 00	2 00
W. G. Tice.	For advertising and printing	15 50	15 50
Geo. T. Chapman & Co.	Poor Bill	20 15	20 15
Geo. H. Slocum	Constable	17 55	17 55
Levi Cornell	Constable	16 55	16 55
T. W. Stark	Justice of the Peace, Criminal Business	1 25	1 25
T. W. Stark	Justice of the Peace, Bill .	18 00	18 00
Theron M. Green	Justice of the Peace	20 00	20 00
H. S. Haviland	Justice of the Peace	30 05	30 05
Geo. S. Norton.	Justice of the Peace	18 00	18 00
Wm. C. Dodge.	Excise Commissioner	3 00	3 00
J. B. Dutcher	One year rent for Town Room	300 00	300 00
Wyman Roselle	Constable, Election Dist. No. 2, (made over to G. S. Norton	2 00	2 00
Chas. F. Denton.	Commissioner of Excise	3 00	3 00
F. S. Merwin	Poor Bill.	6 80	6 80

PAWLING—Continued.

Geo. W. Slocum............	10 00	10 00
Patrick Lennon.............	3 00	3 00

                                          $3,819 02

We certify the above to be correct.

G. F. LEE,
THERON M. GREEN,
G. S. NORTON,
T. W. STARK,
GEO. A. DANIELS,
Auditors.

PINE PLAINS.

Statement of Accounts, Charges and Claims payable by the Town of Pine Plains, in the County of Dutchess, audited and allowed by the Board of Town Auditors, at a meeting of said Board, held at the Town Room, in the Town of Pine Plains, on Thursday, the 6th day of November, in the year 1890.

Name of Person.	Nature of the Demand.	Asked.	Allowed.
John A. Herrick............	Supervisor, town business.	$ 26 80	$ 26 80
John A. Herrick............	For election booths furnished........	37 27	37 27
James P. Morgan............	Town Clerk Business........	89 02	89 02
James P. Morgan..........	Secretary Board of Health	25 50	25 50
William H. Scutt......	Justices Bill and Inspector	33 60	33 60
John Rowe.................	Justices Bill.................	18 00	18 00
Frank Eno..............	Justices Bill.................	14 00	14 00
Geo. H. Knickerbocker..	Justices Bill and Inspector	19 40	19 40

PINE PLAINS—Continued.

John W. Briggs................	Inspector of Election........	16 00	10 00
A. S. Barton...................	Inspector of Election and returning certificate to County Clerk............	17 40	17 40
Horace Bowman.............	Inspector of Election.......	16 00	10 00
Peter Weaver.................	Inspector of Election and returning ballots to County Clerk........	23 80	17 40
Samuel T. Hoag.............	Inspector of Election and returning ballots to County Clerk.....	23 80	17 40
Albert L. Keller.............	Inspector of Election and returning ballots to County Clerk................	17 52	17 40
George G. Titus..............	Inspector of Election and returning certificate to County Clerk.....	19 08	17 40
Lafayette Tripp.............	Inspector of Election..	10 00	10 00
Fred. Tripp..............	Poll Clerk..........	4 00	4 00
Irving B. Pulver.......	Poll Clerk....	4 00	4 00
Henry C· Hedges...........	Poll Clerk....	4 00	4 00
Charles W. Frost.............	Poll Clerk at Spring and Fall Election...............	8 00	8 00
George C. Pulver.............	Justice's bill, assigned to J. S. Bowman...............	8 00	8 00
Adam A. Strever.............	Assessor's bill..................	34 00	34 00
Robert D, Hicks.............	Assessor's bill..................	38 00	38 00
Willard W. Hicks...........	Assessor's bill................	32 00	32 00
Barton & Hicks............	For use of room for 4 days for election purposes......	'25 00	25 00
Lawrence Barrett...........	Overseer of Poor bill......'	28 00	28 00
Carl Schults...................	Commissioner of Highway.............................	30 00	30 00
Anthony H. Barton........	Commissioner of Highway	30 00	30 00
Henry C. Wilber............	Health Physician.............	25 00	25 00
Edward Place................	Constable bill.................	6 25	6 25

PINE PLAINS—Continued.

Jacob W. Tipple	Police Officer	4 00	
Samuel T. Hoag	Printing bill	16 00	16 00
Charles S. Wilber	Printing bill	12 00	12 00
Albert Bowman	For use of Town Room	50 00	50 00
Henry Pitcher	Excise Commissioner	3 00	3 00
Charles Turpin	Excise Commissioner	9 00	9 00
William Sadler	Excise Commissioner	3 00	3 00
Alexander B. Vedder	Excise Commissioner	9 00	9 00
A. O. Mattice	Bounty on foxes in year 1888	2 00	2 00
Amount voted for Commissioners of Highways		250 00	250 00
Pine Plains Free Library, by statute		147 50	147 50
Seymour Smith Academy		100 00	100 00
J. H. Lyke		2 00	2 00
J. S. Hinsdale	Com. of Highway	30 00	30 00
J. A. Herrick	Disbursing money	16 81	16 81

$1,337 75 $1,307 15

We certify the above to be correct.

J. A. HERRICK, Supervisor,
JOHN ROWE, Justice of the Peace,
FRANK ENO, Justice of the Peace,
W. H. SCUTT, Justice of the Peace,
G. H. KNICKERBOCKER, Justice of the Peace.
J. P. MORGAN, Town Clerk,

                                   Auditors.

PLEASANT VALLEY.

Statement of Accounts, Charges and Claims, payable by the Town of Pleasant Valley, in the County of Dutchess, audited and allowed by the Board of Town Auditors, at a meeting of said Board, held at the Hall of W. C. Armstrong, in the Town of Pleasant Valley, on the sixth day of November, in the year 1890.

Name of Person.	Nature of the Demand.	Asked.	Allowed.
Orlando Van Wagner..	Services as Road Commissioner	$70 00	$70 00
Ed. C. Drake	Services as Board of Health	2 00	2 00
Orlando Van Wagner...	To pay note given for money to build new road from N. Holmes to Geo. Formans	1,575 00	1,575 00
Thos. J. Drake	Clerk at Town Meeting	4 00	4 00
Thos. J. Drake	Clerk at Election District No. 1	4 00	4 00
M. P. Vandewater	Services as Poll Clerk, District No. 2	4 00	4 00
W. J. Larry	Services as Officer at Election District No. 2	4 00	4 00
Abram Devine	Clerk at Election	4 00	4 00
Harvey Bullock	A. G. Tobey's bill	4 00	4 00
Chas. J. Bower	Excise Commissioner two years	6 00	6 00
W. H. Smith	Excise Commissioner	3 00	3 00
A. V. Haight	Bill for Printing	9 50	9 50
John M. Edwards	Services as Supervisor	8 88	8 88
M. P. Vandewater Adm'r, W. A. V.	Services as Road Commissioner	54 00	54 00
Harvey Bullock	Services as Town Clerk...	90 02	90 02
Joseph Doty	Services as Assessor	54 00	54 00
W. C. Armstrong	Use of Hall	40 00	40 00
Dr. Irving Le Roy	Services as Health Officer.	20 00	20 00

PLEASANT VALLEY—Continued.

S. J. Hicks	Services as Assessor	54 00	54 00
S. J. Hicks	For furnishing Posts Town Division	3 00	3 00
Irving Le Roy	For Recording Births and Deaths	3 75	3 75
E. R. Newcomb	As Excise Commissioner	3 00	3 00
E. R. Newcomb	Voting Booths and Ballot Boxes	49 75	49 75
W. H. Sheldon	Board of Registry and Ballot Clerk	16 00	16 00
Jno. S. VanKeuren	Board of Registry and Inspector of Election	16 00	16 00
Harvey Halstead	Board of Registry and Inspector of Election	16 00	16 00
J. J. C. Howe	Board of Registry and Inspector of Election	16 00	16 00
W. H. Bower	Board of Registry and Inspector of Election and Election Returns	21 56	21 56
E. W. Lawton	Board of Registry and Clerk of Town Meeting and Returns	26 00	26 00
Isaac Rogers	Board of Registry and Ballot Clerk and Returns	21 88	21 88
A. M. Laird	Board of Registry and Ballot Clerk and Returns	21 56	21 56
Chas. H. Duncan	Board of Registry and Inspector	16 00	16 00
Calvin G. Smith	Board of Registry and Inspector	16 00	16 00
M. F. Duncan	Services as Town Clerk	30 20	30 20
Richard Cronkrite	Services as Assessor	46 00	46 00
J. P. Sheldon	Rent of Hall for Election	10 00	10 00
Sidney S. Masten	Services as Constable	6 00	6 00
Eli Masten	Services as Constable	15 25	15 25
Geo. T. Lawton	Criminal business as Justice and Clerk of Election	8 50	8 50

PLEASANT VALLEY—Continued.

Geo. T. Lawton..............Services as Justice of the Peace........................	18 00	18 00
Jere Wolven.................Services as Justice of the Peace........................	16 00	16 00
Jere Wolven.................Criminal business............	13 25	13 25
G. F. Davis................ Services as Justice of the Peace........................	20 00	20 00
John H. Bates.................Services as Justice...........	14 00	14 00
E. Wright Vail..............Services as Supervisor......	43 75	43 75
M. F. Duncan...............Recording births, deaths and marriages..............	9 50	9 50
Anthony Briggs.............Surveying to divide town.	10 00	10 00
	$2,517 35	$2,517 35

We certify the above to be correct.

E. WRIGHT VAIL, Supervisor,
G. F. DAVIS,
JEREMIAH WOLVEN,
GEORGE T. LAWTON,
JOHN H. BATES,
HARVEY BULLOCK, Town Clerk,
Auditors.

POUGHKEEPSIE.

Statement of Accounts, Charges and Claims, payable by the Town of Poughkeepsie, in the County of Dutchess, audited and allowed by the Board of Town Auditors, at a meeting of said Board, held in the Town of Pougkeepsie, on the 6th, 7th and 8th days of November, in the year 1890.

Name of Person.	Nature of the Demand.	Asked.	Allowed.
James W. Sinsabaugh	Inspector of Election, Dist. No. 3	4 00	4 00
John V. Vermilyea	Inspector of Election, Dist. No. 3	4 00	4 00
John H. Van Sicklen	Inspector of Election, Dist. No. 3, and filing returns	21 80	21 80
Frank R. Ferris	Inspector of Election, Dist. No. 3, and filing returns	22 00	22 00
Chas. Wicks	Inspector of Election, Dist. No. 3	8 00	8 00
Wm. H. McLean	Inspector of Election, Dist. No. 3	4 00	4 00
M. V. Griffin	Clerk of Election, Dist. No. 3	4 00	4 00
Wm. Baker	Clerk and Inspector of Election. Dist. No. 3	8 00	8 00
Wm. A. Lawson	Inspector of Election and filing returns. Dist. No. 3,	18 00	18 00
John G. Harris	Inspector of Election, Dist. No. 3, and furnishing voting booths	105 25	105 25
H. Van Nostrand	Inspector of Election, Dist. No. 3, and use of room for election purposes	33 00	33 00
John Feighrey	Clerk of Election, Dist. No. 2	4 00	4 00
Chas. Howard	Inspector of Election and filing returns, Dist. No. 2,	22 00	22 00

POUGHKEEPSIE—Continued.

Henry Allen..................Inspector of Election and filing returns, Dist. No. 2,	22 00	22 00
Newton J. Ollivett.........Clerk and Inspector of Election, Dist. No. 2......	20 00	20 00
Isaac P. Flagler...........Inspector of Election and delivering returns, Dist. No. 2......	25 00	25 00
C. J. Carey.. ....Clerk of Election, Dist. No. 2............................	8 00	8 00
J. H. Lawrence.............Inspector of Election and delivering returns, Dist. No. 1	28 14	28 14
Michael J. Lyons............Inspector of Election and delivering returns, Dist. No. 1............................	6 00	6 00
John A. Pardee.............Inspector of Election,Dist. No. 1.....	18 00	18 00
James McCloskey.........Clerk Board of Registry Dist. 1, assigned to A. B. Gray...........................	12 00	12 00
John A. Bagley..............Clerk of Election, Dist. No. 1, assigned to A. B. Gray...........................	4 00	4 00
Dennis Hurley, Jr.........Inspector of Election,Dist. No. 1, assigned to A. B. Gray............	22 00	22 00
John A. Bagley..............Clerk of Election, Dist. No. 1 (Spring), assigned to A. B. Gray...............	4 00	4 00
John J. Hughes.............Inspector of Election,Dist. No. 1, and filing returns	21 64	21 64
Peter Downey, Jr.........Inspector of Election, Dist. No. 1...........................	16 00	16 00
Peter LeRoy...............Inspector of Election,Dist. No. 3 and filing returns	11 80	11 80
J. V. Overocker.............Inspector of Election, Dist. No. 4 and filing returns	18 00	18 00

POUGHKEEPSIE—Continued.

Samuel I. Robinson.......Inspector of Election, Dist. No. 4 and filing returns	18 00	18 00
Chas. W. Palmer............Clerk of Election Dist. No. 4.................................	4 00	4 00
Hezekiah C. Gardner......Inspector of Election,Dist. No. 4 and delivering returns, assigned to A. B. Gray...........................	18 00	18 00
J. E. Cartier................Inspector of Election, Dist. No. 4.............................	10 00	10 00
James McLaughlin........Clerk and Inspector of Election, Dist. No. 4, assigned to A. B. Gray......	8 00	8 00
John G. Duncan............Inspector of Election, Dist. No. 4.............................	16 00	16 00
Jas. Brouthers..............Officer at polls, Dist. No. 1, assigned to A. B. Gray	4 00	4 00
Zachariah Chase............Officer at polls, Dist. No. 3,	4 00	4 00
Sydney W. Longfield .....Officer at poll and burying dead dog, assigned to A. B. Gray................	6 00	6 00
Caleb Ballard..............Use of room, Town meetings.................................	36 00	36 00
H. H. Owen..................Use of room, Town meetings.................................	39 00	39 00
St. Mary's T.A.B.Society. Use of room, Town meetings, assigned to John McCann, treasurer........	48 00	48 00
Marvin Van Anden.. .....Use of room, town meetings.................................	6 00	6 00
Cyrus Baker................Use of room, Town meetings.................................	3 00	3 00
D. B. Herrington.... ......Use of room, election purposes............................	24 00	24 00
P. Kennedy estate.........Use of room, Town meetings.................................	9 00	9 00
Mrs. Catharine Perrine..Use of room, Town meetings.................................	3 00	3 00

POUGHKEEPSIE—Continued.

John W. Myers	Use of room, election purposes	15 00	15 00
Aug. B. Gray	Services as Supervisor	51 64	51 64
Aug. B. Gray	Disbursing officer and Board of Health	86 65	86 65
J. F. Pardee	Services as Assessor	14 00	14 00
H. R. Ferdon	Services as Assessor, assigned to Emma Jane Schofield	58 00	58 00
Chas. R. Robinson	Services as Assessor	64 00	64 00
Henry Worrall	Services as Assessor	110 00	110 00
Samuel P. Ellis	Services as Commissioner of Highways	124 00	124 00
John G. Duncan	Services as Commissioner of Highways	120 00	120 00
Alonzo Rynders	Services as Commissioner of Highways	132 00	132 00
S. A. Phelps	Services as Commissioner of Highways, assigned to Alonzo Rynders	82 00	82 00
John H. Ollivett	Services as Justice of Peace	97 35	97 35
John H. Ollivett	Member Board of Health, assigned to Aug. B. Gray	78 00	78 00
John H. Ollivett	Town business, assigned to Aug. B. Gray	31 75	31 75
Thos. A. Gurney	Services as Justice of Peace	36 55	36 55
Thos. A. Gurney	Member Board of Health	10 00	10 00
Thos. A. Gurney	Town business	• 22 50	22 50
John G. Harris	Services as Justice of Peace	3 30	3 30
John G. Harris	Member Board of Health	13 00	13 00
John G. Harris	Town business	24 00	24 00
Martin Croak	Services as Justice of Peace	34 00	34 00
Thos. H. Stuart	Services as Town Clerk	63 63	63 63
Thos. H. Stuart	Services as Registering Officer and Board of Health	64 68	64 68
Warren C. Woodin	Services as Overseer of the Poor, assigned to A. B. Gray	41 00	41 00

POUGHKEEPSIE—Continued.

J. F. Crosier	Services as Overseer of the Poor	25 00	25 00
John W. Hevener	Member Board of Health and Inspector of Election Dist. No. 4, assigned to Sidney H. Austin	33 00	33 00
G.H.Van Wagner, M.D.	Member Board of Health	11 00	11 00
John W. Rose	Excise Commissioner	24 00	24 00
D. W. Jackson	Excise Commissioner	24 00	24 00
Byron D. Baker	Excise Commissioner	24 00	24 00
M. V. Griffin	Services as Town Clerk	29 19	29 19
M. V. Griffin	Services as Registering Officer	23 75	23 75
W. H. Le Roy	Burying dead horse	4 00	4 00
Robert Lawson	Burying dead dogs	4 00	4 00
Flagler & Co.	Stationery	5 03	5 03
Manford Brower	Burying dead dogs, assigned to John G. Harris	4 00	4 00
John Hoolihan	Constable	43 85	43 85
Zachariah Chase	Constable	2 75	2 75
" "	Burying dead dog	2 00	2 00
Joseph Seymour	Constable, assigned to J. E. Andrews	9 15	9 15
Egbert Ferris	Constable, assigned to R. Baker	6 00	4 00
Hiland Rose	Constable	39 10	39 10
Wappingers Chronicle	Printing and stationery, assigned to John O'Farrell	17 37	17 37
Alonzo Rynders	Overseer of the Poor	14 00	14 00
Milton A. Fowler	Counsel services	23 00	23 00
John H. Dakin	Stationery	3 49	3 49
Richard Kennedy	Overseer of the Poor	31 50	31 50
Chas. W. Stone	Constable	33 60	33 60
J. P. Ambler	Stationery	11 60	11 60

POUGHKEEPSIE—Continued.

J. P. Wilson. M. D.......Professional services	3 00	3 00
L. B. Sacket............ ...Counsel services.....	15 00	15 00

$2,594 06 $2,592 06

We certify the above to be correct.

AUG. B. GRAY, Supervisor,
THOS. H. STUART, Town Clerk,
JOHN H. OLLIVETT,
THOS. A. GURNEY,
JOHN G. HARRIS,
MARTIN CROAK,

Auditors.

I hereby certify the foregoing to be a true copy as audited and allowed.

THOS. H. STUART,
Town Clerk.

RED HOOK.

Statement of Accounts, Charges and Claims, payable by the Town of Red Hook, in the County of Dutchess, audited and allowed by the Board of Town Auditors, at a meeting of said Board, held at the Martin Lasher Hotel, in the Town of Red Hook, on Thursday and Friday, the 6th and 7th days of November, in the year 1890.

Name of Person.	Nature of the Demand.	Asked.	Allowed.
William Wurmuth.........Inspector of Election, Dist. No. 4........	$ 18 00	$ 18 00

RED HOOK—Continued.

William S. Massenneau..Inspector of Election, Dist. No. 4................	23 00	23 00
Charles F. Schaffer........Inspector of Election, Dist. No. 4......................	16 00	16 00
John W. Hedges.............Inspector of Election, Dist. No. 4...........................	23 00	23 00
Claud E. Hicks...............Inspector of Election, Dist. No. 4.. ..;.......................	18 00	18 00
F. C. Burnett....................Clerk of Election Dist. No. 4.........	4 00	4 00
H. J. Curtis.. ....Clerk of Election Dist. No. 4................................	4 00	4 00
Robert Nevins................Inspector of Election, Dist. No. 5............................	23 16	23 16
James D. Wood.............Inspector of Election, Dist. No. 5...	16 00	16 00
Alexander Fulton..........Inspector of Election, Dist. No. 5.............................	23 24	23 24
C. R. Coon....................Inspector of Election, Dist. No. 5...	18 00	18 00
William H. Plass............Inspector of Election, Dist. No. 5.................	18 00	18 00
F. D. Lown....................Clerk of Election, Dist. No. 5...	4 00	4 00
Ashley. G. Couse............Clerk of Election, Dist. No. 5...............................	4 00	4 00
Dewitt Coon, Jr.............Clerk of Registry, 1 day's service, Dist. No. 5........	2 00	2 00
Henry Miller...................Inspector of Election, Dist. No. 2...............	23 24	16 00
C. L. Moore...................Inspector of Election, Dist. No. 2...	23 24	23 24
Geo. W. Fingar.............Clerk of Election and Inspector of Registry, No. 2...	12 00	12 00
Albert P. Smith. ....Inspector of Election, Dist. No. 2.........................	14 00	14 00

RED HOOK—Continued.

John L. Teats	Inspector of Election, Dist. No. 2	23 24	23 24
Walter H. Woolsey	Clerk of Election, Dist. No. 2	4 00	4 00
Montgomery Marshall	Inspector of Election, Dist. No. 2	6 00	6 00
F. H. Burnett	Inspector of Election, Dist. No. 1	23 24	23 24
Luke Carey	Inspector of Election, Dist. No. 1	16 00	16 00
Oliver Warranger	Inspector of Election, Dist. No. 1	18 00	18 00
Charles K. MacNiff	Inspector of Election, Dist. No. 1	16 00	16 00
Henry S. Stall	Inspector of Election, Dist. No. 1	18 00	18 00
John H. Hagar	Clerk of Election, Dist. No. 1	4 00	4 00
John Weikert	Clerk of Election, Dist. No. 1	4 00	4 00
Beekman Rhynders	Digging 2 graves	6 00	6 00
Electrus Teats	Assessor's time	91 00	63 00
Electrus Teats	Poor Order	5 00	5 00
Albert Piester	Printing notice	20 50	20 50
Richard E. Fraleigh	Bounty on foxes	7 00	7 00
Alonzo Ring	Late Town Clerk	72 75	72 75
Village of Tivoli	Use of engine room for election,	15 00	15 00
Charles K. Hoffman	Constable	37 27	37 27
John H. Boice	Bridge Plank	14 44	14 44
J. P. Ambler	Stationery	7 24	7 24
William E. Hutton	Medicine for the Poor	10 00	10 00
Georges S. Aucock	Poor orders	20 00	20 00
Peter A. Harris	Commissioner of Highways	116 00	116 00
C. H. Massonneau	Temporary relief	25 75	25 75
Burnett Bros	Furnishing coffins	30 00	30 00

RED HOOK—Continued.

William Wood	Excise Commissioner	24 00	24 00
B. F. Gedney	Temporary relief and sundries and polling place	82 86	82 86
Peter Troy	Poor Master	104 00	104 00
D. W. Wilbur	Coal for poor	129 25	129 25
D. C. Coon	Use of room for election, and stationery	15 50	15 50
Edward Feller	Use of room for election	15 00	15 00
Andrew Ham	Use of room for election assigned to F. G. Vosburgh	15 00	15 00
Charles Hopton	Excise Commissioner	12 00	12 00
Walter H. Woolsey	Constable bill of 1889	3 60	3 60
C. L. Moore	Temporary relief	5 00	5 00
Teator & Potts	Temporary relief	5 00	5 00
P. Peelor's Sons	Temporary relief	53 75	53 75
Peter Feroe	For putting up rails for 5 districts	3 00	3 00
Douglas H. Teats	Excise Commissioner	15 00	15 00
Douglas H. Teats	Temporary relief	15 00	15 00
John S. Minkler	Delivering booths to election districts	5 00	5 00
J. H. Feroe	Temporary relief	22 75	22 75
J. H. Feroe	For making booths and furnishing Guard rails	87 57	87 57
Robert Teator	Inspector of Election, Dist. No. 3	18 00	18 00
Geo. W. Moss	Inspector of Election, Dist. No. 3	23 24	22 24
Alfred Folmsbee	Constable	38 70	38 70
Alfred Folmsbee	Temporary relief	2 25	2 25
Daniel Minkler	Constable	108 22	108 22
DeWitt Clinton	Inspector of Election, Dist. No. 3	23 24	23 24
Philetus S. Traver	Clerk of Election, Dist. No. 3	4 00	4 00

RED HOOK—Continued.

Charles Van Steenburgh.Deputy Sheriff, Assigned			
	to Benj. Teats.	105 08	105 08
Charles E. Feller.	Inspector of Election, Dist.		
	No. 3.	16 00	16 00
Martin Lasher.	Use of house for Town		
	Meeting.	15 00	15 00
R. Dudley Kerley.	Bounty on foxes.	5 00	5 00
Orlando Doyle.	Bounty on foxes.	1 00	1 00
Joseph Malloy.	Deputy Sheriff.	143 28	143 28
E. C. Perrine.	Temporary relief.	55 00	55 00
Hackett & Williams.	Counsel for Excise Com-		
	missioners.	35 00	35 00
Osborn Kelmer.	Temporary relief.	10 00	10 00
John A. Potts.	Clerk of Election, Dist.		
	No. 3.	4 00	4 00
Campbell W. Hicks.	Late Overseer of the Poor.	53 00	53 00
William S. Teator.	Inspector of Election, Dist.		
	No. 3.	18 00	18 00
Losee Feller.	Bounty on fox.	1 00	1 00
Silas Saulpaugh.	Bounty on fox, Assigned		
	to E. Sturgess.	1 00	1 00
J. R. Kerley.	Temporary relief.	3 90	3 90
Geo. Scism.	Late Excise Commissioner	3 00	3 00
Clinton J. Rockefeller.	Late Supervisor.	51 68	51 68
Philip H. Moore.	Overseer of the Poor.	85 52	85 52
Dr. John E. Losee.	Physician	97 00	97 00
Dr. H. L. Cookingham	Physician	122 75	122 75
Edgar L. Traver.	Justice of the Peace.	34 50	34 50
Christian Allendorf.	Justice of the Peace.	39 65	39 65
Andrew J. Gedney.	Justice of the Peace.	91 65	91 65
Walter Sheldon.	Justice of the Peace.	153 35	153 35
Frederick Cotting.	Assessor	58 00	58 00
Campbell W. Hicks.	Town Clerk.	178 64	178 64
Edward Sturgess	Supervisor.	16 00	16 00
Alonzo Ring	Late Town Clerk and		
	Member of the Board of		
	Health.	17 96	17 96

RED HOOK—Continued.

Campbell W. Hicks......Town Clerk and Member of Board of Health........	51 68	51 68
Phillip H. Stickle...........Citizen, Member of Board of Health..................	2 00	2 00
Christian Allendorf........Justice of the Peace, Member of Board of Health..	10 00	10 00
Edgar L. Traver...............Justice of the Peace, Member of Board of Health...	8 00	8 00
Andrew J. Gedney.........Justice of the Peace, Member of Board of Health..	19 50	19 50
Edward Sturgess.............Supervisor, Member of Board of Health............	8 00	8 00
Dr. John E. Losee..........Health Officer....	18 25	18 25
Clinton J. Rockefeller....Late Supervisor. Member of Board of Health........	4 00	4 00
Dr. H. L. Cookingham..Filing certificate and late Health Officer...............	13 00	13 00
Walter Sheldon.............Justice of the Peace and Member of Board of Health.,.................	10 75	10 75
Thos. J. Barton.............Poor, medical attendance.	77 00	77 00
Peter Rifenburgh............Assessor........................	60 00	60 00

$3,426 38 $3.394 14

We certify the above to be correct.

EDWARD STURGESS,
CAMPBELL W. HICKS,
C. ALLENDORF,
A. J. GEDNEY,
WALTER SHELDON,
E. L. TRAVER,

Auditors.

RHINEBECK.

Statement of Accounts, Charges and Claims, payable by the Town of Rhinebeck, in the County of Dutchess, audited and allowed by the Board of Town Auditors, at a meeting of said Board, held at the Town Hall, in the Town of Rhinebeck, on Thursday, the sixth day of November, in the year 1890.

Name of Person.	Nature of Demand.	Asked.	Allowed.
Harry Pottenburgh..	....Inspector of Election and and Registry Board, taking ret. to Pokeepsie......	$22 60	$22 00
Frank Cramer............	...Clerk of Town Meeting of Election and Registry Board,taking ret. to Pok	28 60	28 60
James H. Snyder	...Clerk Town Meeting, &c.	16 00	16 00
Wm. V. C. Ostrom........	" " " "	16 00	16 00
A. C. Noxon.................	" " " "	22 60	22 60
John H. Brown.............	" " " "	22 00	22 00
A. L. Ostrom..............	" " " "	16 00	16 00
P. H. Weckesser...........	" " " "	16 00	16 00
F. G. Cotting.................	" " " "	16 00	16 00
Roswell Beach...............	" " " "	16 00	16 00
R. H. Randolph.............	" " " "	16 00	16 00
George Tremper.............	" " "	16 00	16 00
M. S. Frost..................	" " "	22 60	22 60
C. V. Coon............	" " "	22 36	22 36
James Leary, Jr............	" " "	22 36	22 36
George Esselstyn............	Ex-Supervisor................	20 00	20 00
Charles Butler...............	To use of house for Election, assigned to Roswell Beach................	20 00	20 00
Edward P. Wheeler.......	Constable.......	38 90	38 90
Frank A. Marquet.........	"	4 00	4 00
Thomas Coyle.'.	Poll Clerk............	4 00	4 00
James N. Hester............	" "	4 00	4 00
Wm. R. Tremper.........	" "	4 00	4 00

RHINEBECK—Continued.

T. A. Traver............ .....Prll Clerk	4 00	4 00
Lee VanVredenburgh ... " "	4 00	4 00
Thomas Owens............... " "	4 00	4 00
Wm. Carroll & Son.. .....Coffin for Poor and Goods furnished.....................	70 80	70 80
Jacob Heebe ....Goods for Poor...............	18 05	18 05
Williams & Traver......... " "	38 00	38 00
Wm. R. Tremper............Excise	7 25	7 25
Wilson H. Butler............ "	6 00	6 00
A. L. Ostrom................ "	6 00	6 00
Walter J. Sleight............Overseer of Poor..............	66 64	66 64
F. H. Roof, M. D............Medical Services..............	41 25	41 25
R. E. Asher, M. D.........Medical services..............	65 00	65 00
B. N. Baker, M. D......... " "	63 35	63 35
Jas. F. Goodell, M. D.... " "	22 25	22 25
James H. Kipp......... .....Assessor.	48 00	48 00
John A. Traver............ "	54 00	54 00
Jacob L. VanWagenen.. "	40 00	40 00
Weckesser Bros.............To Painting and Work at Town Hall..................	28 90	28 90
S. G. Talada...................Constable.....................	8 00	8 00
S. G. Talada..................Digging Grave for Poor....	3 00	3 00
Charles Fero..................Supplies......	1 90	1 90
James A. Monfort. ......Justice of Peace, assigned to John C. Milroy........	120 45	120 45
Jacob F. Teal ....Goods for Poor.	8 25	8 25
Ostrom & Cornwell........ " "	7 00	7 00
Ann Mahar...... ....Keeping Tramps..............	127 00	127 00
C. P. Pultz.....................Supplies.	4 31	4 31
A. Lee Wager................Assignee of F. C. Parker..	1 50	1 50
C. S. VanEtten, M. D....Medical Services............	62 50	62 50
Jerome Traver.............Constable......................	12 65	12 65
Rhinebeck News.............Printing, assigned to Jas. Hogan	35 10	35 10
Rhinebeck Gazette ......Printing, assigned to Jas. Hogan	6 00	6 00

RHINEBECK—Continued.

Rosenkranze & Thorn...Supplies furnished and Work......	4 86	4 86
D. E. Ackert & Son........Poor Account and Orders.	61 40	61 40
Sherwood & Herrick...... " " "	58 75	58 75
Ackert & Brown..........For Booths, &c..............	98 53	98 53
Lewis Asher..............For Work, &c..............	4 00	4 00
Peter M. Fulton............For Lumber furnished,&c.	22 36	22 36
Wm. M. Sleight...........Constable......................	57 60	57 60
Wm. M. Sleight............Constable, assigned to J. C. Hamlin............	30 00	30 00
E. M. Haines..............Commissioner of Highway	91 04	91 04
J. C. Hamlin..............Poor Orders	342 86	342 86
Mathias Wortz............Horse Hire by Order of Overseer......................	33 00	33 00
Ackert & Brown........... For Work and Material furnished	108 77	108 77
John Heebe...............Constable	9 95	9 95
Henry Welch..............Vise for Crusher.............	2 50	2 50
James Brice, Jr............Goods for Poor.	10 00	10 00
John J. Bauch.............For Work...................	3 40	3 40
J. H. Acker & Co.........Goods furnished.............	102 29	102 28
J. C. Hamlin.................Poor Orders, assigned to John C. Hamlin............	100 00	100 00
Hoffman Tripp & Co......Goods for Poor, Coal.......	190 00	190 00
John C. Milroy........ ......Supervisor.................	91 44	91 44
Jacob H. Pottenburgh....Town Clerk.................	163 30	163 30
Walter W. Schell........Justice of Peace..............	74 00	74 00
C. V. Coon................ " "	144 40	144 40
M. V. B. Schryver......... " "	116 25	116 25
Milroy Boas..................For Work, &c............	73 90	73 90
C. S. VanEtten. M. D......Services as Health Officer and Member of Board and return.................	78 25	78 25
J. C. Milroy. ....Meeting of Health Board.	30 00	30 00
Jacob H. Pottenburgh...Clerk Board of Health and Register Clerk............	101 25	101 25

RHINEBECK—Continued.

Frank Rikert................Member Board of Health.		36 00	36 00
E. M. Haines...............Commissioner for Building Bridge at Hutton Hollow, working Stone Crusher and Grading Road............................		1,972 08	1,972 08
Commis'r of Highway...For Operating Stone Crusher, as amount voted at Town Meeting..............		2,000 00	2,000 00
" " ...For Operating Stone Crusher,for Roads and Bridges		500 00	500 00

$8,083 35 $8.083 35

Paid on the above account by Supervisor :

Walter J. Sleight......................................	$21 25		
Ackert & Brown...	75 00		
John Heebe..	5 00		
Jerome Traver..	9 00		
J. H. Pottenburgh......................................	63 54		
C. V. Coon..	3 00	176 79	176 79

$7,906 56 $7,906 56

We certify the above to be correct.

JOHN C. MILROY,
J. H. POTTENBURGH,
WALTER W. SCHELL,
W. V. B. SCHRYVER,
C. V. COONS,
         Auditors.

STANFORD.

Statement of Accounts, Charges and Claims, payable by the Town of Stanford, in the County of Dutchess, audited and allowed by the Board of Town Auditors, at a meeting of said Board, held at the Village of Bangall, in the Town of Stanford, on Thursday, the 6th day of November, in the year 1890.

Name of Person.	Nature of the Demand.	Asked.	Allowed.
Chas. H. Humphrey.......Supervisor........		$ 63 69	$ 63 69
Thad. Knickerbocker .....Town Clerk.		94 09	94 09
Edwin Knickerbocker...Justice of the Peace........		23 55	23 55
William Carroll............ " " "		16 00	16 00
A. M. Harrison......... ... " " "		16 00	16 00
Willett Hicks....... .... " " "		10 00	10 00
Sanford Adams.............Ex-Justice of the Peace...		6 00	6 00
Frank Germond.............Assessor........................		34 00	34 00
R. A. Husted... .... "		36 00	36 00
John H. Cox................. "		42 00	42 00
William P. Ferris..........Commissioner Highways..		326 00	326 00
Eugene Bullis...............Ex-Com. Highway...........		38 00	38 00
Sanford Allen...............Ex-Overseer of Poor.......		5 00	5 00
Newton Barlow.............Insp'r of Election, Dist. 1.		18 00	18 00
John Cookingham.......... " " " 1.		16 00	16 00
Homer Robinson............ " " " 1.		16 00	16 00
L. E. Harrison.............. " " " 1.		23 00	23 00
S. K. Germond.............. " " " 1.		22 00	22 00
E. L. Walters...............Clerk " " 1.		4 00	4 00
E. B. Sackett............... " " " 1.		4 00	4 00
J. H. Haight.................Insp'r " " 2.		18 00	18 00
Henry Ackert.............. " " " 2.		16 00	16 00
Geo. E. Rogers... .... " " " 2.		16 00	16 00
Chas. Anson........... ...... " " " 2.		22 60	22 00
Fred. Case.................. " " " 2.		22 60	22 60
Sanford Adams.............Clerk " " 2.		8 00	8 00
S. K. Winans..,............. " " " 2.		4 00	4 00
S. H. Williams.............Constable......................		4 40	4 40

STANFORD—Continued.

M. Knickerbocker.........Constable..................	27 85	27 85
V. P. LeRay...................Watcher at polls, 1889 and		
1890....	8 00	8 00
J. L. Marvin...................Hall for election and regis-		
try......................	47 00	47 00
Samuel G. Tripp..............Com. Highway's note........	1,575 00	1,575 00
William P. Ferris............Commissioner Highways..	825 00	825 00
Dr. M. T. Pultz.. ....Health Officer.....	3 00	3 00
Virgil G. Winans..............Fox Bounty..	6 00	6 00
John H. Davis.. .... " "	1 00	1 00
Willard J. Briggs. .... " "	5 00	5 00
Frank Haight................ " "	2 00	2 00
Duncan Millis.. .... " "	11 00	11 00
J. W. Holsipple....... ..... " "	8 00	8 00
Keifer Millis................ " "	2 00	2 00

$3,445 18

We certify the above to be correct.

CHAS. H. HUMPHREY, Supervisor,
EDWIN KNICKERBOCKER, Justice of the Peace.
WILLIAM CARROLL, Justice of the Peace,
ALMON M. HARRISON, Justice of the Peace,
WILLETT HICKS, Justice of the Peace,

Auditors.

UNION VALE.

Statement of Accounts, Charges and Claims, payable by the Town of Union Vale, in the County of Dutchess, audited and allowed by the Board of Town Auditors, at a meeting of said Board, held at the House of Reuben L. Coe, in the Town of Union Vale, on Thursday, the 6th day of November, in the year 1890.

Name of Person.	Nature of the Demand.	Asked.	Allowed.
Henry L. Campbell.........	Excise Commissioner.......	\$ 6 50	\$ 6 50
Wm. V. Coe...............	Registrator for Board of Health..........................	11 75	11 75
David V. Knapp.............	Inspector of Election.......	23 36	23 36
Wm. M. Bostwick.........	'' ''	16 00	16 00
Charles E. Cronk.........	Poll Clerk at Election.......	4 00	4 00
James E. Way..............	Inspector of Election.......	16 00	16 00
Charles E. Dennis.........	Excise Commissioner.......	9 00	9 00
George I. Vincent	Assessor..........................	34 00	34 00
Orlin B. Abel....	''	36 00	36 00
George H. Uhl.............	Commissioner of Highway	42 00	42 00
John E. Houghtaling......	Ballot Boxes...................	5 00	5 00
Albro Davis.................	Justice of the Peace....... .	4 00	4 00
Edgar Hustis..................	Inspector of Election.......	18 36	18 36
Alanson B. Abel.............	Constable.....................	30 90	30 90
John V. Shaffer..	Assessor	34 00	34 00
Frank T. Hall..	Justice of the Peace.........	22 45	22 45
Frank T. Hall..	Inspector of Election........	16 00	16 00
John V. Shaffer.............	Justice of the Peace.........	14 00	14 00
Frank P. Cromwell........	Constable	30 00	30 00
Wm. V. Coe............	Town Clerk, one day as Registrar.................	53 95	53 95
M. M. Vincent..	Excise Com.. ....'...	6 00	6 00
Frank Coffin..................	Justice of the Peace........	14 00	14 00
James D. Vail................	Clerk at Town Meeting....	4 00	4 00
Wm. G. Vincent...........	Overseer of Poor............	17 15	17 15
David A. Knapp, M. D..	Vital Statistics...............	5 15	5 15
David A. Knapp, M. D..	Medical Attendance to Poor, 1889...................	22 87	22 87

UNION VALE—Continued.

Smith Dunkin............Bounty on foxes.............	8 00	8 00
Eli June..... .... " " "	3 00	3 00
Wm. Gregory..... ....Com. of Highway............	49 25	49 25
Henry Bostwick.............Ex-Supervisor.................	8 20	8 20
John U. Abel............ ....Booths for Election, Etc...	25 68	25 68
Reuben L. Coe.............Use of House for Town Meeting and Election..	30 00	30 00
John U. Abel............ ....Supervisor	17 36	17 36
Edward M. Husted........Com. of Highway............	56 00	56 00
For working Highways..	700 00	700 00
Dr. J. M. Julian............		30 00

$1,423 93

We certify the above to be correct.
JOHN U. ABEL,
WM. V. COE,
JOHN V. SHAFFER,
FRANK T. HALL,
FRANK COFFIN,
Auditors.

WAPPINGER.

Statement of Accounts, Charges and Claims, payable by the Town of Wappinger, in the County of Dutchess, audited and allowed by the Board of Town Auditors, at meetings of said Board, held at the Town Clerk's office in the Town of Wappinger, on the 6th and 7th days of November, in the year 1890.

Name of Person.	Nature of the Demand.	Asked.	Allowed.
George Wood, Supervis'r.	Wappingers bridge bonds and interest...............	$1,490 00	$1,490 00

WAPPINGER—continued.

George Wood	Supervisor	64 15	64 15
J. W. Cornell	Town Clerk	183 22	183 22
Gilbert B. Wood	Commissioner of Highways	90 00	90 00
John Sturgess	Commissioner of Highways	28 00	28 00
R. J. Vandewater	Commissioner of Highways	54 00	54 00
W. H. H. Stoutenburgh	Ex-Commissioner of Highways	22 00	22 00
John B. Conover	Ex-Commissioner of Highways	62 00	56 00
Chas. D. B. Montfort	Assessor	62 00	62 00
G. D. F. Underhill	Assessor	64 00	64 00
E. O. Whitman	Assessor	40 00	40 00
Charles J. Schmidt	Overseer of the Poor	40 00	40 00
David Y. Kent	Overseer of the Poor	7 00	7 00
Eugene Johnson	Ex-Overseer of the Poor	26 00	26 00
William Lambert	Excise Commissioner	9 00	9 00
J. Edward Hicks	Excise Commissioner	9 00	9 00
George H. Abbott	Justice of the Peace	4 00	4 00
William H. Parker	Justice of the Peace	16 00	16 00
C. W. Hignell	Justice of the Peace	59 70	59 70
Edmund Tanner	Justice of the Peace	28 30	28 30
C. W. Clapp	Justice of the Peace, assigned to Mrs. C. W. Clapp	20 00	20 00
Thos. Maher	Constable, assigned to Geo. Wood	4 80	4 80
John St. George	Constable, assigned to M. Croak	9 65	9 65
Uriah Wallace	Constable	5 05	5 05
E. M. Goring	Inspector of Election, Dist. No. 1	8 00	8 00
A. W. Armstrong	Inspector of Election, Dist. No. 1	10 00	10 00
Thomas J. Cashin	Inspector of Election, Dist. No. 1	10 00	10 00

WAPPINGER—Continued.

C. W. Hignell.........Inspector of Election, Dist. No. 1............	10 00	10 00
John M. Goring.........Inspector of Election, Dist. No. 1............	15 64	12 00
E. M. Goring.........Inspector of Election and delivering returns to County Clerk............	5 64	5 64
William J. Dawson........Inspector of Election, Dist. No. 2............	18 00	18 00
C. W. Clapp.........Inspector of Election, Dist. No. 2, assigned to W. A. Brewster............	19 64	19 64
J. W. Bartram.........Inspector of Election, Dist. No. 2............	15 64	11 00
James S. Roy.........Inspector of Election, Dist. No. 2............	15 64	11 00
Matthew Vandermark...Inspector of Election, Dist. No. 2............	10 00	10 00
W. H. H. Stoutenburgh.Inspector of Election, Dist. No. 3............	15 56	11 00
Willis Van Voorhis........Inspector of Election, Dist. No. 3............	21 56	21 56
Jacob R. Cornwell........Inspector of Election, Dist. No. 3............	14 00	14 00
John Owens.........Inspector of Election, Dist. No. 3............	16 00	16 00
C. E. Segar.........Inspector of Election, Dist. No. 3............	15 56	11 00
E. B. Van Dyne.........Inspector of Election, Dist. No. 3............	4 00	4 00
Isaac V. A. Smith........Inspector of Election, Dist. No. 4............	19 72	19 72
Schenck Van Nosdall...Inspector of Election, Dist. No. 4............	16 00	16 00
Edmund Tanner.........Inspector of Election, Dist. No. 4............	12 00	12 00
Oakley I. Norris.........Inspector of Election, Dist. No. 4............	10 00	10 00

WAPPINGER—Continued.

Joseph B. Pulling.......Inspector of Election, Dist. No. 4........................	10 00	10 00
John J. Hasbrook .....,...Inspector of Election, Dist. No. 4	6 00	6 00
Jay Hignell................,...Clerk of Election, Dist. No. 1........	4 00	4 00
Joseph D. Thompson......Clerk of Election, Dist. No. 1........................	8 00	8 00
J. J. Croak................Clerk of Election, Dist. No. 1, assigned to J. W. Cornell........................	4 00	4 00
C. B. Winne ....Clerk of Election. Dist. No. 2......	4 00	4 00
A. S. Peacock..............Clerk of Election, Dist. No. 2........................	4 00	4 00
G. D. F. Underhill........Clerk of Board of Registry Dist. No. 3...................	4 00	4 00
G. D. F. Underhill........Clerk of Election, Dist. No. 3........................	8 00	8 00
E. B. Van Dyne..............Clerk of Election. Dist. No. 3........................	4 00	4 00
James H. Smith...........Clerk of Election, Dist. No. 4........................	4 00	4 00
William H. Losee.........Clerk of Election. Dist. No. 4........	4 00	4 00
W. H. Ryan................Clerk of Election. Dist. No. 4, assigned to O. I. Norris	4 00	4 00
John A. Burnett............16 Election booths..........	88 00	88 00
E. M. Goring............... 1 Election booth..............	5 50	5 50
Village of Wappinger.. ...Use of room for election purposes, Dist. No. 1......	40 00	40 00
Charlotte M. Clapp........Use of room for election purposes, Dist. No. 2	25 00	25 00
Mrs. John Weisner..... ..Use of room for election purposes, Dist. No. 4......	10 00	10 00

WAPPINGER—Continued.

Phebe Vanderbilt	Use of room for election purposes, Dist. No. 3	40 00	40 00
S. S. Hoyt	8 ballot boxes, assigned to W. A. Brewster	36 00	36 00
J. W. Cornell	Use of room for Town meetings	30 00	30 00
J. W. Cornell	Disbursements, postage, expressage, blanks	13 79	13 79
J. H. Dakin	Stationery	3 15	3 15
E. M. Goring	Stationery	13 55	13 55
Farrell & Winne	Stationery, assigned to J. W. Cornell	11 52	11 52
Gates & Fitzgerald	Printing, assigned to John O'Farrell	65 49	65 49
Frank C. Bacon	Printing	8 75	8 75
George Anderson	Killing four foxes	4 00	4 00
Margaret E. Budd	Road tax refunded	6 00	6 00
Maria M. Hulty	Road tax refunded	9 00	9 00
James E. Phillips	Constable	7 75	7 75
C. E. Seger	Health Officer	50 00	50 00
J. W. Cornell	Registering Officer, Secretary Board of Health and Disbursements	42 59	42 59
C. W. Clapp	Board of Health, assigned to W. A. Brewster	10 00	10 00
Edmund Tanner	Board of Health	10 00	10 00
William Rowe	" "	9 00	9 00
William H. Parker	" "	8 00	8 00
C. W. Hignell	" "	10 00	10 00
George Wood	" "	8 00	8 00
Gilbert B. Wood	Com'r Highways, Roads	64 00	64 00
John Sturgess	" " "	24 00	24 00
R. J. Vandewater	" " "	52 00	50 00
John P. Conover	" " "	44 00	32 00

WAPPINGER—Continued.

W. H. H. Stoutenburgh.. ·· ·· ..		12 00	12 00
R. J. Vandewater........ ...Board of Health.............		4 00	4 00

$3.493 77

We certify the above to be correct and the amount above stated is to be levied on the Town of Wappinger outside of the corporate limits of the Village of Wappingers Falls. N. Y.

GEORGE WOOD, Supervisor.
J. W. CORNELL, Town Clerk.
EDMUND TANNER, Justice of the Peace.
CLINTON W. CLAPP, Justice of the Peace,
C. W. HIGNELL, Justice of the Peace.
W. H. PARKER, Justice of the Peace.

Auditors.

WASHINGTON.

Statement of Accounts, Charges and Claims payable by the Town of Washington, in the County of Dutchess, audited and allowed by the Board of Town Auditors, at a meeting of said Board, held at the Town Clerk's Office, in the Town of Washington, on Thursday, the 6th day of November, in the year 1890.

Name of Person.	Nature of the Demand.	Asked.	Allowed.
J. T. Smith.....................	Services as Poor Master....	$ 12 00	$ 12 00
David S. Tallman....... ...Services as Commissioner	of Highways............. ..	464 00	464 00

WASHINGTON—Continued.

Drs. Henry and Mac-			
kenzie................................Certificates of births and			
	deaths.............................	7 75	7 75
John Tompkins.............Poor orders...........................		12 00	12 00
Philip Blinn, Jr...............Services Overseer of Poor.		9 00	9 00
L. W. Hungerford ......"Poor orders.....................		24 00	24 00
S. Van Vlack................... " "		24 00	24 00
John Palmatier..................Services as constable.........		75 95	75 95
W. Records................. " "		7 95	7 95
W. S. Tripp....................Poor orders.....................		6 50	6 50
Charles C. Olivet............Services as inspector and			
	clerk.............................	8 00	8 00
James D. Swift..............Services as inspector. re-			
	turns to Town Clerk.		
	Dist. No. 2....................	18 00	18 00
George W. Merritt....... Services as inspector, re-			
	turns to Supervisor, Dist.		
	No. 1..............................	18 00	18 00
John B. Horton. ....Services as inspector, Dist.			
	No. 1..............................	12 00	12 00
Chas. Welling...............Services as attendant, Dist.			
	No. 1	4 00	4 00
Chas. Bullis....................Services as Excise Com'r...		3 00	3 00
S. D. Travis ....Services as Assessor.........		42 00	42 00
Enoch Tompkins........... " "		42 00	42 00
Chas. J. Swift............... " "		42 00	42 00
Perry Sherow...............Services as constable.........		1 50	1 50
Dr. J. O. Pingry........... Certificates of deaths and			
	births	10 50	10 50
M. D. Andrews..............Services as inspector elec-			
	tion and returns to		
	County Clerk, Dist. No. 2	21 70	21 70
Henry H. Tripp..............Services as inspector and			
	returning to Town Clerk	18 00	18 00
Albert B. Smith..............Services as inspector and			
	returning to County Clerk,		
	Dist. No. 1.....................	22 60	22 60

WASHINGTON—Continued.

H. S. Tripp	Services as Poll Clerk, Dist. No. 1	4 00	4 00
Walsh & Griffen	Printing election notices	1 00	1 00
Frank Welling	Services as Town Sealer	10 00	10 00
Enoch Wilber	Six booths, Dist. No. 1	29 10	29 10
Rhoda A. Swift	Use of hall and storing booths. Dist. No. 1	40 00	40 00
Harriett Losee	Use of hall, Dist. No. 2	25 00	25 00
Charles Whaley	Services as inspector, Dist. No. 2, return to County Clerk	21 70	21 70
J. F. Tripp	Services Town Clerk, furnishing ballot boxes	144 06	144 06
R. C. Van Vlack	Services as Justice of the Peace	15 00	15 00
R. T. Monfort	Services as Justice of the Peace	46 50	46 50
Stephen Robinson	Services as Justice of the Peace	12 00	12 00
Philip J. Sherman	Services as Justice of the Peace and Inspector	26 00	26 00
Richard J. Scoles	Services as inspector and and returning to Supervisor	18 00	18 00
Homer W. Fitch	Services as Clerk of Election, Dist. No. 2	4 00	4 00
Stephen H. Merritt	Services as Clerk of Election, Dist. No. 2	4 00	4 00
Leander Sherer	To killing eight foxes	8 00	8 00
William J. Rundall	To killing five foxes	5 00	5 00
David S. Tallman, Com'r.	Appropriation to Com'r. of Highways for roads and bridges	1,600 00	1,600 00
L. D. Germond	Furnishing booths. Dist. No. 2	29 10	29 10
L. D. Germond	Services as Supervisor and school money	63 15	63 15

WASHINGTON—Continued.

R. T. Monfort	Services as Clerk of Election, Dist. No. 1	4 00	4 00
Howard, Haight & Co	Poor orders	32 29	32 29
T. M. Whalen	" "	1 00	1 00
C. B. Reardon	Burial of Jabiz Lewis	12 00	12 00
Edward M. Freer	Services as inspector and returning ballots to County Clerk	22 60	22 60
		$3,083 95	$3,083 95

We certify the above to be correct.

LEWIS D. GERMOND, Supervisor,

R. C. VAN VLACK, Justice,

P. J. SHERMAN,

STEPHEN ROBINSON,

RICHARD T. MONFORT,

J. F. TRIPP, Town Clerk,

Auditors.

Additional Town Allowances.

AMENIA.

I. P. Conklin.................. .... $6 36

BEEKMAN.

Roads and Bridges... .... $250 00
Andrew Pray.............. .... 3 00

CLINTON.

Roads and Bridges........ .... $250 00
C. H. Tripp................ .... 4 00
Solomon Smith....................... .... 4 00
Wilson Sitzer............... .: 12 50
M. E. Rikert........ .... 2 50

DOVER.

W. B. Newton, Est... $2 63

EAST FISHKILL.

Roads and Bridges... $250 00
John L. Hall.. .... 5 15

FISHKILL.

Poor Fund for Soldiers, &c.	$200	00
Hackett & Williams	25	00
Geo. G. Judson.	54	00
Supervisor, for Judgment of Clara Phillips.	9.818	77
Erastus Horton.	46	00
Chas. Rothery.	46	00
C. O. Osborne.	36	00
Wm. H. Peattie.	46	00
D. H. Post.	5	52
Lewis Tompkins.	44	00

HYDE PARK.

For Bridges	$377	30
Dr. John Faust.	10	00
L. S. Wigg.	4	00

LA GRANGE.

Roads and Bridges.	$250	00
John S. Landon.	4	00
Elias Van Benschoten.	4	00
Jay Howard.	4	00
Wm. H. Austin.	15	97

MILAN.

Roads and Bridges.	$259	80
A. L. Husted.	2	20

NORTH EAST.

For Bridges.	$218	00
For Highway.	2,717	09
John Scutt.	10	20
O. W. Wakeman.	5	00
Chas. Corey.	22	00

PAWLING.

Pawling Cemetery	$10 00
Geo. F. Lee	14 00

PINE PLAINS.

Roads and Bridges	$250 00

PLEASANT VALLEY.

Roads and Bridges	$250 00
Poor Fund	100 00
Benj. Lester	2 70

POUGHKEEPSIE TOWN.

Bridge Repairs	$500 00
Bridge Bonds and Interest	1,740 00
Highway Assessment	3,500 00
John Hoolihan	13 75

POUGHKEEPSIE CITY.

A. V. Haight	$405 88
Po'keepsie News Co	175 00
Platt & Platt	94 83
A. G. Tobey	75 00
Lansing, Van Keuren & Brown	90 73

RED HOOK.

Roads and Bridges	$250 00
Edward Sturgess	25 69

RHINEBECK.

Roads and Bridges.	$250 00
Insurance on Town Hall............	130 00
Wilson Sitzer..	12 50
Rikert Bros.....	6 00

UNION VALE.

Roads and Bridges.	$250 00
M. M. Vincent..	6 00
Judson A. Denton..	10 65

WAPPINGER.

Roads and Bridges.	$250 00
Thos. Fitzpatrick..	18 45

WASHINGTON.

John S. Wing..	6 00
Poor Fund.............	50 00
Geo. Sackett..	3 00

COUNTY ALLOWANCES.

Extra Compensation of Supreme Court Judges.	$2,044 55
Red Rook, for deficiency..	234 00
General Fund............. .... ,........................	10,500 00
Bonds (maturing 1891)...	20,000 00
Interest on Bonds...	2,560 00
Note City National Bank..	7,000 00
Willard State Hospital..............	11,000 00
Hudson River State Hospital..............	18,500 00
Binghamton State Hospital............	4,365 00
Supervisors Pay Roll..	2,500 00
Court and Jury Fund... ...	7,000 00
State Criminal Asylum. Auburn.....................................	585 00
Homeopathic Asylum. Middletown......	225 00
N. Y. Ins. for Blind. Batavia....................... ...	99 13
" " " Deaf and Dumb, N. Y. City........................	187 50
Colored Orphan Asylum, "	409 50
State Asylum. Utica	260 00
N. Y. Asylum for Idiots, Syracuse................................	64 00
Albany Penitentiary.....:.............	4,510 37
H. D. Hufcut, City.............	342 00
Alms House Commissioners.............................:..............	196 14
Salary of County Judge..................:.................	2,000 00
" Surrogate	2,000 00
" " Clerk ,.............. ....,...........	1,000 00
" Treasurer.	1,250 00
" District Attorney........	1,500 00
" Armorer	400 00

Salary of Jail Physician	100	00
" County Sealer	25	00
" Keeper Drake Draw Bridge	350	00
Rent of Armory	1,600	00
Deficiency—Repairs to Poorhouse	585	00
" " 1891	500	00
Wood & Morschauser	50	00
Poor Fund	8,000	00
Po'keepsie News Co., Po'keepsie City	5	84
A. G. Tobey, " "	2	50
Platt & Platt, " "	3	49
Lansing, VanKeuren & Brown, "	3	02
Home for the Friendless. "	1,300	00
A. V. Haight, "	202	50
Wm. H. Bartlett, Amenia	9	84
Wm. H. Austin, LaGrange	9	68
L. D. Germond, Washington	9	00
Supt. of Poor Salary	1,700	00
Matron "	300	00
Ministers "	100	00
S. D. McIntosh	20	00
J. S. Wilson	55	00
J. F. Lamb	105	00
Uriah Wallace	7	55
M. E. Rikert, Clinton	14	00
Chas. Corey, North East	12	35
Willis VanBuren, Fishkill	24	85
Theo. Moith, "	35	25
Jos. Kelly, "	6	65
John Heeb, Rhinebeck	9	25
A. V. Haight, Poughkeepsie City	1,245	87
H. S. Acker, " "	76	00
W. Wallace Smith, " "	111	50
R. E. Lusk & Son, " "	260	00
Theo. A. Hoffman, " "	2,474	09
Henry Bostwick, Union Vale	46	00
J. H. Russell, Beekman	42	00
D. E. Howatt, Hyde Park	17	50
C. J. Rockefeller, Red Hook	36	00

Geo. Wood, Wappinger	18 20
Wm. H. Krieger. City	30 00
John J. Mylod, "	135 00
P. A. M. Van Wyck. "	111 84
J. W. Van Tassell. "	8,670 54
J. P. Ambler. "	346 05
Smith Heroy, "	810 00
L. K. Strouse & Co.. "	21 85
John P. Wilson. "	155 00
F. J. Decker, "	1,074 20
Hugh Morgan. "	969 90
Eli Mastin, Pleasant Valley	6 85
A. J. Thayer, Pawling	26 00
S. L. Buckley, Amenia	131 43
James J. Dowd, City	21 30
Frank J. Cromwell. Union Vale	4 00
A. P. Able, " "	183 10
Geo. W. Slocum, Pawling	15 20
Chas. W. Stone, Po'keepsie Town	17 55
John St. George, " "	5 65
Hilend Rose, " "	26 40
John Hoolihan, " "	72 25
Isaac Kilmer, Milan	10 25
J. C. Ferguson, City	6 00
J. H. Malloy, Red Hook	9 80
E. P. Wheeler, Rhinebeck	7 30
Wm. M. Sleight, "	17 75
F A. Ross, Red Hook	10 25
Chas. Schumacker, Hyde-Park	17 95
M. Knickerbocker, Stanford	5 80
S. H. Williams, "	9 50
Thos. Maher. Wappinger	57 65
Thos. Fitzpatrick. "	171 15
J. G. Porteous, City	40 00
Robt. K. Tuthill. "	45 00
H. R. Powell, "	120 00
A. Hasbrouck, "	10 00
Po'keepsie Cemetery, "	24 00
C. E. Seeger, "	5 00

J. L. Melhado,	City	165 00
J. W. Poucher,	"	30 00
F. A. Faust,	"	65 00
Wm. Cramer,	"	140 00
E. H. Parker.	"	10 00
J. C. Payne.	"	15 00
J. E. Sadlier,	"	20 00
E. A. Wood,	"	5 00
E.V.Vincent, Assignee.	"	5 00
W. R. Case.	"	10 00
C. E. Lane,	"	10 00
Van Dyne & Mellady. Fishkill		70 00
J. C. Otis.	"	5 00
J. P. Ambler,	"	26 35
R. C. Van Wyck,	"	35 00
W. J. Bogardus,	"	30 00
J. T. Schenck.	"	10 00
H. B. Rosa,	"	5 50
E. Moith,	"	110 00
W. J. Conklin,	"	100 00
E. Feller & Son, Red Hook		3 00
R. J. Carroll.	"	20 00
H. L. Cookingham.	"	118 80
Wm. R. Lown,	"	10 00
T. J. Barton,	"	20 00
Alexander Near,	"	5 00
Peter Feroe,	"	25 00
J. E. Losee,	"	5 00
P. H. Potts,	"	5 00
A. Lee Wager. Rhinebeck		15 00
B. N. Baker,	"	5 00
C. S. Van Etten,	"	45 00
H. C. Wilber, Pine Plains		90 83
Geo. Q. Johnson,	"	10 00
Eggleston Bros, Amenia		18 00
G. H. Codding,	"	32 00
Robert Lawson, Po'keepsie Town		5 00
Wm. E. Traver,	" "	5 00
Judson A. Denton, Beekman		27 25
Duane Odell	"	5 00

C. L. Fletcher. Dover		10 00
Thos. Hammond. "		10 00
F. Tallman. "		3 00
M. H. Angell. Pleasant Valley		15 00
A. T. Fink, La Grange		10 00
C. H. Tripp, Clinton		5 00
H. Pearce, Pawling		10 00
M. C. Northrop, Stanford		5 00
D. H. Knapp, Union Vale		20 00
L. C. Wood, Wappinger		55 00
I. M. Cornell, "		10 00
Wm. Baxter. "		10 00
G. H. Van Wagner, "		30 00
T. K. Cruse "		15 00
J. H. Goodale, Rhinebeck		20 00
D. B. Ward, City		25 00
S. K. Phillips, Fishkill		15 00
Dr. D. M. Sheedy, City		70 00
Samuel Rogers, Fishkill		18 00
D. O. K. Strong, "		10 00
J. R. Strong, "		5 00
J. S. Bird, Hyde Park		5 00
W. J. Conklin, Fishkill		885 45
W. S. Watson. "		5 00
D. M. Ormsbee, assignee, Fishkill		134 00
St. Joachim's Church. "		30 00
D. Nickemon, East Fishkill		10 00
J. H. Redfield. Wappinger		20 00
M. T. Tultz, Stanford		10 00
G. M. Wellman. Dover		5 00
E. S. Hoyt. Clinton		5 00
Joseph Morschauser, City		8 00
Reynolds Elevator Co., assignee		33 00
S. Phillips. Fishkill		4 65
John Flannery, "		52 00
William Carroll. Rhinebeck		2 00
R. C. Worden, "		2 00
George Saltford. "		2 00
C. Rikert, "		2 00
J. P. Hermance. "		2 00

Sylvester Hall, Red Hook		4 00
H. E. Moore,	"	2 00
S. R. Burnett,	"	2 00
A J. Howland,	"	2 00
John Morgan,	"	2 00
F. G. Freleigh.	"	2 00
A. J. Gedney,	"	2 00
C. B. Pells.	"	4 00
A. Folmsbee.	"	2 00
W. G. Donaldson,	"	2 00
Peter Troy,	"	2 00
S. W. Coon,	"	2 00
J. A. Stoutenburgh,	"	2 00
R. A. Coon.	"	2 00
Wm. B. Lown.	"	2 00
Walter Sheldon,	"	2 00
T. A. Ross,	"	2 00
W. Rockefeller.	"	2 00
George Coon.	"	2 00
Peter Feroe,	"	2 00
Frank Potts,	"	2 00
Zachariah Minkler.	"	2 00
William Sadler, Pine Plains		1 00
Amos Bryan,	"	1 00
William Husler.	"	1 00
J. S. Bowman.	"	1 00
P. S. Wolven,	"	1 00
Geo. P. Ricketts,	"	1 00
Walter VanBenschoten,	"	1 00
Hoffman Hoysradt,	"	1 00
Fred Bostwick,	"	1 00
Charles M. Benjamin, Amenia		1 00
David Rundall,	"	1 00
Geo. F. Dennis.	"	1 00
Geo. H. Sutherland,	"	1 00
John M. Haskin,	"	1 00
Geo. Middlebrook.	"	1 00
P. A. Barr.	"	1 00

Jerry Pearce.	Pawling		2 00
Wm. R. Lee.	"		2 00
Geo. F. Lee.	"		2 00
Geo. W. Chase.	"		2 00
Thos. Elbott.	"		2 00
Jno. J. Arnold.	"		2 00
S. J. Baker.	"		2 00
Peter Gorey.	"		2 00
John Trowbridge,	City		25 00
S. J. Farnum.	"		29 00
John A. Bayly.	"		27 00
Fred Boos.	"		25 00
T. Lampert.	"		26 00
Wilson Hicks.	"		22 00
E. V. Vincent.	"		26 00
Robt. W. Frost.	"		29 00
Jos. H. Titus,	"		35 00
James H. Ward.	"		24 00
S. A. Perkins.	"		33 00
D. C. Anderson.	"		37 00
E C. Adriance.	"		27 00
Geo. R. Fitchett.	"		13 00
Chas. E. Butts.	Pleasant Valley		6 00
Jas. I. Marshall.	"	"	6 00
Emanuel Briggs.	"	"	6 00
Wm. Lary.	"	"	6 00
John D. Odell.	"	"	6 00
Wm. Sheldon.	"	"	6 00
Wm. Bedell.	"	"	6 00
Isaac Hewlett.	"	"	6 00
Silas Downing.	"	"	6 00
Frank J. Traver.	"	"	6 00
Geo. W. Doty.	"	"	6 00
John G. Harris.	Po'keepsie Town		2 00
Wm. E. Powell.	"	"	2 00
John G. Harris. Assignee.	"	"	2 00
John S. Myers.	"	"	2 00
John R. Matthews.	"	"	2 00
C. M. Clark.	"	"	2 00

Frank Frost.	Po'keepsie Town	2 00
Patrick Fahey.	" "	2 00
A. Doughty,	Assignee, of J. G. Frost. City	38 50
A. B. Lewis.	" " " "	140 00
P. B. Hayt.	" " " "	300 00
Reed & Forman.	" " " "	212 00
J. P. Heath.	" " " "	193 56
Wm. R. Brown.	Fishkill	5 00
Sherwood Phillips.	"	33 00
Wm. Brown.	"	5 00
H. C. Ormsbee.	"	4 00
Jos. C. Sawyer,	"	7 00
Geo. Wilson.	"	2 00
E. Knickerbocker.	Stanford	9 05
Thos. A. Gurney,	Po'keepsie	10 50
Martin Croak.	"	11 35
John H. Olivett.	"	16 40
C. V. Coon,	Rhinebeck	2 00
Edmund Tanner,	Wappinger	3 75
City of Po'keepsie		80 43
Levi Ellis,	Fishkill	5 00
Chas. H. Hoysradt,	"	5 00
Samuel Rogers.	"	12 00
John T. Smith.	"	1 00
Wm. H. Aldridge.	"	1 00
John C. Bassett.	"	7 00
Chas. E. Martin,	"	1 00
Wm. H. Rogers,	"	1 00
Benjamin Hammond	"	3 00
E, S. Phillips	"	14 00
John B. Whitson,	"	16 00
Conrad S. Bevier.	"	3 00
Benj. Sullivan,	"	4 00
A. G. Ormsbee.	"	6 00
L. L. Inman,	"	2 00
Samuel Leith,	"	2 00
John L. Hall,	"	11 00
Wm. H. Miller,	"	2 00

W. F. Weston,	Fishkill	5 00
A. W. Underhill.	"	2 00
D. M. Ormsbee,	"	4 00
Theo. Moith,	"	8 00
John Flannery	"	2 00
T. I. McGlasson,	"	2 00
D. E. Colwell,	"	5 00
Alfred Kemp,	"	2 00
F. D. Spaight	"	2 00
S. H. Tillman,	"	2 00
H. B. Schenck,	"	6 00
Jas. E. Shurter,	"	3 00
Chas. H. Ticehurst,	"	3 00
Edward Lasher, East Fishkill		1 00
Geo. F. Horton,	"	1 00
Chas. E. Knapp,	"	1 00
Andrew Biker,	"	1 00
John C. Dockerty,	"	1 00
Chas. Underhill,	"	1 00
Moses C. Sanford,	Fishkill	5 00
Albert Townsend,	"	4 00
L. W. Perrine,	"	4 00
S.K. Phillips	"	4 00
Wm. H. Gifford,	"	1 00
Chas. Reeves,	"	6 00
Benjamin F. Freen,	"	1 00
John F. Mase.	"	1 00
Roswell S. Judson.	"	1 00
John F. Gerow.	"	1 00
B. J. Hubbell,	"	1 00
Herman Greene,	"	2 00
Greenwood Ammerman,	"	2 00
E. J. Kelley,	"	2 00
H. B. Bevier.	"	2 00
George Harris,	"	2 00
John G. Harris, Pokeepsie Town		2 00
Robert Lawson	"	2 00
John Albertson.	"	2 00
George Albertson,	"	2 00

Wm. G. Ferris, Pokeepsie Town	2	00
Cyrus Baker, "	2	00
Frank Myers, "	2	00
J. A. Redfield, Wappinger	2	00
Chas. Whitman, "	2	00
Edgar G. Greene, Fishkill	2	00
Geo. M. Harding, "	5	00
N. W. Purdy, "	5	00
James E. Dean, "	2	00
D. C. Smith, "	2	00
Chas. W. Carey, "	2	00
W. F. Wakeman, "	2	00
Willet Pearce, "	2	00
L. D. W. Bogardus, "	2	00
Peter Russell, "	2	00
C. Ed. Taylor, "	3	60
Wm. H. Southard, "	6	00
B. Frank Greene, "	3	00
Wm. H. Burlingame, "	2	00
C. R. James, "	2	00
W. J. Pralatowski, "	2	00
Frank Luther, "	3	00
F. T. Hopkins, "	35	00
Pokeepsie News Company, City	1,297	00
A. G. Tobey, "	59	00
Platt & Platt, "	1,227	01
Lansing, Van Keuren & Brown, "	145	80
Pokeepsie Publishing Co., "	32	85
Amenia Times	30	50
Fishkill Printing Association	20	50
" Standard	30	50
" Journal	24	00
Pine Plains Herard	35	00
" Register	32	00
J. Hogan, Assignee, Rhinebeck	39	50
Red Hook Journal	29	00
Wappingers Chronicle	21	00
Millerton Telegram	21	00
Po'keepsie News Co.	68	20

J. Benjamin & Son,	City	38 00
Barnes Bros.,	"	67 62
D. H. Stringham,	"	7 00
W. R. Farrington,	"	18 30
Reynolds & Spink,	"	104 50
W. S. Reynolds & Co.,	"	200 50
J. J. Herley,	"	7 00
Wm. Moore,	"	8 50
Wetzel Bros.,	"	33 00
Chas. Joseph,	"	6 55
Wm. E. Scott & Co.,	"	12 00
John Eley,	"	29 15
Levy Melhado, Assignee,	"	10 00
Wood & Tittamer,	"	11 32
Perkins Bros.,	"	120 54
Timmins Bros.,	"	2 25
Diossy & Co,	"	8 25
W. C. Little & Co.,	"	18 00
C. B. Cunley,	"	3 60
Frank Germond,	"	4 00
W. D. Hicks,	"	4 00
John H. Cox,	"	4 00
Jno. P. Ambler,	"	27 70
Elsworth & Dudley,	"	5 05
Otto Faust,	"	39 00
Geo. Dunwoody,	"	7 00
James Myers,	"	8 00
Henry Stibbs,	"	5 37
D. C. Foster & Sons,	"	202 00
Jerome Paper Co.,	"	9 00
S. S. Peloubet,	"	17 50
Luckey, Platt & Co.,	"	156 31
W. F. German,	Dover	55 00
Chas. W. Vincent,	"	43 00
Marten Heermance,	City	139 57
Chas. Kirchner,	"	33 50
Daniel Sullivan,	"	15 00
W. Haubennestel,	"	150 00
H. E. Haubennestel,	"	19 60

J. P. Ambler,	City	294	54
M. H. Barlow,	"	17	50
H. A. Brown,	"	8	00
P. H. Ward,	"	63	15
Frank Shay,	"	134	67
Andrew Bilyou,	"	227	64
Shurter & Briggs,	"	156	33
Geo. Hughes & Son,	"	104	10
Wm. Gibson,	"	15	00
L. B. Stanton,	"	15	65
Owen Cook, Agt.,	"	8	35
Diossy & Co		20	25
Po'keepsie Gas Co		32	80
James Mahar		12	35
Geo. Worrall		15	00
I. W. Sherrill		200	00
J. P. Ambler		40	58
N. Ball		2	00
W. R. Anderson, Washington		200	00
J. A. Vandewater, Po'keepsie Town		200	00
State Tax		109,987	94

Appropriations Payable by Treasurer.

Extra Compensation of Supreme Court Judges.	$2,044 55
Red Book, for deficiency	234 00
General Fund	10,500 00
Court and Jury Fund	7,000 00
Interest on Bonds	2,560 00
Bonds (maturing 1891)	20,000 00
Note City National Bank	7,000 00
Supervisors Pay Roll	2,500 00
Hudson River State Hospital	18,500 00
Willard State Hospital	11,000 00
Binghamton State Hospital	4,365 00
Homeopathic Asylum, Middletown	225 00
State Criminal Asylum, Auburn	585 00
State Asylum, Utica	260 00
N. Y. Ins. for Blind, Batavia	99 13
" " " Deaf and Dumb, N. Y. City	187 50
N. Y. Asylum for Idiots, Syracuse	64 00
Colored Orphan Asylum	409 50
Rent of Armory	1,600 00

SALARIES.

Salary of County Judge	2,000 00
" Surrogate	2,000 00
" " Clerk	1,000 00
" Treasurer	1,250 00
" District Attorney	1,500 00
" Armorer	400 00
" Jail Physician	100 00
" Keeper Drake Draw Bridge	350 00
" County Sealer	25 00

COUNTY EXCLUSIVE OF CITY.

Repairs to Poorhouse	500 00
Deficiency—Repairs to Poorhouse 1891	485 18
Poor Fund	8,000 00
Supt. of Poor Salary	1,700 00
Matron "	300 00
Ministers "	100 00

LIST OF PERSONS
In Asylums and Charitable Institutions
Chargeable to Dutchess County.

HUDSON RIVER STATE HOSPITAL.

Beatta Martin, age 47, white, residence Rhinebeck, committed by Supt. Wodell, March 8, 1876.

B. G. Smith, age 35, white, Wappinger, Judge Carpenter, July 2, 1877.

Minerva J. Conklin, age 46, white, Hyde Park, Supt. Russell, June 15, 1884.

Charity C. Sackett, age 41, white, Union Vale, Judge Guernsey, Dec. 13, 1884.

Francis Odell, age 38, white, Pleasant Valley, Judge Guernsey, Oct. 29, 1884.

John A. Lambert, age 57, white, Red Hook, Judge Guernsey, May 7, 1885.

Mary A. Mawha, age 20, white, Amenia, Judge Guernsey, Dec. 8, 1885.

Amelia Hilliker, age 70, white, Pleasant Valley. Supt. Russell, March 16, 1886.

Peter Woodfield, age 52, white, Wappinger, J. F. Barnard, Jan. 25, 1886.

Catherine E. Proctor, age 52, white, Wappinger, D. W. Guernsey, Oct. 26, 1886.

John Grant, age 37, white, Hyde Park, D. W. Guernsey, March 18, 1887.

Annie M. Horton, age 35, white, Washington, D. W. Guernsey, July 9, 1887.

Fred. G. Ebert, age 19, white, Fishkill, Supt. Russell, Aug. 8. 1887.

Kate H. Murphy, age 52, white, LaGrange, D. W. Guernsey, Nov. 30, 1887.

Mary E. Hall, age 36, white, Union Vale, Supt. Russell, Dec. 19, 1887.

Alfred Hyatt, age 27, white, Stanford, D. W. Guersey, Dec. 21, 1887.

Gertrude Halsted, age 37, white, Stanford, D. W. Guernsey, Dec. 21, 1887.

Magdalena Heldebrant, white, Pok. City, D. W. Guernsey, Feb. 10, 1888.

Catherine O'Brien, age 22, Pok. City, Supt. Dutcher, July 3, 1886.

Daniel Mack, age 45, white, Pok City, D. W. Guernsey, Oct. 5, 1887.

Henry Doyle, age 23, white, Pok. City, Supt. Dutcher, Dec. 22, 1887.

Anna Mackey, age 34, white, LaGrange, D. W. Guernsey, April 14, 1888.

Jane A. Stanton, age 72, white, Pok. City, D. W. Guernsey, May 4, 1888.

Jane Strong, age 37, white, Pok. City, D. W. Guernsey, May 4, 1888.

Isaac B. Myers, white, Wappinger, D. W. Guernsey, Feb., 1888.

Lewis A. Teator, age 40, white, Red Hook, D. W. Guernsey, June 16, 1888.

Albert Kriosky, age 25, white, LaGrange, D. W. Guernsey, June 22, 1888.

Theodore G. Chambers, age 65, white, Fishkill, D. W. Guernsey, July 6, 1888.

Mary Kimlim, age 80, white, Pok. City, D. W. Guernsey, Aug. 2, 1888.

Mary A. Kane, age 22, white. Pok. City, D. W. Guernsey, Aug. 13. 1888.

Bridget Sweeney, age 65, white, Pok. City, D. W. Guernsey, April 22, 1888.

Mary Trainor, age 66, white, Red Hook, D. W. Guernsey, Oct. 4, 1888.

Virgil E. Coon, age 46, white, Red Hook, D. W. Guernsey, Oct. 6, 1888.

John H. Traver, age 49, white, Pleasant Valley, D. W. Guernsey, Oct. 11, 1888.

Ella Gray, age 20, white, Fishkill, D. W. Guernsey, Nov. 7, 1888.

Susan Todd, age 45, white, Pok. City, D. W. Guernsey, Dec. 31, 1888.

James McManus, age 23, white, Pok. City, D. W. Guernsey, Jan. 30, 1889.

Louis Freyberg, age 26, white, Pok. City, J. F. Barnard, Feb. 2, 1889.

John Cunningham, age 30, white, LaGrange, D. W. Guernsey, Feb. 23, 1889.

Gilbert E. Vail, age 22, white, Stanford, D. W. Guernsey, April 5, 1889.

Margaret Clinton, age 40, white, Pok. City, J. F. Barnard, April 1, 1889.

Willis O'Rourk, age 28, white, Pok. City, J. F. Barnard, April 5, 1889.

Doretta Damn, age 22, white, Pok. City, D. W. Guernsey, April 11, 1889.

Lizzie Fischer, age 20, white, Pok. City, D. W. Guernsey, April 11, 1889.

Benjamin Keech, white, Pok. City, D. W. Guernsey, April 18, 1889.

Helen Bouar, age 80, white, Hyde Park, Supt. Smith, May 4, 1889.

Raymond Bullis, age 24, white, Amenia, D. W. Guernsey, May 4, 1889,

Rebecca E. Risley, age 46, white, Hyde Park, D. W. Guernsey, June 8, 1889.

Amanda J. Commack, age 65, white, Pok. City, D. W. Guernsey, June 8, 1889.

Mary Donnelly, age 43, white, Amenia, Supt. Smith, June 11, 1889.

James Calligan, age 28, white, Pok. City, Supt. Smith, June 28, 1889.

Sarah Ann Murray, age 55, white, Beekman, D. W. Guernsey, July 26, 1889.

Wm. H. Platt, age 58, white, Pok. City, D. W. Guernsey, July 31, 1889.

Ida Powell, age 32, white, Milan, D. W. Guernsey, Sept. 18, 1889.

Ida Moore, age 22, white, Red Hook, D. W. Guernsey, Sept. 23, 1889.

Mary Flanagan, age 22, white, Hyde Park, J. F. Barnard. Sept. 24, 1889.

Hannah Lucy, age 22, white, Pok. City, D. W. Guernsey, Oct. 1, 1889.

Thos. Hefferan, age 48, white, Pok. City, D. W. Guernsey, Oct. 11, 1889.

Mary Howell, age 80, white, Pok. City, Supt. Smith, Oct. 15, 1889.

Fred. McCord, age 60, white, Pok. City, D. W. Guernsey, Oct. 19, 1889.

Patrick Miles, age 36, white, Fishkill, D. W. Guernsey, Oct. 26, 1889.

Emily Buys, age 65, white, Pok. City, D. W. Guernsey, Oct. 29, 1889.

John McLean, age 27, white, Pok. City, D. W. Guernsey, Dec. 23, 1889.

Wm. Hockett, City, D. W. Guernsey, Jan. 17, 1890.

Lousia Hyland, City, D. W. Guernsey, Feb. 10, 1890.

James Cable, City, D. W. Guernsey, Feb. 12, 1890.

Frank Bonamaker, City, Myron Smith Feb. 14, 1890.

Patrick Kennedy, City, Myron Smith, Feb. 14, 1890.

Wm. Dryer, City, D. W. Guernsey, Feb. 19, 1890.

Sarah Rogers, Stanford, D. W. Guernsey, Apr. 10, 1890.

B. Myers, Red Hook, D. W. Guernsey, Apr. 18. 1890.

Peter Rourke. Washington, D. W. Guernsey, Apr. 26. 1890.

Wm. S. Rowe, City, D. W. Guernsey, Apr. 26, 1890.

James Cooper, City, D. W. Guernsey, May 1, 1890.

Mary Gilmartin, City, D. W. Guernsey, May 5, 1890.

John D. Smith, City, D. W. Guernsey, May 9, 1890.

Mary J. Moran, Wappinger, D. W. Guernsey, May 12, 1890.

Alex Simon, Stanford, D. W. Guernsey, May 12, 1890.

Vanie V. Odell, Fishkill, D. W. Guernsey, May 27, 1890.

M. Mitzka, Fishkill, M. Smith Jan. 14, 1890.

Ruth C. Lovelace, City, D. W. Guernsey, Jan. 16, 1890.

Julia Lang, Hyde Park, D. W. Guernsey, Jan. 18, 1890.

Ellen Higgins, City, D. W. Guernsey, Jan. 27, 1890.

M. Supritz, City, D. W. Guernsey, July, 9, 1890.

Arthur Jaycox, City, D. W. Guernsey, July 9, 1890.

Amelia C. Mitchell, Washington, D. W. Guernsey, July 9, 1890.

Albert B. Miller, Pawling, D. W. Guernsey, July 12, 1890.

John Bonicou, City, J. F. Barnard, July 18, 1890.

Arthur Powers, Wappinger, J. F. Barnard, July 28, 1890.

Chas. E. Mosher, Union Vale, D. W. Guernsey, Aug. 4, 1890.

Rachel A. Cole, Rhinebeck, D. W. Guernsey, Aug 4, 1890.

Julia Weeks, Amenia, Myron Smith, Aug. 9, 1890.

Mary F. Feeney, Fishkill, D. W. Guernsey, Aug. 21, 1890.

Bridget Whelan, Fishkill, D. W. Guernsey, Sept. 6, 1890.

Amanda Secor, East Fishkill, D. W. Guernsey, Sept. 17, 1890.

Henry Freleigh, Rhinebeck, J. F. Barnard, Sept. 20, 1890.

Catherine Kelley, City, D. W. Guernsey, Oct. 10, 1890.

Phillipena Tray, City, D. W. Guernsey, Oct. 10, 1890.

Rose Tone, City, D. W. Guernsey, Oct. 10, 1890.

Nancy Strang, City, D. W. Guernsey, Oct. 10, 1890.

Mary Donnelly, City, D. W. Gnerusey, Oct. 10, 1890.

Lavina F. Weed, Amenia, D. W. Guernsey, Oct. 14, 1890.

Julia Goodheim, City, D. W. Guernsey, Oct. 22, 1890.

H. A. Distin, City, D. W. Guernsey, Oct. 25, 1890.

Daniel Garvey, Rhinebeck, Myron Smith, Oct. 31, 1890.

Mary A. B. McCavara, City, D. W. Guernsey, Nov. 6, 1890.

Julia Schroh, City, D. W. Guernsey, Nov. 11, 1890.

Sarah R. Doughty, City, D. W. Guernsey, Nov. 18, 1890.

M. K. Mulcox, City, D. W. Guernsey, Nov. 21, 1890.

LeGrand Curtiss, Red Hook, D. W. Guernsey, Dec. 5, 1890.

R. M. Ostrander, City, D. W. Guernsey, Dec. 9, 1890.

Mary Dorsey, City, D. W. Guernsey, Dec. 15, 1890.

Eliza Pultz, Rhinebeck, Myron Smith, Dec. 11, 1890.

Louisa Pultz, Rhinebeck, Myron Smith, Dec. 11, 1890.

John Miller, LaGrange, D. W. Guernsey, Dec. 17, 1890.

F. R. Griffen, Beekman, D. W. Guernsey, Dec. 20, 1890.

Chas. P. Greensword, City, D. W. Guernsey, Dec. 27, 1890.

Elizabeth Rogers, City, D. W. Guernsey, Dec 27, 1890.

HOMEOPATHIC ASYLUM.
Middletown, N. Y.

Chas. H. Hale, age 33, white, Fishkill, Supt. Russell, May 22, 1885.

AT WILLARD ASYLUM.

Reuben Lasher, age 46, white, residence unknown, committed by Supt. Vanderburgh, Oct. 20th, 1869.

Wm. Hulse, age 45, white, Fishkill, Supt. Vanderburgh, Oct: 20, 1869,

Richard F. Bloodgood, age 48, white, Pok. Town, Supt. Vanderburgh, Oct. 20, 1869.

Sarah McKay, aged 42, white, Washington, Supt. Vanderburgh, Oct. 20, 1869.

Wm. Burton, age 37, white, unknown, Supt. Vanderburgh, Oct. 20, 1869.

Patrick Welch, age 55, white, unknown, Supt. Vanderburgh, Oct. 20, 1869.

Tamar Purdy, age 44, white, Hyde Park, Supt. Vanderburgh, Oct. 20, 1869.

Patrick Burke, age 42, white, unknown, Supt. Vanderburgh, May 18, 1870.

Lucy L. Scott, age 45, white, Supt. Utica Asylum, Dec. 5, 1870.

Gertrude Osterhout, age 60, white, unknown, Supt. Utica Asylum, Dec. 5, 1870.

John Cronin, age 37, white, Pawling, Supt. Wodell, Nov. 11, 1872.

Edgar Bartram, age 34, white, Wappinger, Supt. Wodell, Nov. 11, 1872.

Alfred Germond, age 36, white, Washington, Supt. Wodell, Nov. 11, 1872.

Elizabeth Bates, age 57, white, Washington, Supt. Wodell, Nov. 11, 1872.

Isaac Green, age 39, unknown, Judge Taylor, May 9, 1873.

Charles Shaver, age 35, white, Red Hook, Supt. Wodell, July 3, 1874.

Patrick McMenomy, age 44, white, Hyde Park, Supt. Wodell, July 3, 1874.

Michael Rowen, age 37, white, Amenia, Supt. Wodell, July 3, 1874.

Georgiana Mills, age 24, colored, Pleasant Valley, Supt. Wodell, July 3, 1874.

Ellen Cronin, age 47, white, unknown, Supt. Wodell, July 3, 1874.

Caroline Hill, age 27, white, Clinton, Supt. Wodell, June 11, 1875.

Mary Waters, age 42, unknown, Supt. Wodell, June 11, 1875.

Josephine Pralatowski, age 30, white, Fishkill, Supt. Ladue, April 27, 1877.

Catharine Lyons, age 30, Wappinger, Supt. Ladue, April 27, 1877.

Sarah Palmer, age 41, white, Hyde Park, Supt. Ladue, April 27, 1877.

Susan O'Connor, age 38, white, Wappinger, Supt. Ladue, April 27, 1877.

Fanny Sedore, age 43, white, LaGrange, Supt. Ladue, April 27, 1877.

Charles S. Mosher, age 24, white, Fishkill, Supt. Ladue, June 25, 1878.

Wm. Hedges, age 37, white, Amenia, Supt. Ladue, June 25, 1878.

Aaron DuBois, age 28, white, Washington, Supt. Ladue, June 25, 1878.

Charles H. Husted, age 42, white, Pine Plains, Supt. Ladue, June 25, 1878.

Harvey Pierce, age 31, white, Wappinger, Supt. Ladue, July 2, 1879.

Edward Eddy, age 54, white, Wappinger, Supt. Ladue, July 2, 1879.

Mary Hefferin, age 47, white, unknown, Supt. Ladue, July 2, 1879.

Abbie Wellman, age 51, white, Dover, Supt. Ladue, July 2, 1879.

Laura Wellman, age 39, white, Dover. Supt. Ladue, July 2, 1879.

Caroline Overocker, age 56, white, Pok. Town, Supt. Ladue, July 2, 1879.

Rosanna Rock, age 48, white, Fishkill, Supt. Ladue, July 2, 1879.

John H. Shoemaker, age 36, white, Milan, Supt. Tallman, July 2, 1880.

Garrison Horton, age 28, white, East Fishkill, Supt. Tallman, July 2, 1880.

Wellington E. Vail, age 30, white, Union Vale, Supt. Tallman, July 2, 1880.

Chas. T. Burhans, age 37, white, Hyde Park, Supt. Tallman, July 2, 1880.

Ann D. Reed, age 61, white, Fishkill, Supt. Tallman, Feb. 1, 1881.

Theresa M. Haines, age 28, white, Amenia, Supt. Tallman, Feb. 1, 1881.

Bridget Moonan, age 40, white, Pok. Town, Supt. Tallman, Feb., 1881.

Dorothy Volk, age 49, white, Wappinger, Supt. Tall-man, Feb. 1, 1881.

Margaret P. Blythe, white, Wappinger, Supt. Tall-man, Feb. 1, 1881.

Rose McGrane, age 25, white, Wappinger, Supt. Tall-man, Feb. 1, 1881.

Annie Williams, age 45, white, Wappinger, Supt. Tallman, Feb. 1, 1881.

Catherine Morey, age 40, white, Amenia, Supt Tall-man, June 15, 1881.

Ann Davis, white, Pok. City, J. B. Jewett, Dec. 25, 1870.

Francis Nesbitt, age, 41, Pok City, white, A. Ward, March 28, 1872.

Edward O'Harra, age 32, white, Pok. City, A. Ward, June 8, 1874.

Lucinda Sutton, age 51, white, Pok. City, Supt. Dutcher, April 17, 1875.

Charlotte A. Fox, age 33, white, Pok. City, Supt. Dutcher, Jan. 31, 1877.

Anna M. Wetzell, age 33, Pok. City, Supt. Dutcher, April 17, 1877.

Margaret Connor, age 37, white, Pok. City, Supt. Dutcher, June 8, 1877.

A. J. Coxhead, age 31, white, Pok. City, Supt. Dutcher, June 8, 1877.

Geo. W. Tattan, age 43, white, Pok. City, Supt. Dutcher, July 20, 1877.

Mary Foster, age 44, white, Pok. City. Supt. Dutcher, Dec. 6, 1877.

Mary A. Tanner, age 47, white, Pok. City, Supt. Dutcher, June 12, 1878.

Edward Lottner, age 22, white, Pok. City, Supt. Dutcher, June 12, 1878.

Bettie Koeble, age 30, white, Pok. City, Supt. Dutcher, Sept. 30, 1878.

Matthew Benhart, age 40, white, Pok. City, Supt. Dutcher, Oct. 17, 1878.

Elizabeth Sexton, age 33, white, Pok. City, Supt. Dutcher, Oct. 17, 1878.

Isaac F. Burger, age 31, white, Pok. City, Alson Ward. Oct. 17, 1879.

Julia Cramer age 45, white, Pok. City, Alson Ward, Oct. 17, 1879.

Samuel Deyo, age 34, colored, Pok. City, Alson Ward, Feb. 14, 1880.

Henry Germond, white, Pok. City, Alson Ward, Jan. 13, 1881.

Catharine Dean, age 33, white, Pok. City, Alson Ward, Jan. 13, 1881.

Wm. C. Foster, age 24, white, Pok. City, Adam Caire, Oct. 14, 1886.

Ella Burger, age 25, white, Pok. City, Adam Caire, May 12, 1887.

Alice C. Husted, age 37, white, Clinton, Supt. Russell, Sept. 18, 1888.

Pauline LeRoy, age 34, white, Pok. City, Supt. Russell, Sept. 18, 1888.

Catharine E. Griffith, age 42, white, Fishkill, Supt. Russell, Sept. 18, 1888.

Elizabeth Cramsey, age 70, white, Pok. City. Supt. Russell, Sept. 18, 1888.

Charlotte Bell, age 37, white, Pok. City, Supt. Russell, Sept. 18, 1888.

Wm. P. Schlosser, age 33, white, Pok. City, Supt. Russell, Sept. 18, 1888.

John Moore, age 49, white. Red Hook, Supt. Russell, Sept. 18, 1888.

Michael Gordon, age 36, white, Pawling, Supt. Russell, Sept. 18, 1888.

James Marigla, age 50, white, Pok. City, Supt. Russell, Sept. 18, 1888.

James Fitzgerald, age 74. white, Pok. City, Supt, Smith, Feb. 11, 1889.

Emma Gedney. age 22, white, Red Hook, Supt. Smith, April 12, 1889.

Johanna Barney, age 35, white, Pok. City, Supt. Smith, April 12, 1889.

Abram Boice, age 35, white, Fishkill, Supt. Smith, April 12, 1889.

David R. Perkins, age 45, white, Pok. City, Supt. Smith, April 12, 1889.

John Nugent, age 54, white, Pawling, Supt. Smith, April 12, 1889.

BINGHAMTON ASYLUM.

Mary Hennesey, age 35, white, residence Amenia, Committed by Supt. Tallman, Nov. 10, 1881.

Barbara Lutz, age 27, white, Rhinebeck, Supt. Tallman, Nov. 10, 1881.

Richard Livingston, age 57, white, Wappinger, Supt. Tallman, Nov. 10, 1881.

Thos. Toohey. age 19, white, Wappinger, Supt. Tallman, Nov. 10, 1881.

Louis Loesch, age, 46, white, Red Hook, Supt. Tallman, Nov. 10, 1881.

James Todd, age 43, white, not known, Supt. Tallman, Nov. 10, 1881.

Isaac Chatterton, age 63, white, La Grange, Supt. Tallman, Nov. 10, 1881.

Chas. Henderson, age 30, white, Hyde Park, Supt. Tallman, Jan. 6, 1882.

Mary L. Hoover, age 43, white, Red Hook, Supt. Russell, March 10, 1885.

Annie Ledson, age 34, white, Po'keepsie Town, Supt. Russell, March 10, 1885.

John Seeley, age 30, white, Supt. Russell, March 10, 1885.

Peter Griffen, age 27, white, Dover, Supt. Russell, Mach 10, 1885.

Harriet Bowman, colored, Fishkill, Supt. Russell, March 10, 1885.

Eliza A. Ferris, white, Pawling, Supt. Russell, March 15, 1887.

Mary Ostrander, white, Red Hook, Supt. Russell, March 15, 1887.

Lydia Shoemaker, white, Red Hook, Supt. Russell, March 15, 1887.

Mary Moran, white, Pleasant Valley, Supt. Russell, March 15, 1887.

Margaret H. Gittens, white, Fishkill, Supt. Russell, March 15, 1887.

Elizabeth Kipp, white, Red Hook, Supt. Russell, March 15, 1887.

John O'Neil, white, Rhinebeck, Supt. Russell, March 15, 1887.

Peter Gibeau, white, Fishkill, Supt. Russell, March 15, 1887.

John Flood, white, Po'keepsie Town. Supt. Russell. March 15, 1887.

John Couch, white, North East, Supt. Russell, March 15, 1887.

John McGinn, white, Fishkill, Supt. Russell, March 15, 1887.

Katie Wiest, aged 45, white, Po'keepsie City, Supt. Dutcher, Jan. 11, 1882.

Margaret J. Holtizer, age 33, white, Po'keepsie City, Supt. Dutcher, Jan. 11, 1882.

Minnie Devoe, aged 26, white, Po'keepsie City, Supt. Dutcher, Aug. 2, 1882.

Hannah P. Vail, age 45, white, Po'keepsie City, Supt. Dutcher, Aug. 1882.

Joseph Cary, age 37, white, Po'keepsie City, Supt. Dutcher, April 21, 1883.

Mary Stansfield, age 23, white, Po'keepsie City, Supt. Dutcher, June 4, 1883.

Emily Armstrong, age 40, white, Po'keepsie City, Supt. Dutcher, April 16, 1885.

John White, age 33, white, Po'keepsie City, Supt. Dutcher, April 16, 1885.

John Murray, age 23, white, Po'keepsie City, Supt. Dutcher, April 16, 1885.

John Doyle, age 39, white, Po'keepsie City, Supt. Dutcher, Oct. 8, 1887.

Ettie Todd, age 31, white, Po'keepsie City, Supt. Dutcher, Oct. 8, 1887.

BRUNSWICK HOME.

Amityville, N. Y.

Charles E. Yeoman's white, committed by Supt. Russell, March 10, 1888.

UTICA ASYLUM.

Catherine Hayes, age 49, white, residence Amenia, committed April 21, 1870.

Wm. Loyall, age 19, white, Ulster Co., Oct. 21, 1863.

AUBURN ASYLUM.

John D. Jackson, white, residence Po'keepsie City, committed by W. J. Bacon. S. J.

Chas. Flannagan, white, Pleasant Valley, J. F. Barnard.

Chas. Briero, white, unknown, M. H. Mervin.

NEW YORK INS. FOR THE INS. OF THE DEAF AND DUMB.

New York City.

Chas. J. Sanford, age 9, white, residence Rhinebeck, committed by J. H. Kipp, Sept. 28, 1885.

C. H. Hall, aged 5, white, Red Hook, H. E. Miller, Dec. 6, 1886.

Lester Woodin, age 2, white, Supt. of Instruction, April 1, 1879.

Millie J. Sanford, age 16, white, Supt. of Instruction, Oct. 15, 1879.

Cora L. Millard, aged 16, white, Supt. of Instruction, Sept. 10, 1885.

B. B. Millard, age 14, white, Supt. of Instruction, Sept. 22, 1886.

Terry Fallon, age 12, white, Supt. of Instruction, 1889.

COLORED·ORPHAN ASYLUM.

Mary Jackson, age 7, Red Hook, F. E. Ackerman, Aug. 19, 1883.

Edward J. Jackson, age 7, Red Hook, F. E. Ackerman, Aug. 19, 1883.

Herbert Bowman, age 9, unknown, Supt. Russell, Oct. 10, 1884.

Otis Bruce, age 8, unknown, Supt. Russell, Dec. 24, 1887.

Henry Call, age 7, unknown. Supt. Russell, Dec. 10, 1888.

NEW YORK STATE INSTITUTION FOR BLIND.

Batavia, N. Y.

Fred. Thomas, Rhinebeck, age 8, white, Supt. of Instruction, 1877.

W. C. Harrison, Pawling, age 14, white, Supt. of Instruction, 1882.

Julia A. Silvernail, Pleasant Valley, age 32, white, Supt. of Instruction, 1886.

Albert Litzendorf, Pine Plains, white, Supt. of Instruction, 1886.

Thekla Becke, Po'keepsie, white, Supt. of Instruction, 1887.

LIST OF PERSONS

SELECTED BY THE SUPERVISORS OF THE TOWNS AND WARDS OF THE
COUNTY OF DUTCHESS AT THEIR ANNUAL SESSION IN 1890,
TO SERVE AS GRAND JURORS FOR THE YEAR 1891.

AMENIA.

Name and Occupation.	Post Office Address.
M. K. Lewis, merchant,	Wassaic.
I. N. Mead, merchant,	Amenia.
E. J. Preston, farmer.	Amenia.
W. H. Tanner, farmer,	Wassaic.
M. J. Potts, merchant,	Amenia.
Albert Cline, farmer,	South Amenia.
Jas. S. Chaffee, farmer,	South Amenia.
Frank Van Hovenburgh, farmer,	Smithfield.
Edward L. Lambert, gentleman,	Amenia.

BEEKMAN.

Henry Dodge, farmer,	Beekmanville.
Wm. H. Dutcher, farmer,	Beekmanville,
Henry Ludington, miller.	Poquag.
C. H. Slocum, merchant,	Poquag.

CLINTON.

LeGrand Graham, miller,	Clinton Hollow.
John Budd, farmer,	Bulls Head.
Ira Hadden, "	Ruskey.
William White, butcher,	Shultzville.
Alfred Wildey, farmer,	Clinton Corners.
Manderville Burger, farmer.	Pleasant Plains.

DOVER.

Charles Belding, farmer.	Dover Plains.
Abraham Denton, farmer.	Dover Furnace.
Myron Tabor, farmer,	Dover Furnace.
Jackson A. Aldriag, farmer.	Webotuck.
H. W. Stevens, farmer,	Wings Station.
Wing J. Martin, farmer,	Wings Station.
Myron Edmans, farmer,	Dover Plains.

EAST FISHKILL.

Richard Ostrom, farmer.	P. O. Stormville.
Morgan, L. Vail, farmer,	P. O. Stormville.
D. R. Robinson, farmer.	Fishkill Plains.
Alfred Bonney, farmer,	Hopewell Junction.
Adriance Bartow, farmer,	East Fishkill.
Frank Ketcham, farmer,	East Fishkill.
Richard Van Wyck, farmer,	East Fishkill.
Stephen C. Van Wyck, farmer,	Fishkill Plains.

FISHKILL.

John P. Ryder, manufacturer.	Fishkill-on-Hudson.
Samuel Verplanck, farmer.	Fishkill-on-Hudson.
John T. Smith, merchant,	Fishkill-on-Hudson.
John B. Leverich, gentleman,	Fishkill-on-Hudson.
John W. Spaight, editor,	Fishkill-on-Hudson.
George A. Member, merchant,	Fishkill-on-Hudson.
William A. Peattie, livery,	Fishkill-on-Hudson.
William H. Aldridge, merchant,	Fishkill-on-Hudson.

FISHKILL.—Continued.

Charles W. Brinckerhoff, farmer.	Fishkill-on-Hudson.
Amos Jones, builder,	Fishkill-on-Hudson.
Alonzo S. Wiltsie, merchant,	Fishkill-on-Hudson.
Willard H. Mase, manufacturer.	Matteawan.
William Rothery, manufacturer,	Matteawan.
William H. Jackson, manufacturer,	Matteawan.
Addison G. Ormsbee, merchant,	Matteawan.
Silas Terwilliger, merchant,	Matteawan.
Benjamin Hall, builder,	Matteawan.
James Forrestal, builder,	Matteawan.
William H. Burlingame, manufacturer,	Matteawan.
Benjamin Sullivan, merchant,	Matteawan.
Lyman Robinson, manufacturer,	Matteawan.
B. Frank Greene, druggist.	Matteawan.
Abram Brett, merchant,	Matteawan.
Albert Townsend, merchant.	Matteawan.
Moses C. Sandford, insurance.	Matteawan.
John Clifton, gentleman,	Matteawan.
William Brown, merchant,	Matteawan.
John Gracy, manufacturer,	Glenham.
Samuel Marsh, manufacturer,	Glenham.
Charles E. Bartow, farmer,	Glenham.
Frank R. Benjamin, merchant.	Fishkill.
Halsey F. Walcott, merchant,	Fishkill.
Dewitt C. Smith, druggist,	Fishkill.
Samuel L. Van Voorhis, farmer,	Brinckerhoffville.
William F. Sage, manufacturer,	Fishkill-on-Hudson.
John Creagan, builder,	Fishkill-on-Hudson.
Frank H. Brett, merchant,	Matteawan.
Robert B. Darragh, merchant,	Fishkill-on-Hudson.
Preston Greene, druggist,	Fishkill-on-Hudson.
Samuel H. Sandford, manufacturer.	Matteawan.
Charles D. Sherwood, farmer.	Fishkill.
James Hart, manufacturer,	Glenham.
William H. Haight, farmer,	Fishkill.
Joseph E. Scofield, farmer,	Fishkill.

HYDE PARK.

Edgar A. Briggs,   Hyde Park.
I. D. C. Prichard, wheelwright,   Hyde Park.
Albert E. Jones, gentleman,   Hyde Park.
A. B. Schryver, book maker,   Hyde Park.
James Porter, gentleman,   Hyde Park.
Wm. A. White, farmer,   Staatsburgh.
Howard W. Rowe, farmer,   Staatsburgh.
James Cummings, farmer,   Staatsburgh.
George D. Cronk, farmer,   Staatsburgh.
George S. Halstead, farmer,   Cream street.
Myers Fitchett, farmer.   Cream street.

NORTH EAST.

Darwin Morse, farmer,   Amenia.
Lorin J. Eggleston, merchant,   Millerton.
John Clark, farmer.   Millerton.
James R. Pain, merchant,   Millerton.
Leonard L. Barton, farmer,   Millerton.
Henry A. Cook, gentleman,   Millerton.
Calvin Bryant, farmer,   Shekomeko.
John Winchell, farmer,   Millerton.

MILAN.

John D. Hedges, farmer,   Jackson Corners.
Uriah Teator, farmer,   Cokertown.
Sacket L. Case, farmer,   Lafayetteville.
Nathaniel L. Morehouse, gentleman,   Rock City.

LA GRANGE.

John S. Landon, farmer,   Noxon.
Thomas Wright, farmer,   Arthursburgh.
Charles E. Davis, merchant,   Moore's Mills.
Eugene Storm, farmer.   Overlook.
J. Howard, farmer.   Overlook.
Smith Upton, farmer,   La Grangeville.

PAWLING.

Charles Brownell, farmer,	Pawling.
John G. Dutcher, farmer,	Pawling.
Robert Hurd, farmer.	Pawling.
William Merwin, merchant.	Pawling.
John Watts, farmer,	Pawling.
Nelson Denton, merchant.	Pawling.
Isaac Ferris, farmer,	Pawling.
Geo. T. Chapman, merchant,	Pawling.

PINE PLAINS.

John Van Tassel, miller and merchant,	Mount Ross.
Jacob Hinsdale, farmer.	Mount Ross.
Anthony H. Barton, farmer,	Pine Plains.
William B. Jordan, farmer,	Pine Plains.
Adam A. Strever, farmer.	Pine Plains.

PLEASANT VALLEY.

Anthony Briggs,	Pleasant Valley.
Samuel J. Landis.	Pleasant Valley.
John M. Edwards.	Pleasant Valley.
Bartlett Devine.	Pleasant Valley.
Sylvanus Hicks.	Pleasant Valley.
Orlando Van Wagner.	Pleasant Valley.

POUGHKEEPSIE TOWN.

Jacob V. Overocker, farmer,	Arlington.
John W. Rose, brickmaker,	Arlington.
Henry P. Titus, manufacturer.	Pokeepsie City.
Henry Allen, brickmaker,	Arlington.
Albert Flagler, farmer.	Vassar College.
Sydney H. Austin, manufacturer,	Pokeepsie City.
John J. Hughes, merchant,	Wappingers Falls.
John McCann, manufacturer.	Wappingers Falls.
Daniel S. Baright, farmer,	Van Wagners.
Harvey H. Owen, hotel keeper,	Arlington.

POUGHKEEPSIE TOWN—Continued.

Charles Millard, merchant,	New Hamburgh.
George T. Klump, farmer,	Wappingers Falls.
P. A. M. Van Wyck, farmer,	New Hamburgh.
Wm. G. Ferris, agent,	New Hamburgh.
Benjamin P. Wayne, retired,	Wappingers Falls.
Daniel W. Jackson, farmer,	Wappingers Falls.
Clinton V. R. Jaycox, farmer,	Wappingers Falls.
James Sloane, gardener,	Pokeepsie City.

POUGHKEEPSIE CITY.

FIRST WARD.

Patrick McNulty, merchant,	Mill street.
Frank Cramer, laborer,	Bayeaux street.
John Corcoran, grocer,	Mill street.
Charles Murphy, "	Dutchess avenue.
Philip Mylod, merchant,	N. Bridge street.
Thomas F. Plunkett, clerk,	Albany street.
John Cosgrove, moulder,	Gifford avenue.
Matthew Heffernan, laborer,	Gifford avenue.
James Purcell, printer,	N. Bridge street.
Charles O'Connor, grocer,	Gifford avenue.
Timothy Haggerty, hotel,	Main street.
Patrick H. Ward, merchant,	Mill street.
William Maher, gardener,	N. Bridge street.
John Cahill, laborer,	Charles street.
John Mellady, undertaker,	Mill street.
John Pickett, painter.	N. Clover street.

SECOND WARD.

Seneca Lake, barber,	1 Bellevue avenue.
W. J. Wolff, hotel,	68 Church street.
M. V. B. Wetmore, painter,	2 Gate street.
J. W. Sky, hotel,	10 Gate street.
C. H. Bahret, salesman,	134 Main street.
W. H. Velie, salesman,	11 S. Clover street.
A. W. Moore, shoe dealer,	57 S. Clover street.
John H. Goetz, shoe dealer,	61 S. Clover street.

Grand Jurors. 113

W. H. Lapaugh, livery.
C. G. Bauman, hotel.
T. G. Kelly, grocer.
Jas. Carroll, butcher.
P. B. Cusack, shoe dealer.
Henry Winter, painter.
Val. Boecher, grocer.
Wm. Coffey, grocer.
Thos. McPartland, hotel.
Peter Becker, mason,

60 S. Clover street.
Main street.
Church street.
Jefferson street.
66 Church street.
Perry street.
Union street.
Union street.
Tulip street.
Perry street.

THIRD WARD.

James H. Ward, merchant.
Edwin L. Bushnell, manufacturer.
Peter Shields,
Wm. B. Carpenter, gentleman.
B. S. Bayly, merchant.
Isaac Marks, merchant.
Court B. Cunley, merchant.
Geo. W. Cluett, merchant.
Oliver S. Atkins, merchant,
Edgar C. Adriance, merchant.
Jas. Luckey, Jr., insurance agent.
Henry R. Hoyt, merchant.
Chas. L. Dates, merchant.

320 Mill street.
23 Washington st.
15 Mansion street.
305 Mill street.
283 Mill street.
329 Main street.
37 Marshall street.
217 Main st.
228 Mill street.
111 Garden street.
23 Marshall street.
18 Balding avenue.
265 Mill street.

FOURTH WARD.

E. B. Taylor, merchant.
J. R. Monfort, carpenter and builder.
C. C. Lansing, clerk.
J. I. Vail, builder.
Andrew Smith, confectioner.
H. J. Vail, liveryman.
Jas. E. Dorland, gentleman.
J. F. Hull, Jr., manufacturer.
Charles Joseph, clothier.
Jas. A. Thompson, merchant.
A. M. Doty, druggist.
Geo. W. Scott, liveryman.
Thos. Madden, gentleman.

FIFTH WARD.

William H. Sheldon, merchant,	Catharine street.
James H. Hickok, merchant,	Catharine street.
Charles J. Schwartz, merchant,	Catharine street.
Nelson J. Boyce, merchant,	Mansion square.
George Hughes, merchant,	Smith street.
Eliphalet P. Bogardus, bookkeeper,	Smith street.
Kernan Lawlor, teamster,	Bartlett street.
Wm. E. Gurney, teamster,	Harrison street.
Thomas Weaver, carman,	E. Mansion street.
Andrew J. Spencer, mason,	Harrison street.
Joseph D. Neal, builder,	Jewett street.
James E. Deyo, confectioner,	E Mansion street.
Oliver A. Green, builder,	N. Clinton street.
Charles E. Dobbs, merchant.	N. Clinton street.

SIXTH WARD.

Wm. M. Quintard, merchant.	S. Clinton street.
John Lyke. gentleman,	Montgomery street.
Franklin Sutton, insurance,	Academy street.
Peter B. Hayt, merchant,	Church street.
James E. Dutcher, ex-sheriff,	S. Clinton street.
Horace Sague, carriages,	S. Clinton street.
Samuel C. Chase, printer,	Church street.
Paul Flagler, gentleman,	S. Clinton street.
George Bartholomew, gentleman,	Church street.
Chas. P. Angel, gentleman,	Church street.
B. H. Trowbridge, merchant,	Church street.
James B. Platt, editor.	S. Hamilton st.
P. F. Spalding, broker.	S. Hamilton st.

RED HOOK.

Philip N. Stickles, farmer.	Upper Red Hook.
Robert Teator, farmer,	Upper Red Hook.
John A. Boice, farmer,	Upper Red Hook.
Olando P. Doyle farmer,	Upper Red Hook.
Andrew J. Gedney, merchant.	Red Hook.
John S Thompson, farmer,	Red Hook.

Andrew E. Teal, farmer,	Red Hook.
Edward Shook, farmer.	Red Hook.
Henry E Miller, gentleman,	Red Hook.
William Hass, farmer,	Annandale.
Clinton J. Rockefeller, farmer,	Madalin.
Charles Sturges, farmer.	Madalin.
Peter Rifenburgh, farmer.	Madalin.
Edward O Benton, farmer.	Madalin.
Henry Feller, merchant.	Madalin.
George Washington Fingar, gentleman,	Madalin.
Philip N. Potts, hotel keeper,	Madalin.

RHINEBECK.

John A. Traver, farmer.	Rhinebeck.
Philip J. Ackert, farmer,	Rhinebeck.
John P. Hermance, farmer,	Rhinebeck.
George Fellows, insurance.	Rhinebeck.
James H. Kipp, farmer.	Rhinebeck.
Wm. A. Traver, musician,	Rhinebeck.
Duncan Monroe, farmer.	Rhinebeck.
Egbert M. Haines, farmer,	Rhinebeck.
John M. Welch, farmer.	Rhinebeck.
Lewis A. Near, farmer.	Rhinebeck.
Francis Curnan, farmer,	Rhinebeck.
Mandeville S. Frost, farmer,	Rhinebeck.
Walter L. TenBroeck, farmer.	Rhinebeck.

STANFORD.

Robert Sutherland, farmer,	Bangall.
Nathan C. Sackett, farmer.	Bangall.
James E. Hammond, farmer.	Bangall.
Eugene Losee, farmer,	Bangall.
Almond M. Harrison, farmer.	Stanfordville.
Smith Knapp, farmer.	Willow Brook.
Frank Wilbur, farmer.	Stissing.

UNION VALE.

Charles B. Germond, farmer,	P. O. Verbank.
Wm. H. Van Wagner, farmer,	P. O. Billings.
Wm. G. Cox, farmer,	P. O. North Clove.
Geo. Diederick, blacksmith,	P. O. Clove.

WAPPINGER.

Clinton W. Clapp, mechanic.	Wappinger's Falls.
Samuel R. Brown, manufacturer,	Wappinger's Falls.
Thomas Stevenson, mechanic,	Wappinger's Falls.
Edmund Tanner, Justice of the Peace,	Hughsonville.
William Roe. farmer,	New Hackensack.
Alonzo Cole, mechanic,	Wappinger's Falls.
C. W. Hynell, merchant,	Wappinger's Falls.
George H. Abbott, mechanic,	Hughsonville.
John O'Farrell, mechanic,	Hughsonville.
James A. Redfield, merchant,	Wappinger's Falls.
Underhill Budd, farmer,	Wappinger's Falls.
Lewis Adams, farmer,	Hughsonville.
George Anderson, farmer,	New Hackensack.
Hiram Brownell, farmer,	Swartoutville.
John P. Conover, farmer,	Hughsonville.
John Owens, farmer,	New Hackensack.
W. H. H. Stoutenburgh, farmer,	New Hackensack.

WASHINGTON.

Sherman Haight, farmer,	Mabbettsville.
Edwin Clements, auctioneer,	Washington Hollow.
Eugene Ham, farmer,	Verbank.
John P. Anderson, farmer,	Washington.
John Ham, farmer,	Washington Hollow.
Stephen H. Cutler, farmer,	Mabbettsville.
Thomas Smith, farmer.	Millbrook.
Lewis D. Germond, farmer.	Verbank Village.
Myot D. Andrews, farmer.	Mabbettsville.
Henry Shaw, liveryman,	Millbrook.
Stephen Robison, farmer,	Lithgow.

LIST OF INCORPORATED COMPANIES.

A STATEMENT of the names of the several Incorporated Companies liable to taxation in the County of Dutchess, the amount of Real and Personal Estate belonging to each, as the same is set down in the Assessment Rolls, which have been sanctioned by the Board of Supervisors of said County, and the amount of tax assessed upon each in the year 1890.

Towns.	Name of Corporations,	Amount of Real Estate.	Am't of stock taxable, deducting real estate.	Total Valuation.	Amount of Tax.
Amenia......	First National Bank,	$ 5,000	$ 100,000	$ 105,000	$ 871 50
	Amenia Mining Co.,	25,550		25,550	211 65
	N. Y. C. & H. R. R. Co ,	178,000		178,000	1,477 40
	New England Telephone Co.,	165		165	1 37
	Commercial Union Telegraph Co.,	1,420		1,420	11 79
	Postal Telegraph Co.,				
	Western Union Telegraph Co.,	3,738		3,738	31 03
	Sharon Valley Iron Co.,	1,605		1,605	13 32
	New York Condensed Milk Co.,	37,600		37,600	312 08
Beekman.....	Clove Spring I. W. & Dutchess Furnace.	16,000		6,000	48 00
	Clove Branch R. R. Co.	6,000		6,000	48 00
	N. Y. Boston & Montreal R. R. Co.	16,000		16,000	128 00
	N. Y. & New England R. R. Co.,	55,000		55,000	440 00
	Pawling & Beekman Turnpike Co.,	2,000		2,000	16 00

LIST OF INCORPORATED COMPANIES—Continued.

Town	Company				
Beekman	Western Union Telegraph Co.,	425		425	3 40
	American Rapid Telegraph Co.,	1,235		1,235	9 86
Clinton	Western Union Telegraph Co.,	320		320	1 92
	Mutual Union Telegraph Co.,	462		462	2 77
	American Rapid Telegraph Co.,	639		639	3 84
	New York & Mass. R. R. Co.,	11,000		11,000	66 00
	Po'keepsie & Connecting R. R. Co.,	11,666		11,666	70 00
Dover	Dover Plains National Bank,		100,000	100,000	720 00
	Clove Spring Iron Works,	126		126	91
	Dover Furnace Iron Works,	4,600		4,600	33 12
	Western Union Telegraph Co.,	3,281		3,281	23 63
	New York Cen. & Harlem R. R. Co.,	189,200		189,200	1,362 24
East Fishkill	New York & New England R. R. Co.,	93,750		93,750	675 00
	Newburgh, Dutchess & Conn. R. R. Co.,	66,450		66,450	473 37
	Clove Branch R. R. Co.,	9,881		9,881	71 15
	American Rapid Telegraph Co.,	880		880	6 34
	Western Union Telegraph Co.,	1,092		1,092	7 86
	Mutual Union Telegraph Co.,	2,035		2,035	14 66
	American Telegraph and Telephone Co.,	4,494		4,494	32 36
Fishkill	First National Bank,	6,000	85,000	91,000	855 40
	New York Cen. & H. R. R. R. Co.,	374,250		374,250	5,373 73
	New York & New England R. R. Co.,	60,000		60,000	709 70
	New York Rubber Co.,	55,000	120,000	175,000	2,170 00
	Matteawan Manufacturing Co.,	5,000	55,000	60,000	704 00
	Fishkill Landing Machine Co.,	35,000	20,000	55,000	517 00

LIST OF INCORPORATED COMPANIES—Continued.

Towns.	Name of Corporation.	Amount of Real Estate.	Am't of stock tax, deducting real estate.	Total Valuation.	Amount of Tax.
Fishkill......	Western Union Telegraph Co.,	$ 1,690		$ 1,690	$ 21 13
	Hudson River Telephone Co.,	5,000		5,000	61 88
	Fishkill Ld. & Matteawan Water Co.,	46,000		46,000	661 30
	Fishkill Boot & Shoe Co.,	2,500		2,500	23 50
	Fishkill Landing & Matteawan Gas Co.,	6,000		6,000	56 40
Hyde Park..	Newburgh, Dutchess & Conn. R. R. Co.,	48,450		48,450	716 28
	N. Y. C. & H. R. R. R. Co.,	559,550		559,550	3,357 30
	Knickerbocker Ice Co.,	10,000		10,000	60 00
	Mutual Benefit Ice Co.,	6,000	$ 15,000	21,000	126 00
	Mutual Union Telegraph Co.,	2,940		2,940	17 64
	American Rapid Telegraph Co.,	5,507		5,507	33 04
	Western Union Telegraph Co.,	2,486		2,486	14 92
	Central N. E. & Western R. R. Co.,	750		750	4 50
La Grange...	Newburgh, Dutchess & Conn. R. R. Co.,	48,145		48,145	351 31
	Mutual Union Telegraph Co.,	587		587	4 29
	Western Union Telegraph Co.,	110		110	80
	Hudson River Telephone Co.,	637		637	4 65
Milan	American Telephone & Telegraph Co.,	3,375		3,375	24 63
	Hartford & Conn, Western R. R. Co.,	38,887		38,887	349 98

LIST OF INCORPORATED COMPANIES—Continued.

Town	Company				Tax
Milan..........	Western Union Telegraph Co.,	1,075		1,075	9 68
North East....	Millerton National Bank,	61,000		61,000	536 80
	Millerton Iron Co.,	32,156		32,156	385 87
	Hartford and Conn. Western R. R. Co.,	74,350		74,350	874 28
	New York Cen. and Harlem R. R. Co.,	180,000		180,000	2,064 00
	Newburgh, Dutchess & Conn. R. R. Co.,	37,660		37,660	441 92
	Riga Mining Co.,	8,000		8,000	96 00
	Southern N. E. Telephone Co.,	285		285	3 46
	Western Union Telegraph Co.,	6,016		6,016	69 87
	Commercial Telegraph Co.,	2,400		2,400	28 80
	Laflin & Rand Magazine Co.,	100		100	88
Pawling......	Pawling National Bank,		250,300	250,340	1,877 25
	Postal Telegraph Co.,	1,040		1,040	7 80
	Hudson River Telephone Co.,	552		552	4 14
	Western Union Telegraph Co.,	2,936		2,936	22 02
	Pawling and Beekman Turnpike Co.,	2,250		2,250	16 85
	New York & N. E. R. R. Co.,	52,500		52,500	393 75
	New York Cen. & Harlem R. R. Co.,	135,860		135,860	1,018 95
	National Mining Co.,	3,000		3,000	22 50
	Mizzen Top Co., (Limited),	30,000		30,000	225 00
	Clove Spring Iron Works,	360		360	2 70
Pine Plains..	Stissing National Bank,		90,000	90,000	567 00
	Western Union Telegraph Co.,	1,140		1,140	7 10
	New York & Mass. R. R. Co.,	15,973		15,973	100 63
	Hartford & Conn. Western R. R. Co.,	13,040		13,040	82 15

LIST OF INCORPORATED COMPANIES—Continued.

Towns.	Name and Corporation.	Amount of Real Estate.	Am't of stock taxable, deducting real estate.	Total Valuation.	Amount of Tax.
Pine Plains...	Newburgh, Dutchess & Conn. R. R. Co.,	$ 66,629		$ 66,629	$ 419 76
	Central N. E. & Western R. R. Co.,	91,062		91,062	573 69
Pleas. Vall'y.	New York & Mass. R. R. Co.,	40,725		40,725	325 80
	Central N. E. & Western R.R. Co.,	67,500		67,500	540 00
	Western Union Telegraph Co.,	3,030		3,030	24 24
Po'k Town..	New York Cen. & H. R. R. R. Co.,	297,000		297,000	3,861 03
	Dutchess Company,	80,470		80,470	1,042 54
	Mutual Telegraph Co.,	1,458		1,458	18 96
	American Telegraph & Telephone Co.,	1,136		1,136	14 78
	New York & Mass. R. R. Co.,	5,750		5,750	78 74
	Phœnix Horse Shoe Co.,	30,000		30,000	390 00
	Central N. E. & Western R. R. Co.,	3,750		3,750	48 75
	Poughkeepsie Horse R. R. Co.,	1,000		1,000	13 00
Po'k City...	Fallkill Lodge, I. O. of O. F.,	4,500		4,500	23 40
	Fallkill Iron Works.	90,200	$ 35,000	125,200	651 04
	Hudson River Boot and Shoe Co.,	19,000	31,000	50,000	260 00
	Knickerbocker Ice Co.,	6,500		6,50	33 80
	New York Cen. & H. R. R. R. Co.,	318,900		318,900	1,658 28
	New York & Mass. R. R. Co.,	15,100		15,100	78 52

LIST OF INCORPORATED COMPANIES—Continued.

Po'k City...	Poughkeepsie City R. R. Co.,	12,800	50,000	17,800	30 89
	Poughkeepsie Lodge, I. O. of O. F.,	13,000		13,000	67 60
	Poughkeepsie Transportation Co.,	63,000	25,000	88,000	399 27
	Poughkeepsie Gas Light Co.,	69,000	25,000	94,000	430 47
	Poughkeepsie Savings Bank,	79,700		79,700	414 44
	Poughkeepsie Glass Works,	20,000	37,000	57,000	206 40
	Po'keepsie Electric Light & Power Co.,	6,300	40,000	46,300	147 43
	Poughkeepsie Steam Cooperage Mfg.Co.	5,500	2,000	7,500	39 00
	Poughkeepsie Bridge Co.,	246,500		246,500	1,281 80
	New York Life Insurance Co.,	11,500		11,500	
	City National Bank,	10,500	105,000	115,500	600 60
	Farmers & Manufacturers National Bk.,	14,000	230,000	244,000	1,268 80
	First National Bank,		115,000	115,000	598 00
	Fallkill National Bank,	17,500	400,000	417,500	2,171 00
	Poughkeepsie National Bank,	18,000	165,000	183,000	951 60
	Merchants National Bank,	28,000	250,250	278,250	1,446 90
	Dutchess Mutual Ins. Co.,	5,000		5,000	26 00
Red Hook...	First National Bank,	5,000	145,000	150,000	840 00
	Western Union Telegraph Co.,	3,570		3,590	19 99
	Cheney Towing Co.		100,000	100,000	560 00
	American Telegraph & Telephone Co.,	3,391		3,391	18 99
	New York Cen. & H. R. R. Co.,	455,000		455,000	2,548 00
	Hartford & Conn. Western R. R. Co.,	72,696		72,696	407 10
	Mutual Benefit Ice Co.,	67,700		67,700	379 12
Rhinebeck...	New York Cen. & H. R. R. R. Co.,	487,120		487,120	3,409 84

LIST OF INCORPORATED COMPANIES—Continued.

Towns.	Name and Corporation.	Amount of Real Estate.	Am't of stock taxable, deducting real estate.	Total Valuation.	Amount of Tax
Rhinebeck ..	Rhinebeck & Kingston Ferry Co.,	$ 25,000		$ 25,000	$ 175 00
	Rhinebeck Gas Co.,	5,000		5,000	35 00
	Hartford & Conn. Western R. R. Co.,	94,750		94,750	663 25
	Knickerbocker Ice Co.,	14,000		14,000	98 00
	Western Union Telegraph Co.,	2,155		2,155	15 09
	Mutual Union Telegraph Co.,	1,760		1,760	12 32
	American Union Telegraph Co.,	977		977	6 84
	Hudson River Telephone Co.,	1,540		1,540	10 78
	Rhinebeck Savings Bank,	7,000		7,000	49 00
	Rhinebeck Mining Co.,	3,051		3,051	21 36
	First National Bank,	7,000	$ 125,000	132,000	924 00
Stanford	Newburgh, Dutchess & Conn. R. R. Co.,	75,400		75,400	542 88
	New York & Mass. R. R. Co.,	75,050		75,050	540 36
	Central N. E. & Western R. R. Co.,	172,523		172,523	1,242 16
	Western Union Telegraph Co.,	1,905		2,345	16 89
Union Vale..	Newburgh, Dutchess & Conn. R. R. Co.,	14 000		14,000	114 80
	Western Union Telegraph Co,	112		112	92
	Bankers and Merchants Telegraph Co.,	1,800		1,800	14 76
Wappinger...	New York Cen. & H. R. R. R. Co.,	152,250		152,250	983 54

LIST OF INCORPORATED COMPANIES— Continued.

Wappinger..	Western Union Telegraph Co.,	582	582	3 76
	Mutual Union Telegraph Co.	1,108	1,108	7 06
	I. O. of O. F.,	3,500	3,500	24 80
	Dutchess Company.	399,204	399,204	2,475 07
	Clinton Company,	190,650	190,650	1,182 03
	Franklindale Company,	6,000	6,000	37 20
Washington..	Newburgh, Dutchess & Conn. R. R. Co.,	50,000	50,000	390 00
	Bankers & Merchants Telegraph Co.,	1,450	1,450	11 31
	Western Union Telegraph Co.	500	500	3 90
				$69,226 03

TABULAR STATEMENT OF TAXES OF 1890,

in and for the County of Dutchess, New York, and the apportionment of the same to the several Towns and City therein.

TOWNS.	Town Allowances.	Roads and Bridges.	School Commissioners.	School Tax.	State Tax with School Tax.	General County Tax.	County Tax Exclusive the City.
Amenia	3,713 54	$250 00	$15 06	$1,609 00	$3,619 00	$4,350 46	$584 00
Beekman	1,451 33	250 00	7 58	797 00	1,793 00	2,155 54	289 64
Clinton	684 79		14 44	995 40	2,239 00	2,692 16	361 68
Dover	1,734 70		11 86	1,239 00	2,786 09	3,349 89	459 00
East Fishkill	2,033 08	250 00	12 56	1,322 00	2,974 19	3,575 17	480 23
Fishkill	23,851 75	4,000 00	48 47	5,074 00	11,415 00	13,721 36	1,842 81
Hyde Park	1,521 30	877 30	32 14	2,226 00	5,007 40	6,019 25	808 38
La Grange	1,144 67	250 00	11 37	1,182 70	2,661 00	3,198 68	429 69
Milan	1,627 75	250 00	8 85	620 35	1,395 00	1,677 25	225 43
North East	834 46	2,717 09	15 40	1,610 00	3,681 00	4,352 39	584 58
Pawling	3,843 02		15 05	1,584 38	3,564 00	4,284 12	575 41
Pine Plains	1,307 15	250 00	8 38	875 00	1,968 00	2,364 87	317 75
Pleasant Valley	2,620 05	250 00	16 25	1,135 60	2,555 00	9,071 00	412 53
Poughkeepsie Town	4,845 81	3,500 00	41 06	2,853 00	6,418 46	7,714 91	1,086 43
Poughkeepsie City	841 44			13,972 70	31,451 30	38,071 91	
Red Hook	3,417 83	250 00	45 80	3,172 70	7,137 00	8,579 17	1,152 42
Rhinebeck	8,055 66	250 00	41 46	2,861 40	6,437 00	7,737 07	1,039 36
Stanford	3,445 18		13 60	1,431 00	3,221 00	3,872 82	520 07
Union Vale	1,440 58	250 00	6 45	668 00	1,501 50	1,804 91	242 56
Wappinger	3,519 97	250 00	18 70	2,019 00	4,544 00	5,462 12	733 68
Washington	3,142 95		15 52	1,639 00	3,680 00	4,428 91	394 17
	$75,077 01	$13,844 39	$400 00	$45,883 53	$109,987 94	$182,478 96	$12,681 05

TOWNS.	Surplus 1889.	Deficiency 1889.	Total Tax.	Surplus 1890.	Deficiency 1890.	Tax List includ'ing Surplus & Deficiencies.	Ratio in Mills.
Amenia		$120 76	$12,403 15	$84 78		$12,487 96	8.3
Beekman		42 36	5,989 45	6 43		5,995 88	8.-
Clinton		3 42	6,245 49	53 14		6,298 63	6.
Dover		54 36	8,380 90		$44 68	8,342 22	7.2
East Fishkill		20 34	9,345 57	10 47		9,356 04	7.2
Fishkill		421 41	55,300 80		469 99	54,832 91	9.4
Hyde Park	$ 14	21 65	14,287 42		44 55	14,242 87	6.
LaGrange			7,695 27	13 16		7,708 43	7.3
Milan	2 40	11 65	5,195 93		11 86	5,184 07	9.
North East	72 51		12,122 52	29 10		12,151 62	8.8
Pawling			12,209 09	40 85		12,249 94	7.5
Pine Plains		13 57	6,229 72	52 51		6,282 23	6.3
Pleasant Valley		27 12	8,951 95	11 48		8,963 43	8.
Poughkeepsie Town	286 11	119 68	23,676 35	82 96		23,759 37	10.9
Poughkeepsie City		142 29	70,506 94		356 87	70,150 07	5.2
Red Hook			20,296 11	84 32		20,380 43	5.6
Rhinebeck		205 86	23,766 41		92 80	23,673 61	7.
Stanford	186 85	26 31	11,098 98		41 42	11,058 56	7.2
Union Vale			5,039 15		11 99	5,027 16	8.2
Wappinger	55 21	25 95	14,554 32	69 91		14,624 13	6 20-100
Washington			11,801 34		39 41	11,761 93	7.8
	$603 22	$1,256 73	$345,102 86	$539 11	$1,110 97	$344,531 49	

SUPERVISORS' PAY ROLL.

TOWNS.	NAMES.	No of Days.	No of Miles.	Footing Tax Roll.	Amount.
Amenia	Wm. H. Bartlett	26	216	$13 38	$108 66
Beekman	Kromline Andrews	26	176	7 84	99 92
Clinton	Edward Herrick	26	80	10 52	94 92
Dover	Sheldon Wing	26	280	13 00	111 60
East Fishkill	Isaac S. Genung	27	140	12 78	101 98
Fishkill	Samuel B. Rogers	26	128	32 80	124 02
Hyde Park	D. E. Howatt	26	38	11 76	93 56
La Grange	Wm. H. Austin	26	144	8 42	97 94
Milan	Cyrus F. Morehouse	26	112	8 21	95 17
North East	John Scutt	26	180	14 90	107 30
Pawling	Geo. F. Lee	26	288	17 34	118 38
Pine Plains	John A. Herrick	26	120	8 00	95 60
Pleasant Valley	E. Wright Vail	26	44	10 16	91 68
Pokeepsie Town	A. B. Gray	27	16	15 76	95 04
Pokeepsie City, 1st Ward	John J. Mylod	26			81 00
" 2d "	Wm. H. Krieger	26			78 00
" 3d "	Guilford Dudley	26			78 00
" 4th "	Chas. W. Swift	26		63 26	141 26
" 5th "	F. W. Pugsley	26			78 00
" 6th "	Chas. Williams	26			78 00
Red Hook	Edward Sturgess	26	120	17 39	104 99
Rhinebeck	John C. Milroy	26	80	15 22	99 62
Stanford	Chas. H. Humphrey	15	80	9 55	60 95
Union Vale	John U. Able	26	150	9 51	99 51
Wappinger	Geo. Wood	26	36	14 42	95 90
Washington	Lewis D. Germond	26	172	10 76	102 52
				324 98	253 52

STATE OF NEW YORK, }
COUNTY OF DUTCHESS. } ss :

I, Smith Heroy, of the Board of Supervisors of the County of Dutchess, do hereby certify that the foregoing is a correct statement of the Proceedings of the Board of Supervisors of said County. of the Equalization of the Assessment Rolls of the several towns in said County and the City of Poughkeepsie, and also contains the names of every person who has had any account or claim audited by said Board during and for the year ending December 31, 1890, and the amount asked and the amount allowed thereon.

Dated, Poughkeepsie, N. Y., February 20, 1891.

SMITH HEROY,
Clerk of the Board of Supervisors.

ABSTRACT OF FEES.

ABSTRACT OF FEES.

Revised 1887.

References to Revised Statutes to Seventh Edition of Same.

No Town Officer shall be allowed any per diem compensation for his services unless expressly provided by law.

1st Revised Statutes. 845, §23.

No account shall be audited by any Board of Town Auditors, Supervisors or Superintendents of the Poor, for any services or disbursements unless such account shall be made out in items, and accompanied with an affidavit attached to and be filed with such account, made by the person presenting or claiming the same, that the items of such accounts are correct, and that the disbursements and services charged therein, have been in fact made or rendered, or necessary to be made or rendered, at that session of the board, and stating that no part thereof has been paid or satisfied.

1st Revised Statutes, 845, § 24.

§ 25. Nothing in the preceeding section shall be construed to prevent any such Board from disallowing any account in whole or in part when so rendered and verified, nor from requiring any other or further evidence of the truth and propriety thereof as such Board may think proper.

1st Revised Statutes, page 846, § 25.

All accounts presented in any year to the Board of Supervisors of any County shall be numbered from one up in the order in which they are presented, and a memoranda of the time of presenting the same, of the names of the persons in whose favor they shall be made out, and by whom they shall be presented, shall be entered in the minutes of the Board, to which they shall be presented, and no such account after being so presented shall be withdrawn from the custody of the Board or its Clerk for any purpose whatever, except to be used in evidence upon a judicial trial or proceeding, and in such case it shall, after being so used, be forthwith returned to such custody.

1st Revised Statutes, page 846, § 28.

ASSESSORS.

[Town Charge.]

Shall receive for each day's services performed by each............... $2 00

Laws of 1870, Chapter 252, § 2.
2d Revised Statutes, page 1218, § 3.

AS FENCE VIEWERS.

[Town Charge.]

For services in examining and certifying in relation to sheep killed or injured by dogs, per day........................ .... $2 00

Laws of 1870, Chapter 242, § 2.
Laws of 1864, Chapter 197, §§ 3, 4 and 7.

[Individual Charge.]

For services in relation to division fences, each day...................... $1 50

Laws of 1866, Chapter 450, § 43.

FOR SERVICES IN RELATION TO STRAYS.

For certificate of damages.. 25
For every mile he shall be obliged to travel from his house to
   where the strays are kept, to be paid by owner of strays....... 06
   For service in relation to floating timber, etc., no fees prescribed by
Revised Statutes, but expense to be paid by owner of timber.
   Chapter 242, Laws of 1870, has sometimes been supposed to apply to
services as fence viewers, but it is doubtful.

1st Revised Statutes, page 830, § 22.

For meeting state assessors, county charge, per day and travel fees. $2 00

CLERK OF BOARD OF SUPERVISORS.

Is entitled to a reasonable compensation, to be fixed by the Board.
For a certified copy of every account on file in his office, for every
   folio of one hundred and twenty-eight words........................ 06

2d Revised Statutes, page 927, § 12.

CLERK OF THE POLLS.

[Town Charge.]

Shall receive for each day's service performed by each............ ..... $2 00

Laws of 1870, chapter 242, § 2.
1st Revised Statutes, page 839, § 1.

COLLECTOR OF TAXES.

For collecting and receiving taxes within thirty days from
posting notices required by law...................................1 per cent.
For all taxes collected after expiration of said thirty days......5 per cent.
For all unpaid taxes returned to County Treasurer, to be paid
by the County Treasurer............ ....2 per cent.

Laws of 1876, chapter 96.
1st Revised Statutes, pages 846, 847 and 850, § 16.

[County charge.]

Settling with County Treasurer, per day. $2 00
Settling with County Treasurer, per mile, going only.................. 08

[Town charge.]

Collecting dog tax................... ....10 per cent.
Killing any dog when required by law... .... $1 00

COMMISSIONERS OF EXCISE.

[Town charge.]

For each day......... .... $3 00

Laws of 1874, chapter 444.
3d Revised Statutes, page 1991.

COMMISSIONERS OF HIGHWAYS.

[Town charge.]

For each day actually and necessarily spent in discharge of official
duty.. .... $2 00

Laws of 1870, chapter 242, § 1.
2d Revised Statutes, page 1218, § 2.

6   *Abstract of Fees.*

AS FENCE VIEWERS.

(See Assessors.)

COMMISSIONERS FOR LOANING MONEY OF U. S.

May retain out of the interest of the moneys committed to their charge respectively in each and every year :

Upon $25,000 or a less sum... ....¼ of 1 per cent.
Upon a further sum of $25,000 or less................ ....½ of 1 per cent.
Preparing notices of sale and services............ .... $5 00
If paid before sale, all disbursements, etc............... .... 2 00

1st Revised Statutes, page 514, § 18.

CONSTABLES' SERVICES IN CRIMINAL CASES.

For serving warrants (if an arrest is made). 1 Denio, 658............. 75
For every mile travelled, going and returning.................... 10
For taking defendant into custody on mittimus........................ 25
For every mile travelled in taking a prisoner to jail, going and returning 10
For taking charge of a jury........................ 50
For attending court pursuant to notice from sheriff, for each day.. 2 00
For each mile travelled, going to and returning, from such court, payable by county treasurer, on clerk's certificate, &c.. (and mileage as allowed by law to trial jurors in courts of record). Code, §3312, as amended in 1881.
For serving every subpœna........................ 25
For every mile travelled in serving each subpœna, going and returning ...... (5

§ 1. Such officer shall be allowed for mileage only for the distance going and returning, actually travelled to make such service upon all the witnesses in such case of complaint, and not separate mileage for each witness, unless the Board of Supervisors auditing accounts for such services shall deem it equitable to make a further allowance.

3d Revised Statutes, page 2580.

For notifying complainant........................ 25
For every mile travelled in notifying complainant, going and returning ...... (5
For keeping a prisoner after being brought before a justice and by his direction in custody, per day........................ 1 00

3d Revised Statutes, page 2585.

The Board of Supervisors may allow such further compensation for the services of process, and the expense and trouble attending the same, as they shall deem reasonable.

CORONERS.

[County Charge.]

Mileage to place of inquest and return, per mile.................................. $	10
Summoning and attendance upon jury..	3 00
Viewing body...	5 00
Serving a subpœna, per mile travelled..	10
Swearing each witness...	15
Drawing inquisition for jurors to sign...	1 00
Copying inquisition for record, per folio, one copy only.............................	25
For making and transmitting statement to Board of Supervisors, each inquisition..	50
For warrant of commitment..	1 00
For arrest and examination of offenders, same as Justice of the Peace in like cases..	
Shall receive for each day and fractional part thereof spent in taking an inquisition, except for one day's service..............................	3 00
For taking an anti-mortem statement, per day, and fractional part thereof...	3 00
Mileage to and from the place, per mile...	10
For taking deposition of injured persons in extremis..............................	1 00
When, in consequence of the performance of official duties, he becomes a witness in a criminal proceeding, he shall be entitled to receive mileage to and from place of residence, per mile....	10
For each day, or fractional part thereof, actually detained as such witness..	3 00

Shall be reimbursed for all moneys actually and necessarily paid out by him in the discharge of official duties, may, when necessary, employ not more than two competent surgeons to make post-mortem examinations and dissections. Compensation, county charge.

3d Revised Statutes, pages 2586, 2587.

When required to perform duties of Sheriff, same fees as Sheriff in like cases.

Code of Civil Proceedure, § 3310.

CORONER'S JURY.

FEES OF.

[County Charge.]

For each day's service, not to exceed, per day............................ $1 00

3d Revised Statutes, page 2586, § 4.

COUNTY CANVASSERS.

(See " Supervisors " and " County Clerk.")

COUNTY CLERK.

AS CLERK OF BOARD OF CANVASSERS.

[County Charge.]

For attendance in canvassing the vote given at an election.......... $2 00
For drawing all necessary certificates of the result of such canvass,
    for each folio.. 18
For every copy, per folio... 09
For recording such certificate, per folio................................ 10

Code, § 3304.

AS CLERK OF COURTS OF OYER AND TERMINER AND COURT OF SESSIONS.

[County Charge.]

For swearing a witness...$ 06
For entering or respiting a recognizance................................ 12½
For calling and swearing a jury... 19
For entering a sentence in the minutes kept by him..................... 12½
For every certified copy thereof.. 12½
For a transcript thereof for the Secretary of State..................... 12½

3d Revised Statutes, page 2579.

For necessary expenses which he may incur in purchase of books
    for indices..
For entering name in general indices of deeds and mortgages, for
    every one hundred names.. 50

3d Revised Statutes, page 2223, § 2.

For renewing records on order of necessity, reasonable compensation,
not to exceed amount certified by County Court.

2d Revised Statutes, 939, § 7.

For duties under census laws, reasonable compensation, audited by Board of Supervisors.

1st Revised Statutes, page 267, § 4.

SERVICES FOR WHICH COMPENSATION IS DISCRETIONARY.

[County Charge.]

The following services are required by various statutes. No fees being prescribed by law therefor, the compensation is a reasonable sum, to be fixed and determined by the Board of Supervisors :

For writing, folding and depositing in a box the names of grand and petit jurors.

In giving notice of drawing juries and publishing the same.

For serving notice on Sheriff and County Judge of drawing juries.

For drawing juries and making list, and delivering to sheriff.

For drawing additional petit jurors on order of the court and making lists thereof.

For receiving and transmitting the duplicate census returns to the Secretary of State.

For arranging, binding and preserving the original census returns.

For swearing justices of the peace.

For giving notice of supervisor of the neglect of justice of the peace to file oath of office.

For transmitting to the Secretary of State statistical information concerning convicts.

For transmitting to the Comptroller the names of all religious societies that were incorporated in the preceding year.

For reporting to district attorney all omissions of town officers to make and transmit returns and certificates, which, by law, they are required to make to such clerk.

For approving the bond of coroner, acting as sheriff.

For approving the bond of surrogate.

For delivering to sheriff copy of order for defaulting juror to show cause.

For delivering to sheriff copy of any person to jail.

For delivering to sheriff copy of sentence of any person to state prison.

For making and printing calendar of causes for courts.

For making a return to a writ of error or certiorari.

For issuing subpœnas to defendants in criminal cases.

For witnessing and certifying the execution of the death penalty.

For making index to books of record and collectors' bonds.

For making certificates for pay of jurors and other officers for attendance at court.

For delivering notice of election to supervisor or assessor.

For causing same to be published.

COUNTY JUDGE AND SURROGATE.

Salary, of, in Dutchess County, paid by County Treasurer quarterly, $2,000

Laws of 1887, chapter 401, § 35.

2d Revised Statutes, page 973, §§ 3 and 4.

A county judge of one county holding a county court or presiding at a court of sessions of another county, shall be paid for his expenses by the county treasurer of such other county the sum of, per day.. $3 00

Provided that such compensation shall be paid only in case of the sickness or disability of the county judge of the county in which such court is held.

CRIER OF COURTS.

[County Charge.]

For each day's attendance at any court of sessions or oyer and terminer,.............................. .... $3 00

For traveling expenses going to and returning from said courts, per mile.. 05

3d Revised Statutes, page 239, 6th edition.

Code, § 91.

IN COURTS OF OYER AND TERMINER.

For calling a jury.. 12¼

For calling and swearing a witness... 06

For making proclamation for the discharge of any person 06

For calling any person on recognizance.. 06

3d Revised Statutes, page 2578, § 5.

FENCE VIEWERS.

(See Assessors.)

GAME CONSTABLE.

Same compensation as is allowed by law to constables of towns, and also one-half of penalties recovered by him, and if he fails to recover on any suit the county shall pay costs of suit.

3d Revised Statutes, page 2108, § 28.

INSPECTORS OF ELECTION.
[Town charge.]

For each day's service performed by each............................ . $2 00
For filing duplicate returns in County Clerk's offices................. 5 00
Travel fee, going and returning, per mile............................. 04
    1st Revised Statutes, pages 408 and 839.

JUSTICES OF THE PEACE.
SERVICES IN CRIMINAL CASES.

For administering an oath..$ 10
Warrant... 25
Bonds in recognizance.. 25
Subpoena, including all names inserted therein...................... 25
Commitment for want of bail.. 25
Examination of the accused where such examination is required
  by law, for each day necessarily spent............................ 1 00
Every necessary adjournment of the hearing or examination....... 25
    3d Revised Statutes, page 2584, § 3.

AS COURT OF SPECIAL SESSIONS.
[Town charge.]

For venire...$ 25
Swearing each witness on the trial................................ 10
Swearing a jury.. 25
Swearing Constable to attend jury................................. 10
Subpoena, including all names inserted therein..................... 25
Trial fee, per day, during actual and necessary continuance of the
  trial... 1 00
Receiving and entering verdict of jury............................ 25
Entering sentence of the Court.................................... 25
Warrant of commitment on sentence................................ 25
Record of conviction, and filing the same......................... 75
But all such charges, in any one case, unless the Court continues
  more than one day, shall not exceed............................. 5 00
In such case, the Court of each additional day may be added thereto.

Return to writ of certiorari, to be paid by the county.............. 2 00
For services when associated with another Justice in case of Bas-
  tardy, for each day actually and necessarily spent............... 2 00
    Code, § 3322.
    3d Revised Statutes, page 2585, § 4.

AS JUSTICE OF SESSIONS.

[County charge.]

For each day's attendance at Oyer and Terminer and Court of Sessions. $3 00

Mileage going and returning, per mile. 05

Laws of 1859, chapter 496.
3d Revised Statutes, page 2365, § 2.

SERVICES FOR TOWN.

For each day employed............. .... 2 00

2d Revised Statutes, page 1218, § 3 sub. 1.

IN HIGHWAY CASES.

For swearing jury in case of proceedings to lay out or alter a highway, paid by applicant. 2 00

Code, § 3322.

OVERSEER OF THE POOR.

[Town charge.]

For each day's service performed............. .... 2 00

2d Revised Statutes, page 1218.

PHYSICIANS.

SERVICES AT INQUEST.

[County charge.]

Reasonable compensation.

Laws of 1868, chapter 833, § 2.
Laws of 1874, chapter 535.
3d Revised Statutes, page 1053.

AT POOR HOUSE.

Reasonable compensation audited by Superintendent of the Poor.

AT JAIL.

Compensation allowed by the Board of Supervisors.

3d Revised Statutes, page 715.

PRINTERS.

For publishing any matter required by law, except session laws and election notices, to be published, not more for first insertion than, per folio.................................... 75

For each subsequent insertion, per folio................................... 50

Code, § 3317.

ELECTION NOTICES.

Election notices and official canvass to be published in not to exceed two papers, and when in two to be of opposite politics, and compensation to be fixed by Board of Supervisors.

1st Revised Statutes, page 878.

SESSION LAWS.

Compensation fixed by the Board of Supervisors, not to exceed, per folio.. 50

Code, § 3317.
See Laws 1887, Chap. 443.

SCHOOL COMMISSIONERS.

Salary payable quarterly by the State Treasurer from free school fund............................... ....$800 00

The Board of Supervisors shall annually audit and allow to each commissioner within the county the fixed sum for his expenses of............................... .... 200 00

2d Revised Statutes, page 1145, § 9.

SHERIFF.

IN CRIMINAL AND OTHER CASES.

[State Charge.]

For conveying a single convict to the State prison, for each mile from the county prison from which the convict shall be conveyed............................... .... $ 20

For conveying two convicts, for each mile. 35

For conveying three convicts, for each mile, each................... 12

3d Revised Statutes, page 2587.

For executing a requisition of the Governor in any other State, a reasonable sum per diem and actual expense, audited by the Comptroller.

3d Revised Statutes, page 1047.

A reasonable compensation for the following services :

Arresting fugitive from justice from another State, paid by such State.

Serving Comptroller's notification upon debtors of the State.

Serving subpœnas of canal board, canal commissioners and canal appraisers.

For making a return of conviction to Secretary of State (county charge.)

Crocker on Sheriffs, pages 480, 481.

Any service rendered for the people of the State, or for their benefit, and not otherwise provided for, a State charge, and audited by Comptroller.

2d Revised Statutes, page 967.

[County Charge.]

For every person committed to prison.. 37½

For every person discharged from prison............................. .... 37½

For conveying juvenile delinquents to House of Refuge, and lunatics to insane asylums, such compensation as shall be fixed and determined by the Board of Supervisors, which compensation shall be fixed annually.

3d Revised Statutes, page 2579, § 11.

IN DUTCHESS COUNTY.

For summoning a grand jury...$10 00

For performing any duty which may be performed by a constable, same fee as constable. (See " Constable.")

3d Revised Statutes, page 2579, § 11.

For returning the precept for the Oyer and Terminer....... .... 12¼

For returning the jury lists each................................. .... 12½

Crocker on Sheriffs, page 483.

For the following services, required by various statutes, the compensation is in the discretion of the Board of Supervisors, and a county charge :

People vs. Supervisors, etc., 12 Wend, 257.

For proclamation of courts.

For attending upon the drawing of a grand and petit jury.

For summoning petit jury in criminal cases.

For execution of the death penalty.

For summoning county officers, physicians and jury to witness execution of death penalty.

For necessary expense of execution.

For preparing statements of prisoners in jail for District Attorney.

For preparing calendar of prisoners in jail for courts of Oyer and Terminer and Sessions.

For any service required by law for which no fee is prescribed, he is entitled to a reasonable compensation under a decision of People vs. Supervisors, 12 Wend. 257.

For board of prisoners, paupers and transient persons, per day....... 50

Proceedings of the Board of Supervisors, 1883.

For bringing up a prisoner upon a writ of habeas corpus to inquire into the cause of detention.. 1 50

And for traveling to and from the jail, for each mile.................. 12

For bringing up a prisoner upon any other writ of habeas corpus, the same fees ; and for attending the court or judge thereupon, each day.. 1 00

For notifying constables to attend a court, for each constable notified.. 50

For attending a term of court which he is required by law to attend, for each day.. 3 00

Code of Civil Precedure, § 3307.

STENOGRAPHER FOR COUNTY COURT.

The Board of Supervisors of any county in this State may provide for the employment of a stenographer in the county court and court of sessions thereof, and may fix the compensation he shall receive, and provide the payment thereof *in the same manner as other county expenses are paid.* Such stenographer shall furnish to any party to a trial in such courts, to his attorney, or to the District Attorney on the trial of an indictment, on request, a copy of the evidence and proceedings taken by him on such trial, or of such part thereof as may be required, on payment *on behalf of such party,* of ten cents for every one hundred words of the copy so furnished. *When the District Attorney of any county* requests such copy, *the amount due therefore shall be a charge against the county, and may be collected as other county charges are collected.*

Code of Civil Procedure, § 3311.

SUPERVISORS.

COUNTY SERVICES.

[County Charge.]

For each day's service of 24 hours at the session of their respective
Boards........................ ....:.......... ....$ 3 00

Mileage at the rate of eight cents per mile for once going and returning from his residence to the place of meeting, for each regular or
special session, and actual expenses on any duty committed to him by
the Board, and which shall require his attendance at any place from
where the Board shall hold its session.

For making copy of assessment roll and making out the bill to be delivered to the collector :

For the first hundred written lines, per line............................$ 04
For the second hundred written lines, per line..................   02
For each written line in excess of two hundred.......................   01

Laws of 1876, § 257.
2d Revised Statutes, pages 933 and 939.

AS COUNTY CANVASSERS.

Discretionary allowance not fixed by statute.

TOWN SERVICES.

[Town Charge.]

Approving Collector's bond... ....$1 00
Going and returning to file said bond, per mile............................   08
Disbursing school moneys............................ .... .1 per cent.
For all services required by law to be performed in the service of
the town, and for which no compensation is otherwise pro-
vided, per day...$2 00

An actual and necessary expense of travel.

Laws of 1876, Chapter 257.
2d Revised Statutes, page 933.

TOWN CLERKS.

For each day's services as a town officer. $2 00

2d Revised Statutes, page 1218.
Laws of 1870, Chapter 242, § 2.

For filing and entering certificate of marriage.......................... 25
For copy of same. 10

3d Revised Statutes, page 2234, §16.

CASES WHERE NO COMPENSATION IS PRESCRIBED.

Services are required in many cases of various officers, especially county clerks and sheriffs, for which no compensation is provided by statute. Whenever such service is required by law and actually performed, the officer is entitled to a reasonable compensation, to be determined by the Board of Supervisors or Board of Town Auditors, as the case may be, unless there be a statutory prohibition express or constructive.

The People ex rel. Hilton vs. Supervisors of Albany, 12 Wendell, 257.

CLAIMS NOT A COUNTY OR TOWN CHARGE BY STATUTE.

' Accounts not made a charge expressly or by implication, by law cannot be allowed by any Board of Auditors.

The People ex. rel. Merritt vs. Lawrence, 5 Hill, 244.

Any allowance of such claim is a mere nullity.

Same case.

WHEN PAYMENT CANNOT BE MADE ON ACCOUNTS AUDITED.

CHAPTER 341.

An Act to amend Chapter 104, of the Laws of 1863, entitled "An Act in regard to certain officers in several counties in this State," passed May 4, 1863. Passed April 23, 1864.

The People of the State of New York, represented in Senate and Assembly, do enact as follows:

SECTION 1. Section one of Chapter four hundred and four, of the laws of eighteen hundred and sixty-one, is hereby amended so as to read as follows :—Each officer in the several counties of this State who shall receive, or is authorized by law to receive any money on account of any fine or penalty, or other matter in which his county or any town or city therein shall have an interest, shall make a report in writing every year, bearing date the first day of November, in which he shall state particu-

larly the time when, and the name of the person or persons from whom
such money has been received, and also the amount, and also on what
account the same was received, and also all sums remaining due or unpaid, which report shall include all receipts of money before mentioned
that he has received during the year next preceding the date of his report, and if no such moneys have been received, his report shall state
such facts. Said report shall be made to the Board of Supervisors of his
county, duly verified by oath, and filed with the clerk of said Board on
or before the fifth day of November in each and every year, and no officer shall be entitled to receive payment for services, salary or otherwise, from the Supervisors or from a City or County Treasurer, unless he
shall file with the Supervisors his affidavit that he has made such report
and has paid over all moneys which he is bound to pay over.

§ 2. This act shall take effect immediately.

2d Revised Statutes, page 980.

COUNTY CHARGES.

The compensation of the members of the Board of Supervisors, of their
Clerk and of the County Treasurer.

The salary of the District Attorney, and all expenses necessarily incurred by him in criminal cases arising within the County.

The compensation of Criers of Court.

The compensation of Sheriffs for the commitment and discharge of
prisoners on criminal process within their respective Counties.

The compensation allowed by law to Constables for attending Courts
of Record, and reasonable compensation to Constables and other officers
for executing process on persons charged with criminal offences, for the
service of subpoenas issued by the District Attorney, for conveying prisoners to jail, and for other services in relation to criminal proceedings
for which no specific compensation is provided by law.

The expenses necessarily incurred in the support of persons charged
with or convicted of crimes and committed therefor to the county jail.

The sums required by law to be paid by prosecutors and witnesses in
criminal cases.

The moneys necessarily expended by any County officer in executing
the duties of his office in cases in which no specific compensation for such
services is provided by law.

The accounts of County Clerks for services and expenses under Chapter six, part one, of the Revised Statutes.

Abstract of Fees. 19

All charges and accounts for services rendered by any justice of the peace, under the laws for the relief and settlement of the poor of such county, and for their services in the examination of felons, not otherwise provided by law.

The sums necessarily expended in each county in the support of county poor houses and of indigent persons whose support is chargeable to the county.

The sums required to pay bounties for destruction of noxious animals when chargeable to the county.

The sums necessarily expended in repairing court house and jails of the respective counties.

The contingent expenses necessarily incurred for the use and benefit of a county.

Every other sum directed by law to be raised for any county purpose under the direction of the Board of Supervisors.

> 2d Revised Statutes, pages 978 and 979.

The compensation of coroner's jury.

> 3d Revised Statutes, page 2586.

Salary of county judge and surrogate.

> 2d Revised Statutes, page 973.

Compensation of justices of sessions.

> Constitution. Article VI., § 15.

Expenses of printing calendars for courts of record.

> Code, § 20.

Expenses incurred in insuring county buildings.

> 1st Revised Statutes, page 884, 6th edition.

Services of counsel employed by district attorney according to law.

> 2d Revised Statutes, page 972.

Services rendered as counsel for Board of Supervisors.

> 10 N. Y. Reports, 260.

Compensation of stenographer in supreme and county courts.

> 3d Revised Statutes, page 2384.

The sum of $30 annually for each pupil in State asylum for idiots.

> 3d Revised Statutes, page 1937.

In regard to State institution for the blind at Batavia, see

> 2d Revised Statutes, pages 43, 101, 102, 103, 104, 105, 6th edition.

20 *Abstract of Fees.*

In regard to State institution for instruction of deaf and dumb, see 2d Revised Statutes, pages 43, 106, 107, 6th edition.

Accounts for county charges of every description shall be presented to the Board of Supervisors of the county, to be audited by them.

Willard Asylum for insane.
3d Revised Statutes, page 1915.

Trial of indictment in another county.
3d Revised Statutes, page 2569.

And see the various heads of the abstract fees and the sub-divisions thereof.

DISTINCTION BETWEEN TOWN AND COUNTY CHARGES IN CRIMINAL CASES.

All fees and accounts of magistrates and other officers for criminal proceedings, including cases of vagrancy, shall be paid by the several towns and cities wherein the offence shall have been committed, and all accounts rendered for such proceedings shall state where such offence was committed, and the Board of Supervisors shall assess such fees and accounts upon the several towns or cities designated by such accounts. But when any person shall be bound over to the oyer and terminer or court of sessions, or committed to jail to await trial in either of said courts, the costs of the proceedings had before the single magistrate shall be chargeable upon the towns or cities aforesaid, and the costs of the proceedings had after the person shall have been so bound over or committed shall be chargeable to the county. But nothing herein contained shall apply to cases of felonies, nor where the proceedings or trial for the offence shall be had before any court of oyer and terminer, or courts of sessions of the county ; and the fines imposed and collected in any such cases shall be credited to such towns or cities respectfully.

1st Revised Statutes, page 846.

The term "felony" means an offence for which the offender, on conviction, shall be liable by law to be punished by death, or by imprisonment in a State prison.
3d Revised Statutes, page 2539.

The term "criminal proceedings" includes, among other things :
1. Proceedings against beggars and vagrants.
2. Proceedings to prevent the commission of crimes.
3. Proceedings against disorderly persons.
4. Search warrants and proceedings thereon.

People ex. rel. Post vs. Supervisors Ontario, 4 Denio, 260.

CHAPTER 402.

AN ACT to amend "An Act authorizing the confinement of convicts from Dutchess County in the Albany Penitentiary," etc., passed April fifteenth, one thousand eight hundred and fifty-four.

Passed April 13th, 1885, three-fifths being present.

The People of the State of New York, represented in Senate and Assembly, do enact as follows:

SECTION 1. The second section of the act entitled "An act to authorize the confinement of persons convicted of certain offences in the County of Dutchess in the Penitentiary of the County of Albany, and to prescribe the punishment of certain offences," passed April fifteenth, eighteen hundred and fifty-four, is hereby amended so as to read as follows : It shall be the duty of every court, police justice, justice of the peace, or other magistrate by whom any person may be sentenced in the County of Dutchess, for a term of not less than two months, for any crime or misdemeanor punishable by imprisonment in the county jail, to sentence such person to imprisonment in the Albany County Penitentiary, there to be received, kept and employed in the manner prescribed by law ; and such court, justice or other magistrate, shall cause such person so sentenced to be conveyed forthwith, by some proper officer, to said penitentiary ; and the officers thus conveying such convicts shall be paid such fees and expenses therefor as the Board of Supervisors of the said County of Dutchess shall direct.

§ 2. This act shall take effect immediately.

It will be seen from the above section that all costs in cases of misdemeanor are town charges up to the commitment; after commitment, the fees of officers for transporting to jail or penitentiary are county charges. Nothing is a town charge after the prisoner is committed.

Chapter 261 of the Laws of 1854, as amended by Chapter 402 of the Laws of 1855, applies specially to Dutchess County, and the fees and expenses for transporting prisoners are such as the Board of Supervisors of Dutchess County shall allow and direct.

The fees of officers as fixed by the General Statues do not apply, this being a special act authorizing the Board of Supervisors to fix the amount of the fees, and are county charges.

TOWN CHARGES.

The compensation of town officers for services rendered for their respective towns.

The contingent expenses necessarily incurred for their use and benefit of the town.

The moneys authorized to be raised by the vote of a town meeting for any town purpose.

Every sum directed to be raised by law for any town purpose.

1st Revised Statutes, page 841.

Judgments against towns or against town officers in actions prosecuted by or against them in their name of office.

1st Revised Statutes, page 842.

Accounts of Boards of Health (town charge).

2d Revised Statutes, page 1085.

For town charges in criminal cases, see distinction between town and county charges.

Support of roads and bridges.

Support of indigent inebriates and lunatics, if town charge, at State asylum.

See references under "County Charges."

See the various heads.

FORMS.

[Report under chapter 341, Laws of 1864.]

To the Board of Supervisors of Dutchess County:

The undersigned, a justice of the peace in and for said county, respectfully reports that Schedule A, hereto annexed and forming a part of this report, contains a true and correct statement of all moneys received by him for any fine or penalty, or any other matter in which said county or town therein has any interest, during the year ending Nov. 1, 1890, together with the names of persons from whom, the time when, and on what account such moneys have been received. That such moneys have been duly paid to the officers empowered by law to receive them, as appears by the receipts which are hereunto annexed.

Dated November 1st, 189......

....

Justice of the Peace.

SCHEDULE A.

Name.	Time.	On what account.	Amount.

DUTCHESS COUNTY, SS.:—

.,.................. ....being duly sworn, says the foregoing report, by him subscribed, is true and correct.

....

Subscribed and sworn to before me this 1st day of November, 189..

....

No. 2.

To the Board of Supervisors of Dutchess County :

The undersigned, a Justice of the Peace in and for said County, respectfully reports that, during the year ending November 1, 189.., he
has received no moneys for any fine or penalty, or any other matter in
which said County or any Town therein has any interest.

Dated, November 1, 189..

....

Justice of the Peace.

(Add verification as in No. 1.)

INDEX.

INDEX.

www.ingramcontent.com/pod-product-compliance
Lightning Source LLC
Chambersburg PA
CBHW032341280326
41935CB00008B/412